GOLDEN AGES
OF THE GREAT CITIES

GOLDEN AGES

OF THE GREAT CITIES

THE AUTHORS:
SIR MAURICE BOWRA · JÉRÔME CARCOPINO
STEVEN RUNCIMAN · DAVID DOUGLAS
HAROLD ACTON · CECIL SPRIGGE
VICTOR CUNARD · R. TREVOR DAVIES
JACQUES CHASTENET · ALAN PRYCE-JONES
ROGER FULFORD · ROBERT WAITHMAN

WITH AN INTRODUCTION BY
SIR ERNEST BARKER
AND A PREFACE BY
ALLAN NEVINS

WITH 95 PICTURES IN
PHOTOGRAVURE

THAMES AND HUDSON
LONDON · NEW YORK

First published 1952

HT
113
, 66

PRINTED IN GREAT BRITAIN
BY JARROLD AND SONS LTD., NORWICH

CONTENTS

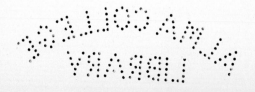

ILLUSTRATIONS

2

PHOTOGRAPHIC SOURCES

ALINARI: Pl. 3 Theatre of Dionysus; Pl. 5; Pl. 6 Drapers Shop; Pl. 9; Pl. 20; Pl. 21 Clement VII; Pl. 34 Louis XIV's Bedroom; ANDERSON: Pl. 1 Sophocles, Thucydides, Aeschylus; Pl. 6 Procession; Pl. 7 Hadrian, Marcus Aurelius; Pl. 17 Lorenzo de' Medici; Pl. 18 Giuliano de' Medici; Pl. 19; Pl. 21 Julius II, Leo X; Pl. 23; Pl. 25; Pl. 26 Procession; Pl. 28; Pl. 29; Pl. 30 Escorial; Pl. 32; FOX PHOTOS: Pl. 45; Pl. 46 Bowery, Wallstreet; GIRAUDON: Pl. 6 Soldiers released; Pl. 7 Trajan; Pl. 15; Pl. 33; Pl. 34 Mazarin; Pl. 35; Pl. 37 Congress of Vienna; DORIEN LEIGH: Pl. 3 Erechtheum; COREIN LEIGHT: Pl. 48 Grand Central Station; MANSELL: Pl. 1 Pericles, Euripides, Aristophanes; Pl. 2; Pl. 4; Pl. 7 Antoninus; Pl. 8; Pl. 16 Lower Chapel; Pl. 21 Paul III; Pl. 24; Pl. 34 Maintenon; Pl. 39 Haydn, Schubert; Pl. 41 Gladstone; Pl. 42; Pl. 43 House of Commons; Pl. 44 Railway Station; PORT OF NEW YORK AUTHORITY: Pl. 46 Bus Terminal; Pl. 48 Lincoln Tunnel; U.S. INFORM. SERVICE: Pl. 46 U.N. Headquarters.

Preface

ALLAN NEVINS

THIS is the Age of the City. By 1900 almost precisely one third of the American population lived in centres of more than eight thousand, and the American trend simply followed the world trend.

For better or for worse—who knew? What is certain is that the change was inevitable and inexorable; that America simply had to adjust itself to the dynamic pressures, confused forces, and social complexities of the urban age. It was clear that the city was changing the character of America as it had altered the character of older lands.

Now what is the special American experience with great cities; and what are the attitudes that have governed and accompanied that experience?

One basic American postulate, if we look at the matter in historical terms, is that a healthy balance ought to be struck between the great cities and the vigorous countryside. Deep in the American heart lurks a feeling that the rural community, if left to itself, stagnates into provincialism and boorishness; that the city, if not constantly revivified by red country blood, becomes "effete". At the beginning of our history we had to take action to encourage towns. In our more recent history, on the contrary, we have had to encourage the countryside.

The pressure against the old balance comes now, and will come in the future, from the side of the city. Jefferson thought that the geographical vastness of the country would keep it predominantly rural for centuries. But by the middle of the last century cities were springing up full-panoplied in the United States, and today the future unquestionably belongs to the city.

Everywhere, after 1850, America witnessed the rise of the Aladdin's-Lamp city. Nothing is more instructive than the contrast between the slowly-maturing cities of the past treated in this book—Rome, Paris, Madrid, London—and the swiftly-rising cities of the newer age—Chicago, Vancouver, Rio de Janeiro, Johannesburg—in the younger nations. The modern economy not merely favours, but even necessitates, the rapid development of cities and their dominion over all modern life.

In America the old desire for a balance between urban and rural elements will no doubt persist; but the idea of balance will be given a new interpretation. It is doubtless true that quite different faculties of mind and character, broadly speaking, appertain to the city and to the country. If the city does more to feed the acquisitive traits of the human mind, the country is kindlier to the ruminative and even creative talents. The rural outlook is the more serene and conservative; the urban outlook the more volatile, alert, and radical. Assuredly more wit is to be found in the cities, and more quiet humour in the countryside. Each type of mind and character has its merits and its defects. But we must make up our minds now to be a preponderantly urban civilization, and try to nurture rural virtues in a citified environment.

Hence the importance to a more and more urbanized America of this book, which demonstrates with compelling interest and the most modern erudition the immeasurable debt which our civilization owes the great cities of the past. The pictures of ancient Athens, Rome, and Constantinople here given us by Sir Maurice Bowra, Jérôme Carcopino, and Steven Runciman, each astonishingly full of touches that we would call modern, describe a heritage which is vital and immediate to New York, Chicago, and San Francisco. The studies of medieval Paris, Florence, Madrid, and Rome, by David Douglas, Harold Acton, Trevor Davies, and Cecil Sprigge, show that if these cities are in one sense centuries dead, in another they are vividly alive and full of significance to our own urban era. So, too, are the vigorous presentations of modern Paris, London, and Vienna in this rich volume.

*

A second great American postulate on cities, historically speaking, may be summed up in three words: No dominating metropolis. By that is meant that Americans believe there should be no city which is both the seat of political government, and also by its size, wealth, and intellectual power the head and centre of the country—the favourite residence of the rich, powerful, and learned, the natural focus of literary and scientific activity. This book deals with cities which dominated the ages in which they flourished, and American readers will find the study of this domination of fascinating interest.

It should not be forgotten that until the year 1776 London was as much a metropolis for America, albeit of a faraway, diluted kind, as for England, and that even after the thirteen colonies became free and independent states the spell of London remained potent in many areas of culture and activity.

But jealousy of and dislike for London, and repugnance to the very idea of any metropolis, was strong throughout the Colonial period. Antagonism to the rise of any metropolis was perpetuated and expanded during the early national period when it long seemed uncertain which of four cities, Boston, New York, Philadelphia, and Baltimore, would take a clear lead in population, wealth, and enterprise; and the belief that America is best served by a congeries of great cities, and not by one super-colossal city, is today more deeply implanted than ever in the breast of the people.

To be sure, for a time in the days of "normalcy" just after the First World War, the United States seemed to be contradicting Lord Bryce's statement that it was a country without a capital. In the days of Harding and Coolidge, political power moved from Pennsylvania Avenue to downtown New York.

The agglomeration of money in Wall Street broke all records. However, the Great Depression and the New Deal shattered that brief era.

Today, the United States can again be said to be without a capital—which is as America would have it. Anyone who visits Chicago, Minneapolis, Denver, or San Francisco, finds himself in a distinct regional metropolis. New York cannot demand the privileges of a national metropolis, and a dozen cities would rise in wrathful dissent if it did. No seat exists which corresponds to what Paris has been to France, London to Britain, Madrid to Spain, Rome to Italy, or Vienna to Austria.

An Englishman or a Frenchman would perhaps think this a disadvantage. Would it not be better, they might ask, if one lordly American city played the part that Paris played in the days of Louis XIV and Racine, or that London played in the era of Queen Victoria? Does not the intellectual and artistic life of a nation gain by concentration? Is it not well to have wealth, and political power, and intellectual activity in such close conjunction that they stimulate and modify one another? For Americans the answer is No; not for the three million square miles and 155,000,000 people in the United States. In a country so large, with such multiform regional differences, and with such sharply differentiated traditions as mark the South, the Far West, the Midlands, and the North Atlantic states, the genius of the land defies concentration.

For this reason American readers will find a special interest in a study of the principle of concentration, its advantages and penalties, in the great cities of older lands. They will profit by comparing with their own cities the picture of an Antonine Rome which was the head and centre of a great empire, the fountain of political, financial, and cultural authority for the whole Mediterranean basin and lands beyond. They will find it equally profitable to study in the record of Louis XIV's Paris, and of Victoria's London, as so ably presented by Jacques Chastenet and Roger Fulford, the qualities of leadership which made these cities the capitals in every sense of monarchist France and imperial Britain. These two cities were lodestones of talent, nurseries of genius, well-organized power-houses of intellectual force, whose influence upon finance, politics, letters, art, manners, fashion, and modes of thought shaped the destinies of two great peoples, and profoundly influenced neighbouring lands as well. Madrid, too, was once mistress not only of Spain but of the vast Spanish-speaking lands across the ocean, today possessed of their own metropolitan cities.

*

We face a new era in the history of our great western cities —the North Atlantic era, in which all the countries fronting on the Atlantic and its main arms will be more closely united culturally as well as politically. As an Atlantic community comes into being—and it *must* be created—New York and Philadelphia will be less American; London will be less English; Paris and Rome will be less French and less Italian.

The great cities of the western world have always had much in common, and in modern life they are not only a standardizing influence, in the healthy sense of the term, but are tending themselves to become more standardized. For one reason, the growth of cities must be correlated with other elements in our changing civilization, and particularly with two of universal influence: the rising employment of machine power, which in advanced countries has grown three or four times as fast as population, and the enlargement of leisure, which has become recognized economically as "consumable", and which is consumed in much the same way in all large Occidental cities. The cities of the past were centres of toil, and heavy toil at that, with little leisure for the labouring class, and great contrasts between the rich and the poor. This volume contains illuminating glimpses of that old class-stratification. Now cities are centres of a widely diffused leisure, which is translated into a crescent interest in the fine arts, science, and letters, into a growing participation in sports, into a wider enrolment in educational institutions, into a greater addiction to travel, and into a growing use of radio, cinema, television, and like mass-media of entertainment and cultivation.

The city of the future will be conscious of the splendid heritage which is so vigorously described in the successive chapters of this book. Each city will owe much to the intellectual glory of Periclean Athens, the administrative efficiency of Antonine Rome, the architectural splendour of Byzantine Constantinople, the learning and piety of medieval Paris, the humanitarian zeal of Victorian London. The finer our urban arts and crafts become, the more conscious we shall be of our debt to the sculptors and painters of Florence, Venice, and Madrid; to the Guildsmen of the medieval French and English towns; to the thinkers and writers who gave humanistic breadth to the outlook of olden cultural centres. This heritage has to be adapted, however, to a social and economic life that is quite new; to a civilization not of restricted classes, but of the multitudinous masses. Whether we regard it as gain or loss, that is the urban future. The masses, now given an ample leisure, and lifted to a high level of health and comfort by the power age and mass-production techniques, will expect to enjoy all the amenities that a city can offer.

Already we have in present-day New York an intimation of what the future city of mass-leisure and mass-culture will be. New York has its free municipal university and college system which in 1951 enrolled about 70,000 students; two great endowed institutions, Columbia and New York University, which are training about 75,000 more; and additional universities, like Fordham, which have raised the total of men and women pursuing higher education to fully 200,000. These students alone are a city within a city. New York provides fine music for the millions: for throngs gathered in the Lewisohn Stadium to hear a symphony orchestra, in Central Park for the Goldman band concerts, in Carnegie Hall, the Metropolitan Opera House, and dozens of smaller auditoriums. The city has

park areas (more than doubled during the 1930's) which, with
flowers, beaches, bathing-pools, and playgrounds, are adequate
for its eight million people. It boasts one of the three or four
finest libraries in the world—and the New York Public Library
is perhaps the most efficiently operated of them all—with
numerous smaller collections. It has not one but a dozen great
art museums: the Metropolitan, the Frick, the Museum of
Modern Art, the Whitney Museum of American Art, the
Brooklyn Museum, and others. It has a towering architecture
all its own; it has 1500 clinics, and 1200 social agencies.

The central task of leaders in the future cities of the western
world will be to lift mass-culture in such a way as to make
mass-leisure truly significant, profitable, and hopeful. In this
undertaking each country can aid its neighbours. They will
learn how much they have to give and to receive.

It is worth noting, as one historical illustration, how much
the United States has borrowed from the urban institutions of
Great Britain. We borrowed the Y.M.C.A., a city organization
for young men placed in a crowded environment where they
needed friendship and moral stay. We borrowed the Charity
Organization Society. We borrowed the Salvation Army. We
borrowed the Boy Scouts, with some contribution of our own.
We borrowed the social survey, which Jacob Riis and others
took from Alfred Booth. We borrowed the Society for the
Prevention of Cruelty to Animals. We borrowed the idea of
model tenements. We borrowed the settlement house, which
Stanton Coit and Jane Addams brought straight from Toynbee
Hall. This list could be much enlarged. These urban institutions of Britain took root instantly in the United States, because
the social, economic, and cultural climate of the American city
so closely resembled that of British municipalities. No American
city planner has failed to look to the work of Haussman in
Paris. No American supervisor of urban schools has forgotten
certain path-breaking innovations of Berlin. Today, in the
middle of the twentieth century, the current tends to set the
other way; European cities learn from American. But the

important fact is that all cities can learn from each other, and all are really integral parts of one great community.

The urban trend seems irresistible, and will doubtless persist through many coming decades. London, Paris, and New York will not shrink, and other great cities will grow. As urbanization continues, it will inevitably make new contributions to the establishment of an ever-finer civilization. We shall learn to think of cities and their place in world culture in broader terms. All great cities, while preserving their separate personalities and characters, will belong more clearly to a single spiritual community. So at least we may hope—and we must strive to make that dream come true.

Separateness was the mark of the older cities treated in chapter after chapter of this remarkably varied book. How diverse they were, and how isolated they stood! The future has a brighter hope. The cities of the North Atlantic community now irresistibly drawing closer together can and should regard themselves as one family. They will become sister cities of a great Atlantic commonwealth which in essentials will have one culture, one common tradition—a tradition largely derived from ancient Athens and Rome, and medieval Paris, and Renaissance Florence and Venice—and one overmastering aim, the maintenance and enlargement of their hard-won freedoms. Rich in their pattern of life, flexible, resilient, and human in their social structure, they will, we may hope, look less to their place as cities of a single nation, and more to their place as cities of the United Nations. Thus closely-linked in comradeship they will bid defiance to tyrannic pressures, atomic bombs, or disruptive philosophies. It may well be that these cities of the future will possess a greater splendour than any of the cities which existed in the two thousand years covered by this admirably planned and admirably written volume.

Introduction

SIR ERNEST BARKER

THE title of this book is "Golden Ages". It might also be "Golden Cities"; and the motto on its title-page might then be "Earth has many a noble city". For the purpose of the book, and the idea by which it has been inspired, has been to assemble (as it were on a necklace or in a coronet) a collection of historical essays on the dozen or so most famous cities of Europe, as they were at the time of their highest civilization and the peak of their cultural influence. There is a reason, and a cogent reason for this concentration on the idea of the city. Etymology is sufficient to teach us that the city (*civitas*) is the nursing mother of civilization. The Greek city-state, or *Polis*, was the original fountain of the notion of a free political society composed of equal citizens living together in fraternity under a system of ordered justice. The city-state, or *civitas*, of Rome was the source of our notions of civilization or "civility" (or in other words the way of life which belongs to cities); and another Latin word for city—the word *urbs*—has produced the tradition of "urbanity", that is to say of grace and good manners in social intercourse. A book on the golden cities of Europe, as they stood at their prime, is accordingly also a book on the sources and springs of European civilization. Sophocles, in a great chorus of the *Antigone*, reflecting on a theme which long afterwards moved Shakespeare to wonder in *Hamlet*—"What a piece of work is a man! how noble in reason! how infinite in faculty!"—sets the city high, if not highest, among all human achievements. These, he says, are the great things which man has taught himself— "language, and wind-swift thought, and city-dwelling habits".

I

Man's city-dwelling habits are a fine theme for any writer. An American author of our own day, Lewis Mumford, has devoted an illuminating work to the theme of "the culture of cities". I have dreamed myself (if I may speak of myself and indulge in a personal confession) of attempting a work on the theme of "the culture-cities of Europe". It was never more than a dream; and I never even succeeded in making a final list of the "culture-cities" which I wished to describe. For the period of antiquity I knew that I must include Athens and Rome and Constantinople (which are all "eternal cities"); but I also wanted to include Alexandria—even though it was not in Europe—because I felt that the thought of Alexandria, from the third century B.C. to the fifth century A.D., was the most stirring and subtle thought which troubled and moved the mind of Europe. For the period of the Middle Ages I was clear about Paris and Florence; but I also wanted to include Cordova (though I knew that I might be condemned as fanciful) because I felt that the Arabic philosophy and general culture of southern Spain could not be forgotten in any account of medieval cities. When I came to modern history I was still more a prey to indecision. I wanted Vienna and Venice and London; but I also wanted Cracow (not only because of Copernicus, but also because of all that it is and has been for so many centuries); I wanted Geneva (not only for Calvin, but also for Rousseau and much besides Rousseau); I wanted Amsterdam; I wanted the Edinburgh of the eighteenth century and the Dublin of the turn of the nineteenth—in fact I wanted far too much, and thus my plan capsized. When once you begin to reflect on the "Golden Cities" of history and on man's "city-dwelling habits" your mind is soon overloaded. Bruges will insist on coming aboard, as it was in the days of the Hansa and the early Flemish painters. Prague and Kiev and Moscow have their claims; and before you know where you are the cities of Asia demand a place by the side of the cities of Europe, and Baghdad and Samarkand and Agra and Pekin are all on the deck.

It was no wonder, therefore, that my plan capsized. I am the more delighted, and the more proud, to have the honour of introducing in this prologue a plan which has not capsized, but has made a successful voyage and safely entered port. There are ten cities in this plan; but two of them, naturally Rome and Paris—*Roma caput mundi* and Paris *la ville lumière*—make a double entry, and thus, though there are only ten cities, there are as many as twelve golden ages. If you look at the cities and ages in terms of space, you will find that three of the cities and four of the ages—Rome, as has just been said, making a double entry, first in the age of the Antonines and then in the age of the Popes of the Renaissance and the Counter-Reformation—belong to Italy. It is not surprising that the cities of Italy, Florence of the Medici and Venice of the sixteenth century as well as the double Rome, should occupy so much space. From the days of the entry of the Etruscans, soon after the year 1000 B.C., down to the days when Venice held "the gorgeous East in fee", Italy was always a mother of cities and of traditions of civility. Indeed it may almost be said that the city is the product of a Mediterranean world of "urbanity", and that Northern Europe in comparison—at any rate down to the emergence of Paris in the thirteenth century of our era—was a home of "rurality" and scattered tribes and the countryside. This is not only a matter of Italy and the middle Mediterranean: it is also a matter of Greece and the wide area of the diffusion of the civilization of Greece in the eastern Mediterranean. Greece was a mother of cities even before Italy was: she spread them from Cyrene to Odessa, and from Marseilles to Miletus; and it is only bare justice to her city-founding and city-dwelling habits that one of the chapters of this book should be devoted to the city of Athens and another to the city of Constantinople, which maintained the speech and the tradition of Greece (in philosophy and law as well as in art and the glories of Byzantine architecture and painting) down to the end of the Middle Ages.

Half of the book is thus devoted, if we consider it in terms of space, to the Mediterranean world. What of the rest? A great part of it—indeed a third of the whole book—is devoted to what may be called the world of the eastern Atlantic, the world which includes France, England, and Spain. This is the world of Paris, London, and Madrid. It is a world which was later in emerging into the light of history than the world of the Mediterranean: indeed its golden ages belong, in the main, to the last five hundred years, and date from that great age of discovery, beginning in the latter half of the fifteenth century, which brought the maritime states of the Atlantic seaboard of Europe into the foreground of action. But Paris had already a golden age in the middle of the Middle Ages, when her University began its life and St. Louis did justice to his subjects under the oak of Vincennes; and later she had another under another Louis, *Le Roi Soleil*, in the palace and the splendours of the park of Versailles. Paris, therefore, like Rome, makes a double entry on the scene. Madrid, a modern city, first chosen as the Spanish capital in the middle of the sixteenth century, makes only a single entry, in the age of its Habsburg rulers and Velasquez and Lope de Vega: London, as old as the Romans, and a city of note as early as Paris (though never the home of a university till the nineteenth century), has also only one entry, in the period of Queen Victoria's jubilees and the gorgeous days—as they seem in retrospect—of the reign of Edward VII. Yet London had earlier golden ages; and if I had been dictator, and could have chosen for myself the *aureum saeculum* of London, I should have thought first of the age of Shakespeare and then of the age of Dr. Johnson (which was also the age of Burke and Garrick and Gibbon and Pitt), and I might have decided finally in favour of the age of Johnson. Happily, I was not dictator; for, if I had been, the readers of this book would have lost the zest and the delight of the chapter on "Jubilee London".

There are two other cities described in this book besides the five cities of the Mediterranean and the three cities of western Europe. They are Vienna of the age of Metternich (which was also the age of Beethoven), and New York of the twentieth century, that is of today and tomorrow. Vienna is an imperial city, where "the ghost of the deceased Roman Empire" still walks for those who have eyes to see: it is a city "built to music",   And therefore built for ever;

it is a city set on the confines of the east: it is a city which must always endure, even if it now endures in decline, by virtue alike of its history and its geographical position. New York is pulsing electricity, and it is becoming the power-house of the world, both in international politics and in international economics. It is not yet one of the golden cities of culture—that will yet come, because political and economic greatness generally fosters, as the history of cities shows, the rise and growth of great art and architecture—but even so it could not be omitted from the plan of this book. The book is to be published jointly in England and America, and it is planned to serve as a link (or intellectual "Atlantic Union") between western Europe and North America. It serves to show to America what Europe has given in the past to the accumulated treasure of civilization, and what, if it is true to its past, it will still continue to give; but it must, as it ends, serve also to show to Europe what America is already giving and will continue increasingly to give. Over and above that, and apart from any weighing and balancing of two separate and several sides, there is still a greater service which the book may render, jointly and in common, to both sides of the Atlantic. It may remind two peoples, who are divided in space but united in spirit, of the riches of the past which they have jointly inherited and which, in this age, they must jointly defend. The great cities of Europe belong to America (they have given their sons for its peopling and contributed their cultures to its making); and conversely the great cities of America—not only New York, but others also, stretched over a continent from Boston and Philadelphia to Los Angeles and San Francisco—belong to Europe, and are contributing to Europe, as well as to their own hemisphere.

The argument hitherto has been an argument mainly in terms of space. Some words must be added, in conclusion, in terms of time and chronology. The essays succeed one another

3

in time, like runners in one of those torch races celebrated by the ancient Athenians: each author receives and hands on the torch, and all are linked by the common theme of the development of western civilization. There is an unbroken continuity, even if at times, and perhaps particularly in the early part of the book, there may seem to be gaps and wide interstices. There is a long span between the Athens of the fifth century B.C. and the Rome of the second century A.D.: there is a still longer span—a span of nearly a thousand years—between Rome in the age of the Antonines and Constantinople in that age of expansion and consolidation which was crowned by the victories of Nicephorus Phocas and John Tzimisces. But the Athens of Pericles reaches forward, in its gifts and the continuous tradition of its culture, to the Rome of Marcus Aurelius; and the Byzantine Empire of the tenth century—with its double tradition, both Greek and Roman—reaches back to, and is the heir of, Athens and Rome alike. The continuity of the spirit overleaps the gaps and intervals of time, even for the earlier ages which seem so widely divided; and when the course of the argument turns to medieval Paris and Medicean Florence, and then proceeds on its steady march from one century to another, the continuity of time is added to continuity of the spirit.

But in matters of the progress of culture and the long chain of civilization the student of history cannot walk, as it were by mile-posts and successive stations, along the slow road of continuous time. He must seek the mountain-tops, and his concern must be with the peaks. He must set out with a guide, or even with a dozen guides, on a spiritual cruise or pilgrimage—not an "Hellenic Cruise", or a cruise by way of the sea (though there is much to be learned by that method), but rather a general cruise over Europe along the great ways of "wind-swift thought" which pass from summit to summit of culture, permitting a bird's-eye view of the heights of men's achievements in the cities which they have built. The aim of this book is to be a guide or itinerary of such a cruise or pilgrimage; and the plan of each of its chapters is to provide for the alert and seeing eye a synoptic view of each age of culture as it reached its height in some great city—a view which takes account at once of the city's history and its political and economic structure, of its art and literature and manners and customs, and of the general pattern of its social system and the general nature of its social life.

It is this general aim of the book, and this general plan of each of its chapters, which give unity and continuity to these studies of twelve "Golden Ages". Each author has followed a general scheme—though authors would not be authors if each did not show his own idiosyncrasy and run off the rails at some point or other in his own individual way—and all have approached their particular subject in common (or at any rate similar) terms, treating it as one of the chapters of a long and continuous story, and so presenting it that it forms a facet or stone, at once reflecting and giving light, in the general sum and chain of influences which has produced and constitutes western civilization. And yet, though the book is thus informed by a spirit of collectivism (or is "co-operation" a better word?), it has also a saving grace of individualism and personality. The picture of each age is a separate picture, painted by a separate painter; and each picture is the more distinct and vivid because each is an individual achievement. The book of cities of which I once dreamed might well have been dull (as it would certainly have been imperfect) because it would all have been in one style and limited to the vision of one pair of eyes. A book which begins with the essays of Sir Maurice Bowra and Jérôme Carcopino (so different and yet of an identical excellence) and then proceeds to the essay of Jacques Chastenet, on Paris and Versailles in *Le Grand Siècle*, and the essay of Roger Fulford on Jubilee London, is very far from dull, and very seldom imperfect. To have read the essays which it contains is an education at once in identity and in difference—the identity of a common scheme and the difference of individual vision.

PLATE I

PERICLES C. 500–429 B.C.

AESCHYLUS 525–456 B.C.

EURIPIDES C. 480–406 B.C.

SOPHOCLES 496–406 B.C.

THUCYDIDES C. 460–400 B.C.

ARISTOPHANES C. 448–380 B.C.

PLATE 2

SILENUS SWINGING A MAIDEN
Attic Vase 5th century B.C.

THE CORONATION OF A BRIDE
Attic Vase 5th century B.C.

Athens: The Periclean Age

5TH CENTURY B.C.

SIR MAURICE BOWRA

IT is a commonplace that the modern world owes the most abiding and most valuable elements in its civilization to Mediterranean lands, that what Palestine did for religion and ethics, or Rome for law and government, Greece did for science and the arts. No doubt these remarkable achievements were largely determined by physical conditions. If the first victories of order and organization were won on vast alluvial plains watered by great rivers like the Nile, the Euphrates, the Indus and the Yellow River, the equilibrium so established between man and nature was so nicely calculated that life followed a fixed pattern with little call to change or enterprise. The greater difficulties of maintaining life round the Mediterranean gave a sterner challenge and elicited a more vigorous response. In Greece above all, natural conditions have not made life easy. Barren marble mountains and a thin soil forbid an extensive agriculture; the never too distant sea calls to adventure on and beyond it; violent differences of temperature between summer and winter discourage religions of resignation or philosophies of inaction; continual winds from the north and months of unbroken sunshine make for lively tempers and swift changes of mood; the limpid outlines of mountains and sea-coast sharpen the taste and discipline the intelligence. If civilization was slower to start here than in Mesopotamia or Egypt, yet once it began, it had a more vigorous impetus and a richer variety of experiment and achievement. If most parts of Greece,

3* 9

both mainland and islands, shared in this development, the finest, most dramatic and most influential success was won in Athens, above all in the fifth century B.C., which includes the period honoured by posterity as the Periclean age.

In 510 B.C. the Athenians expelled their tyrant, Hippias, and the great age began: in 404 B.C., broken by a long war, they surrendered to a Spartan general, and something was lost to the world for ever. Much of importance and significance happened before 510, and much was to happen after 404, but between these dates Athens did what it had never done before and was never to do again. In extent and in quality this achievement has almost no parallel in the recorded history of man. A small state, about the size of Yorkshire or Connecticut, with a population of some 200,000 free men, made contributions to thought, literature, and the fine arts on an unprecedented scale with so sure a touch that much of it has never been replaced or surpassed. If this was an age of experiment, as it certainly was, there is nothing uncertain or tentative or incomplete in what it did. If politically it ended in disaster, that is after all a tribute to the bold scope of its endeavours and the soaring flight of its vision.

The prodigious outburst of energy which followed the expulsion of the tyrants and turned alike to political action and to the creative arts cannot be explained by any materialistic or economic hypothesis. It was due rather to psychological causes, to the Athenians' discovery of themselves, of their own resources and capacities. They found a new confidence in themselves and sought to express it in many activities both public and private and to create a manner of living worthy of their claims and convictions. The history of Athens in the fifth century B.C. is largely that of various attempts to find satisfying forms for powerful creative instincts, to reduce to harmony and order ideas which might otherwise be lost in empty discussion, to give a concrete form to the great issues which troubled men's minds and clamoured for solution. The wonder is that in so short a time so much was done and done so well. The transition from tyranny to an almost complete democracy was matched in the arts by the transition from crude and improvised plays to the ripe glories of tragedy and comedy. Despite its taste for experiments and innovations Athens did not waste its energies in futile experiments but seems to have known from the start in what direction to move and what steps to take. The result is that its history has an air of inevitable, predestined development, but this is really the reflection of determined wills and powerful intellects solving problems with decision and with prescience.

The achievements of this age were based on a very simple economy. Its chief trees are the olive and the vine, its chief animal the goat. While the olive provides the oil which is the basis of all Mediterranean diets, the vine provides the drink which is no less indispensable. The goat gives not only cheese and milk but the staple meat of the country. The remaining chief article of food is fish, which is easy to get in a country which is bounded on three sides by the sea and whose indented coast provides if not good harbours at least adequate anchorage for small craft. Attica grows very little corn, and one of the chief economic problems was its importation from the Black Sea. This simple economy was strengthened in other ways. The mountains give all the marble that any builder could desire. The soil provides a clay which bakes well into pottery and became a notable article of export to places so distant as Etruria, the Crimea, and Egypt. The mines of Laureion produced enough silver for a solid and respected currency. Athenian life was never luxurious, nor by modern standards comfortable. Houses were small and dark; water was scarce in the summer; furniture, if neat and shapely, was spare and simple; horses were the privilege of the rich; the cold of winter was inadequately countered by charcoal fires; agricultural land was full of rocks and stones, had often to be carved in terraces on steep slopes, and was liable to devastation by storms. There must always have been a struggle for existence in most Attic homes, and even the rich never enjoyed the resources of the great magnates of Egypt or Persia. Such conditions called for continual enterprise and improvisation and gave to the Athenian character that toughness and adaptability which were among its salient characteristics.

On the other hand the hardness of life was more than compensated by the unique beauty of the country. Compared with France or Italy Attica looks at first sight austere and naked. It lacks woods or rivers or lush meadows, and indeed its beauty is perhaps more of line than of colour. At every turn the outlines of mountains etch the sky, while the sea seems always to be lurking behind a corner, if it is not already in full view. But though the first impression is of a grave restraint, the eye soon detects a great range of effects within it. The red-brown earth, the grey-green olive-trees, the honey-coloured marble, the white, pearly sand of coves and beaches, the dark gravity of cypresses and pines, form a subtle and splendid harmony which may be unlike that of western Europe but has its own great variety of tones and shades. The whole scene is held together by an air of an unexampled limpidity, from which every foreign matter seems to have been removed, and in the evening the whole sky changes with bewildering and dramatic swiftness from one dazzling effect to another. Life in such a landscape may be hard, but it can never be dull or deadening. It explains why the Athenians were great both in action and in the arts. Their physical setting was both a challenge and an inspiration, since, while it made them work hard to keep alive, it enriched their life with unparalleled delights to the eye.

This country produced a nation of peasant farmers. Even those who lived in towns and engaged in manufactures or in sea-borne trade were close to the soil and knew its ways. Such men tended to treat one another as equals because they shared common interests and despite differences of income lived in much the same fashion. Living in close contact with one another and knowing their neighbours' intimate secrets and idiosyncrasies they developed a remarkable candour and forthrightness in their social relations. Even if they had some respect for birth and breeding, there seem to have been no such formal restraints between men of different social position as we find in more highly organized societies where specialized pursuits tend to promote isolated groups of people. As in most Mediterranean countries, the centre of social life, at least for men, was not the home but the street or the market-place, where all topics, and especially politics, were discussed with the greatest freedom, eloquence, and even knowledge. If such circumstances allow a reasonable degree of decorum and courtesy, they also allow scurrilous abuse, passionate outbursts, and lewd banter. Hieratic stiffness and commercial servility are alike lacking. Such conditions encourage a lively interest in personal traits and peculiarities, with the result that a man is known as he really is without any delusive disguise conferred by office or pedigree, and, though good manners are usual, they do not prevent him or his neighbours from saying at times what they think of each other.

This social life was the real basis of Athenian democracy and of its two great ideals, equal laws and free speech. Men who knew each other so well as this saw no reason why some should have special privileges or others not be free to say what they thought. All that was needed to make a political reality out of the habits of every day was the enactment of laws which gave the male population a part in governing the country. This was done in a series of stages after 510 B.C., and the process was complete before the middle of the century. Henceforth until defeat in war brought reaction, Athens was in a strict sense of the word a democracy. The people, that is all free males, were the sovereign power. They took all political decisions, sat on juries, held public office, and had a right to free speech untrammelled by considerations of public security or laws of libel. This democracy was not representative but complete. It did not elect members to some assembly, but the people really met together, discussed, and decided what should be done. If powers were delegated to generals and public officers, it was only for limited periods, usually for a year, though they might be re-eligible. Though the laws by which Athens was governed were published and known, they could be repealed or altered by the decision of the people, and Pericles spoke the truth when he said that a law was whatever the people decided. This in itself was a great revolution from the old view that laws came from the gods and could not be altered. Of course such a system had its perils, which were in due course to reveal themselves, but none the less it made Athenian democracy what it was and was responsible for most of its triumphs.

It is easy to deride this system and to say that it was not truly democratic because it was based on slavery. Yet this defect is perhaps not so great as it seems to modern moralists. Athens differed from many slave-owning societies in the large proportion of free men to slaves. Indeed it has been calculated that this was about two to one. Poor households would not normally own any slaves, a moderately well-to-do one might have so many as twelve, and a rich one fifty. This is nothing like the scale of slavery in imperial Rome or any Oriental empire, and the reason for it is partly the poverty of Athens which could not afford to buy or maintain slaves in large numbers. Slaves were usually employed not on the land, but in mines and quarries and ships, and slave-women were often nurses in rich homes. They were hardly ever Greeks by origin, since Hellenic sentiment seems to have resisted such an exploitation of Greeks by their fellows, but they might be any kind of foreigners or "barbarians". Of course, like slaves everywhere, slaves in Athens were at the mercy of their masters, and might suffer from their whims and vices, though no doubt good tempers and common prudence assured that usually they were quite well treated. We cannot doubt that Athenian democracy was able to do what it did because it rested on slavery. This provided the free citizens with leisure to do more than spend their time in finding the means of subsistence. Of course the majority of them had still to work hard, but at least there were times when they could leave their work and give their attention to public affairs. However much we may deplore slavery in any form, we must remember that in Athens the variety of origin in slaves and their relatively small number prevented Attica from developing anything like a "colonial" economy, or from becoming like Georgia or Mississippi before the American Civil War. The citizens composed the larger part of the population and almost the whole indigenous part of it. And this was indeed democratic in the extent of its powers and its responsibilities.

One large class of persons was excluded from political life. The Athenians did not anticipate the modern world in allowing woman to manage public affairs. Indeed their whole treatment of women may rather surprise us. If we are to believe their own statements, women, at least in theory, were confined to an almost oriental seclusion, and proverbs stress that their right place is the home and that silence is their noblest part. Such statements need not be taken too literally, since they plainly contain an element of wishful thinking and it is hard to imagine women in any Balkan country keeping silent for long. It certainly seems true that women in the Athenian democracy mixed less freely and less easily with men than they do in Homer, but this does not mean that they were locked up. Not only does Attic tragedy give some of its most important parts to women, and in doing this it can hardly have flown altogether in the face of actual experience, but even comedy, which is far more realistic, makes great play with them. A woman is the leading character in Aristophanes' *Lysistrata* and behaves with a remarkable lack of inhibition. No doubt women worked while men talked, and in humble households did much that might have been done by slaves elsewhere, but that need not have prevented them from speaking freely or assuming responsibility in their own sphere. Indeed the evidence of Attic tombstones and funeral vases suggests that the Athenians were just as capable of deep and lasting affection for their wives as any other men. But what was lacking was any conscious or artificial cult of womanhood, such as existed in the Middle Ages, or even any courtly sentiment about them such as has existed in Europe since the Renaissance. In Athens men played the main part and kept their relations with women in the background, as an essential part indeed of their lives but separate from politics and public affairs. Even in their poetry love plays a very small part in comparison with what other poetry leads us to expect, and no conception of Athenian life is right which does not recognize its essentially male character.

The unusual character of Athenian democracy may be seen in one or two qualities which we do not associate with such a society. In the first place, it inherited an aristocratic tradition of taste and elegance and succeeded in adapting it to a wider circle and in giving it a new strength and solidity. This is clear not only from sculpture and poetry, which show a progressive tendency towards a greater scope and more majestic air until at least the middle of the century, but in the ceremonies and rites of civic or domestic life. The noble art of vase-painting illustrates much of Athenian life to which the written sources do not refer, and on these scenes drawn from the living world we see the Athenians as they saw themselves. In moments of gaiety which the painter has caught there is hardly anything vulgar or unrestrained: style and taste are always dominant, and have an aristocratic distinction, as if they belonged to men who knew almost instinctively how to transform any small occasion with a touch of charm or dignity. Whether it is young men jumping or girls dancing or graver episodes of adventure and war, the same distinction is always present, and of course the artists have learned it from life around them. Here are the ordinary episodes of every day seen with unspoiled eyes and appreciated at their true worth without exaggeration or rhetoric. Here we can see an "unbought grace of life" which is entirely natural and unpremeditated and derives its strength from being an accepted part of any household routine.

The respect and taste for the individual, which is so marked a feature of Athenian democracy, was matched and countered by a deep feeling of national unity, by a conviction that all these different men and women were members of a city which made them what they were and was responsible for their most

PLATE 3

THE CARYATIDES OF THE ERECHTHEUM, C. 420-409 B.C.
On the north side of the Acropolis

THE THEATRE OF DIONYSUS
Built at the foot of the Acropolis in the middle of the 4th century B.C.
It accommodated some 27,000 spectators

PLATE 4

POSEIDON, DIONYSUS AND DEMETER

TWO HORSEMEN
Reliefs from the Parthenon Frieze, 5th century B.C.

cherished traditions. This was of course patriotism as it exists everywhere, but in Athens it took a special shape. The Athenians boasted that in their long history they had never been conquered, and the fifth century was to confirm this confidence until the tragic end destroyed it. In 490 B.C. and again in 480–479 they defeated the Persians, who on the first occasion landed on Attic soil at Marathon and on the second burned the sacred buildings of the Acropolis. Athenian patriotism drew a new strength from danger and throve on a faith that the gods loved Athens and protected her. Above all it made a man feel that, however much he might think about his own rights and individuality, he was part of a larger scheme and proud to belong to it. At the great national festival of the Panathenaea, whose religious purpose was to conduct a simple rite of laying a garment on the knees of the image of Athene, the whole population took part, and the scene in all its dignity and harmony can be seen on the frieze of the Parthenon. Young men on horses, young women walking in stately robes, bulls driven to the sacrifice, and the gods watching in pleased detachment show the Athenian ideal of national solidarity. This is the expression of something very dear to the Athenian heart, a harmony of law and liberty, of ceremony and pleasure, of communal strength and individual contributions to it. It is in this same spirit that at the end of Aeschylus' *Eumenides* the chorus sings of Athens:

> Fare ye well, rejoiced with riches' righteous portion, fare ye well,
> Folk that in this city nigh to God's own Virgin Daughter dwell;
> Dear to her as she to Zeus, beloved and loving timely-wise,
> And, beneath her wings abiding, sacred in the Father's eyes.
> [*Trans*. C. M. Cookson]

The Athenians in their own way felt that they were a chosen people, specially loved by the gods, and that this imposed peculiar obligations upon them.

This love of country was naturally expressed in war. For a large part of the fifth century Athens was at war with some power or other, usually with Persia or Sparta. War, indeed, was an inevitable ingredient in Hellenic life, and what matters is not that it was so common but that at least in Athens attempts were made to justify it and fit it into a philosophy of life. No Athenian would question that the best thing a man can do is to die for his country, but they liked to ask what this means, what, after all, is the significance of a man's country, and why is he glad to die for it. In answer to such questions they pleaded that Athens had something like a mission and did for others what they were unable to do alone. In the main this mission was to secure political freedom against either foreign conquerors like the Persians or selfish cliques at home, but of course the two aims were easily confused and the conception of liberty was wide and adaptable. This ideal received an enormous impetus from the Persian wars, when Athens took a leading part in repelling the invader, and was sanctified in the following years when Sparta abandoned the military hegemony of Greece and let Athens take it over from her. The spirit of this movement can be seen in Aeschylus' *The Persians*, produced in 472 B.C. It is cast in dramatic form but is in spirit a paean of victory for free men over tyrants and slaves. Behind its peals of glory lies that respect for the common man which was the basis of Athenian life and refused to admit any good in tyranny. To die in such a cause was to assert the right of man to be himself and to go his own way, and this passionate conviction gave a special strength to Athenian patriotism.

In the world of affairs this spirit had far-reaching results. When Athens took over from Sparta the leadership of the league against Persia, it was as one free city among others. But by a gradual process this league was transformed into an empire of which Athens was the mistress. Cities who wished to leave the league were compelled by force to stay in it; the money which they paid towards the common costs was taken by Athens as tribute for herself; the democracies established among the allies were kept in power less because they were democracies than because they represented a pro-Athenian element in power. The cause of freedom which Athens had championed for its own sake at the start imperceptibly began to be identified with the cause of Athens and her interests. Once she began to feel the lure of power, she could not resist it, and though it took long for her allies to turn their old trust in her to hatred, in the last quarter of the century the change was complete and Athens, who had begun as the home of liberty, became the tyrant of the Aegean, who might slaughter or enslave a whole male population, as she did at Melos, because it refused to fit in with her plans.

An empire of this kind may be looked at from many angles and is likely to contain many good as well as bad elements. From the practical side Athens certainly did much for Greece at least in the second quarter of the fifth century. The Persian menace was still real, and Athens countered it, not only on the sea with her excellent navy, but by such far-flung adventures as the invasion of Egypt in support of local rebels against the Persians. This ended in an appalling catastrophe in 454 B.C., when 250 ships and a large army were trapped and lost. No one could say that Athens was not prepared to take the leading part and bear the heaviest cost in such undertakings. Equally, it cannot be denied that the democratic regimes which Athens sustained in her allies were probably better equipped for law and liberty than the small aristocratic cliques which opposed them. Even if the payment of tribute to Athens was an in-dubitable burden, it ensured a degree of safety and order. But to argue in this way is to neglect the other side of the picture—the feelings of the allies themselves and of their friends outside the Athenian sphere who saw Athens in a different and more hostile light. If liberty had made Athens great in spirit, it was a disastrous paradox that she should at times be forced to stifle it elsewhere. The great Athenians were conscious of this and did their best to explain and justify their position.

The finest plea for Athenian imperialism was made by

Pericles, who was elected in successive years to the office of general in the years 443–430, and held by virtue of his powerful personality and striking eloquence a special place in the councils and government of Athens. In the speeches which Thucydides ascribes to him and which, though they may not be verbal transcripts of what he said, certainly reflect his views, we see the Athenian justification of imperialism. It is, as we might expect, based on a belief in democracy. He understood with remarkable insight what this meant at Athens and wished Athens to teach it to other cities, regarding her as "the school of Greece" and claiming with justice that her doors were always open to foreigners. But this task, in his view, had almost inevitably to be carried out through force, and in this he saw a special glory. For him Athenian adventures into distant lands were among their greatest glories, which needed no Homer to sing them since they had their own deathless memorials. He knew that such a conception might, if carried out to the letter, win more enemies than friends, but he was not afraid of that and argued that glory was more important and more than compensated for it. So Pericles turned Athenian imperialism into a mission whose task was to make other cities like Athens and whose reward was an undying memory among men. In this way he justified and explained the new and terrible power which had come to Athens and was still not fully understood either in its use or its results.

The imaginative and spiritual side of this ambition was presented in striking visible form in the buildings which Pericles caused to be built on the Acropolis. The rocky hill which dominates Athens and had for centuries been the seat of its sacred shrines became the dazzling and far-seen symbol of Athenian achievement. Since the old temples and works of art had been destroyed by the Persians in 479 B.C., the way was clear to building something new and far more striking. In 447 B.C. the Parthenon was begun from the plans of Ictinus under the supervision of Callicrates. The cost was defrayed from tribute paid by the allies who thus saw their dependence on

Athens in its true reality. Behind the Parthenon and its attendant buildings lay the idea that Athens, guided by her national
goddess, Athene, had through the exercise of power found a
supreme glory which demanded the highest art to express it.
The Parthenon was the temple of the Maiden, Athene, who
was also known as "the Champion" and renowned as a goddess
of war. It was therefore appropriate that her statue should
stand outside and be visible from land and sea for many miles
around as the emblem of her own power and glory, and of the
power and glory of Athens whom she inspired and guided. It
was no less appropriate that the noble gateway and attendant
buildings, the Propylaea, should be built on a scale hardly less
than the Parthenon, since through it went the ceremonial
processions which honoured the national goddess. Both Parthenon and Propylaea were for all purposes completed when
war broke out with Sparta in 431 B.C., and are the ripest and
most revealing monuments of the great age in its ambitions and
its grandeur.

The Parthenon was a temple of a goddess in whose reality
men believed, and the sculptures which adorned it show what
the Athenians thought about themselves. They depict partly
struggles against primitive creatures like centaurs, thus illustrating the rise of Athens from uncouth barbarism, partly events
of cosmic grandeur which underlie the course of Athenian
history. The east pediment shows the birth of Athene on
Olympus. A celestial world of dreaming calm is broken by the
sudden appearance of a fully-grown goddess in its midst, and
wakes with awe and amazement at it. The west pediment
shows the struggle of Athene and Poseidon for the possession of
Attica: two great divinities in conflict, and a fearful sense of
power and effort. Each pediment represents a different aspect
of the national myth. If the east shows what the emergence of
such a power as Athene means even on Olympus, the west
shows what a goddess this must be that even the lord of the sea
quails before her. This is not allegory but mythology in the
truest sense. The gods in their own sphere display in a pure form

4

what happens to the men who live under their sway. Both scenes are concerned with power, either emerging or in full action, and both present to the eye the unexampled force which the Athenians felt at work in themselves and believed to be divine.

Even in their present ruined state the great buildings of the Acropolis stand as a majestic and compelling memorial to the greatness of Athens. We can see that they were a truly national monument, the expression of what the Athenian people as a whole believed and hoped about itself. If they glorify power, it is not the power of individuals but of a people and its goddess, and the expression of this power is not flaunting or boastful but disciplined by something characteristically Hellenic and Athenian. The Parthenon was indeed richly decorated, and in its unspoiled state, with its gold and ivory statue of Athene, may well have startled and dazzled the eyes, but none the less the decoration is subordinated to an austere and dominating design. The sculptures are confined to the frieze, which is not visible from outside, to the two pediments high in air, and the metopes between the tops of the columns. None of them immediately strikes the beholder, who is captured rather by the plain, magnificent, and orderly design of the building with its wonderful proportions, its fine surface of marble turned by sun and rain to a faint colour of gold, and its pillars in their mathematical elegance and harmony. This control is typical of the Athenian genius. However powerful their feelings may have been, whatever ideas and ideals may have stirred them, they reduced them to order, and set them in a design which is at once plain and overwhelmingly majestic. This shows how serious the Athenians were. For all their sense of irony and mockery, for all their outbursts of pride or anger, they felt that their national shrine must conform to the ideal of law which was the foundation of their liberties.

The Acropolis shows the Athenian spirit in its power and glory, but a people with so honest and intelligent a vision of life was not content to rest with this as the only expression of its

national life. Parallel to the great development of architecture
and sculpture came no less great a development in poetry
which was also national and profoundly serious. Because this
appealed to a whole people it had a special strength and scope.
The poet had no need to defend himself against the Philistine or
to justify himself to a society mainly given to other aims; he
drew his ideas, his strength, his public from a people of which
he was himself a characteristic member and whose outlook he
shared. He was not only an interpreter but a critic, not merely
a participant in a national experience but a leader of thought
about it. It is therefore right that the most powerful literary art
of Athens should be drama performed in the open air before a
vast audience in the theatre of Dionysus. Drama was in origin a
religious rite and never quite lost traces of it. It was usually
concerned, sooner or later, with the ways of the gods to men; it
was always profoundly thoughtful; it presented great issues
through individual stories and related them to current problems
of religion and morality; above all it maintained a noble level
of poetry, derived in part from hymns to the gods but enriched
by imaginative speculation and a keen sense of what divine
government means to the conduct of men. It was also a civic
rite. The men and women who make their brief appearances on
the stage are fundamentally not unlike actual figures of the
time; they speak in a rich language, which draws much from the
literary past but also owes some of its strength to a close contact with the living word; they take part in grim and tragic
stories which seem remote enough from actuality but have none
the less an illuminating affinity with it. Greek drama is in
every sense a national art just as much as architecture, and
serves a parallel purpose. Into it men of remarkable genius put
their profound thoughts and imaginative insight, and through
their work we get another view into the thoughts of Athenians
as their interpreters understood them. In some countries it may
be possible to study history without looking at literature, but
in Athens it is not, since the poetry of the age provides some of
the most important evidence about its character.

Greek tragedy is not always tragedy in the modern sense. It need not and does not always end in disaster. But it is tragic in the Greek sense that it is intended for production at a religious ceremony and has to maintain a high seriousness in its subjects. Through tragedy the Athenians expressed the universal aspects of problems which concerned and perplexed them. Though their themes are nearly always taken from a remote, mythical past, that does not prevent them from being highly contemporary. For instance, in the three plays of his *Oresteia* Aeschylus tells a terrible story of murder and vengeance, of a woman who kills her husband and of a son who has to kill his mother. But though all the horror and excitement of the old story is preserved with a remarkable power, the end comes with all the force of a new discovery. The son, Orestes, is in the end purified of blood-guilt by a law-court, which is none other than the high court of Athens. The introduction of this into the plot reflects a deep social change, of which Aeschylus was fully conscious, from domestic vendetta to the rule of law. The splendid and exalted poetry which closes the third play conveys in an imaginative and compelling form what law means to a people like the Athenians and is appropriately associated with the guardian goddess, Athene. It was by such means that Athenian dramatists presented their understanding of political events and of the great issues which lay behind them. The audience, trained to listening to tragedy and able to follow its methods, would see what the dramatist meant and come away all the prouder of the institutions of its city.

Tragedy provided something else than this, a kind of national self-examination and inquiry into the universal aspects of its actions. Though it is dangerous to read any reference to passing events in the plays of Sophocles, there is no doubt that he was keenly interested in them and knew of them from the inside, since he was a friend of Pericles and even held office with him as a general in 440 B.C. His method is to take some universal problem and to present it in vivid drama with a full sense of its human and moral implications. Above all he seems to have been much concerned with the whole question of power, its motives, its means, and its dangers. In an age of growing imperialism, he was well aware of its character and consequences and did not shrink from a dramatic analysis of its exponents. His *Ajax* turns on the conflict between the old heroic individualism and the new claims of civic power to obedience and respect; his *Antigone* on the discord between the immutable laws of the gods, which lay certain inescapable obligations upon men, and the harsh decrees of a tyrant who is too infatuated with power to know what evil he is doing; *King Oedipus* on the great man, who through no real fault of his own, none the less falls from high position to utter misery because the gods decree that he must; *Electra* on a state of human affairs in which law has ceased to work, and men and women have to undertake ugly duties against which their consciences may rebel but which cannot be shirked. Each play presents in a different shape some issue of power and its limits. The implicit criticism of it is penetrating and deeply disturbing. If Creon in the *Antigone* is a poor thing with delusions of grandeur, Oedipus is a magnificent creature, a true shepherd of his people, who none the less falls disastrously. In two of his last plays, *Philoctetes* and *Oedipus at Colonus*, Sophocles portrays in Odysseus and Creon even more advanced cases of the moral insensibility which power breeds in its victims. His conclusions are unanswerable. Power is fraught with dangers not merely to a man's happiness but to his soul. In its very nature it conceals corruptions of which a man must beware, and the typically Greek conclusion is that he is wise to remember that he is as nothing before the gods. These conclusions are all the more remarkable because Sophocles himself knew about power and office from the inside. But in his art he revealed his real feelings about them. If he stressed the need for moderation and the doctrine of the Mean, it was not because he saw them practised around him but because he felt that something of the kind was vitally necessary if his countrymen were not to destroy themselves by attempting too much.

Unlike tragedy in most ways and yet like it in its criticism of life is Attic comedy, itself also a Dionysiac rite, which with reckless fancy and complete candour approached contemporary questions without any attempt to disguise them in mythical dress. The Attic comedians thought nothing of presenting living characters on the stage or of putting them in the most ridiculous positions. Since the greatest age of comedy seems to have come with Aristophanes in the last twenty or so years of the Athenian empire, it is surprising how vigorous and outspoken it is, how in a time of growing violence it speaks for liberty and peace and common sense. Its dazzling jokes and fantastic situations are in their own way as pertinent a criticism of life as the grave conclusion of the tragedians. It works with different weapons, and of course we cannot always be sure how seriously to take it, but its results are often deadly. If Aristophanes' chief butts are the inferior statesmen who came to power after the death of Pericles, he does not altogether spare Pericles himself, and his whole outlook is a comment, by no means favourable, on Periclean ideals. For him imperial power was hostile to the grace and sweetness of life, and he used his whole armoury of nonsense to press his point home. He believed in Athens with a deep love, but the Athens of his dreams was a quiet, rural town, the home of farmers and small traders, of simple pleasures and graceful decorum. If he accepted facts as he was sometimes compelled to, he was ready with wise and far-seeing suggestions, as when in the *Lysistrata* he urged with powerful eloquence that the empire should be turned into a confederacy of equal states. He was certainly popular, not merely for his jokes; he may well have represented a solid body of public opinion which was frightened of the way taken by events. No doubt, too, he awoke great hostility, but despite a fine or two he was allowed to say what he liked, and until its collapse Athens submitted yearly to this merciless criticism of its favourite personalities and approved designs.

A city which could allow itself to be criticised in such ways both by tragedy and comedy had an uncommon share of self-confidence and of respect for the truth, and we need ask for no further proof of the extraordinary spirit which carried Athens through her great adventures to her final doom. Yet we may perhaps ask on what ultimate scheme of beliefs this confidence was based, what religious or metaphysical foundation it had. Though it is hard for us to recapture what the Greeks felt about their gods, no consideration of Athens is complete without some attempt to do so. Perhaps we might say that their greatest, most honoured gods were powers of the spirit, forces which they felt at work in themselves but which, not without logic, they believed to exist outside themselves with an independent divine being. Just as Athene was both the adventurous spirit who inspired her subjects and a real power who guided and guarded them, so Dionysus, the god of intoxication, was both the inspiration which poets know in themselves and something even more incalculable which works in the world. Though the essence of such gods was their power, they were not beyond good and evil, and moralists and poets agree that in the end they punish the wicked. None the less there remained something more frightening about them. Being in the last resort beyond understanding, they cannot be explained by human rules of behaviour or expected to conform to common morality. They may always, without warning or apparent motive, punish or destroy, and a man's task is to be humble and hope to avoid their wrath. Like the sea they allure and amaze and call to action, but also like the sea they are liable to swift changes of mood and often bring death where they seem to have promised success. Greek politics and Greek life were played against this background of glorious, menacing, inscrutable gods. A man might try to resemble them, and even perhaps for a moment succeed, but in the end he was sure to fall. Behind all the reckless activities and the high ambitions of the fifth century lies this uncertainty, and it imparts an almost tragic grandeur to the actors who perform their heroic parts with a full knowledge of what they will cost.

On the other hand these ancient and half instinctive beliefs were countered by a searching spirit of inquiry. Just as Greek art and poetry owe much of their indestructible strength to the hard intellectual labour which has gone into them, so in Greek life there was no lack of hard and vigorous thought. How grand this might be can be seen from the searching pages of Thucydides with their appalling insight into the unchanging ways of political man. Yet we may be sure that he was not alone, that any politician who wished to have his way in public life had to some degree to rely on reasoned argument. The release of Athenian energy meant an enormous impetus for the intelligence, and this process was strengthened by the conditions of life which encouraged talk and forced decisions to be made. When this spirit was combined with the old religious faith, the result was not so precarious as we might expect. Indeed, until late in the fifth century the spirit of inquiry served to clarify and give point to much that was already accepted from tradition. In this period Athens was at her greatest. Just as she was able to infuse an aristocratic elegance into a democratic frame, so she was also able to fortify an ancient religion with serious speculations about the worth of man and his place before the gods. In the last years, when victory receded into the distance and self-confidence ebbed, it may be true that this happy balance was shaken and that questions became more deadly and more destructive. The spirit of Euripides and Socrates was perhaps too strong for a war-worn people to accept without danger to itself, and it is not surprising that it turned against both. Most great civilizations fail in the end from the defects of their virtues, and Athens failed mainly from the superabundance of that energy which had made it great but partly from placing too great a trust in the intelligence, which turned from the clarifying of great issues to undermining their assumptions. Before these processes were completed, Athens found an equilibrium which allowed the whole human being to work in harmony with itself and to discover the full range of its powers. If in this it made mistakes, they are as nothing in comparison with its successes or with the example and inspiration which these still are for us.

Rome under the Antonines

2ND CENTURY A.D.

JÉRÔME CARCOPINO

IN the first two-thirds of the second century of the Christian era, Rome was at the height of her greatness and her prosperity. The pulse of an empire beat in her heart: an empire then at its greatest extent, enjoying an atmosphere of unparalleled serenity and a vitality that drew effortlessly upon the wealth of her provinces and her vassal kingdoms. Both the rich and the poor in the countries that she ruled or protected looked towards her and accepted her sway: the former with the object of confirming their ascendancy; the latter in order to attain the standard of living to which she had raised her own proletariat. Virgil had long since lauded her as the city that dominated all others just as the lofty cypress overtops the rowans.

> *Verum haec tantum alias inter caput extulit urbes*
> *Quantum lenta solent inter viburna cupressi.*

Now she was established as *Urbs Orbis*: *Urbs*—the city of cities —capital of the world—glowing with a beauty that through the genius of her rulers was a reflection of the perfect beauty of the heavenly sphere—*orbis*. She had herself become the goddess whom Martial invoked as "Goddess of continents and nations, Rome, whom nothing equals and nothing rivals."

> *Terrarum dea gentiumque, Roma,*
> *Cui par est nihil et nihil secundum.*

A century earlier Augustus had put an end to civil war but

29

had lost the legions of Varus; a century later, Rome was to tremble before barbarian invasions; but in the second century of our era she enjoyed freedom from fear.

Trajan had enriched her with fresh conquests and fruitful spheres of influence: Dacia, Arabia, Mesopotamia. His successors, Hadrian (117–138) and Antoninus Pius (138–161), avoided the necessity of waging glorious but exhausting campaigns by relying on the strength of their defences, the wisdom of their administration, and the skill of their diplomacy. Their military activity was limited to reviews and manoeuvres and more or less summary police action against local insurrections in remote provinces—Cyrenaica, Judaea and Mauretania. During their reigns Rome enjoyed the most profound and lasting peace that she had ever known: civil peace, social peace, peace at home and abroad. It was the golden age of her history.

*

It was a clear sign of Rome's prosperity and of her magnetic attraction that she has hardly ever been more populous. During the last century of the Republic (150–50 B.C.) the population of the *urbs* had grown slowly and steadily from 322,000 in 147 B.C. to 463,000 in 85 B.C. and to 486,000 in 57 B.C. Since then the increase had become so rapid that in the second century there were more than a million inhabitants. The figure is only approximate, for St. Jerome's vital statistics come to an end too soon to state it exactly; but there can be no question but that the figure is of this order. It is confirmed alike by the topographical measurements of G. Lugli, the consumption of rationed corn studied by Oates, and the lists of houses which I have myself investigated.

In population alone Rome was three or four times the size of the capital cities of Asia and Africa that most nearly approached her: Alexandria, Carthage and Antioch, and was thus comparable with the cities of today. The latest census of Buenos Aires, Rio de Janeiro, Berlin, Paris, Moscow, New York or

London may record two, three, four, or eight times as many inhabitants as Rome held in the age of the Antonines, but a hundred years ago none of these cities was more populous than she was in the second century.

An increasing influx of inhabitants drove the Roman architects, as it has ours, to find, in the words of Vitruvius, "an answer to over-population in the height of their buildings". We too often think of the houses of Rome in terms of the villas of Pompeii or of the House of Augustus (called that of Livia) on the Palatine. These are horizontally developed with state apartments and reception rooms, *atrium*, *triclinium*, and *tablinum*. The glorified villas built on the Esquiline or the Pincian in the middle of large grounds that in their turn enshrined gardens as exquisite and varied as those of Japan, exemplify the *domus*, the private house that offered a measure of isolation to a single family. In the time of the Antonines such houses could no longer be built, except for princes and the great men of the court, who were wealthy enough not to care how much land they occupied. Few men were still rich enough to be so wasteful of space. The very name of *domus* was now used to dignify the best flat on the ground floor of an apartment house, or *insula*, in which the owner of the whole only occupied a single floor and let the rest. In the fourth-century lists of the wards of the city there are only 1,797 private houses as against 46,602 blocks of flats, and this striking preponderance is certainly much older than the drawing up of the relatively late documents which reveal it. Whereas the *domus* was an exception, especially in the recently developed quarters, the *insula* was everywhere the rule. As more and more apartment houses were built, so was their height increased. The ruins of Roman houses at the foot of the Capitol, near the *Porta Tiburtina*, under the Palatine along the *Via nova*, above all in the little suburban town of Ostia, fifteen miles from Rome, redeveloped under Hadrian, all show that they had once two or three or more stories. Such a block as the *insula Felicles* was a veritable skyscraper; its enormous size had won it universal fame by the end

of the second century, and made Tertullian as giddy as the
ascension into heaven of the false angels of the Valentinian
heresy would have done. The ruling powers were conscious of
the danger and the want of elegance of such inordinately tall
buildings. An edict of Trajan strengthened previous legislation
by setting a limit of sixty feet to the height of private buildings.
It goes without saying that cupidity impelled the builders to
accept this maximum as a minimum, very much as the architects of Paris did fifty years ago.

It was another sign of prosperity that these buildings were
resplendent with luxurious decoration. Mosaic floors were a
commonplace, some with geometrical designs (*opus tessellatum*),
others depicting flowers, animals, men, and gods (*opus vermicula-
tum*), forming a gay and glittering pattern in the white ground,
or glowing richly from one of black, as in the house of the Via
dei Cerchi. The houses were solidly built, sometimes of blocks
of ashlar, tufa, or trevertine (*opus quadratum*), most often with
baked brick (*opus latericium*) laid in regular courses to link and
define with their red stripes the no less regular sections of
lozenged brown tufa (*opus reticulatum*). The exterior was sometimes coated with fine-grained white roughcast (*opus tectorium*)
or faced with thin sheets of marble (*opus sectile marmoreum*), but
such additions were not essential, and it was not long before
brickwork itself was decoratively exploited, in the same fashion
as it was later to be in the Versailles of Louis XIII.

The inside walls were covered with delicate stucco work or
with frescoes, either of landscape in Alexandrian style, of scenes
of ordinary life, or of mythological subjects, all treated with
considerable freedom of movement and charm of colour,
whether they adorned a commonplace house like that which lies
below the Church of SS. *Giovanni e Paolo* or in the successive
domus, transitoria and *aurea*, of the extravagant Nero.

The splendid furnishings were in harmony with the decoration of the rooms they adorned. Furniture, however, was
relatively scanty. The Romans, influenced by the customs of
the conquered east, preferred to recline rather than to sit, even

at meals, and left benches and stools to inns and workrooms and shops. The use of high-backed chairs was the privilege of ruler or judge at his official work, of priests at their rites, and of teachers lecturing *ex cathedra*. Apart from these, their use was the mark of scholars such as the younger Pliny, who liked to give a professorial air to their casual conversation, and of a few affected great ladies who loved comfort.

Large tables were little used; chests, *guéridons*, variously mounted shelves, and tripods took their place. The most important pieces of furniture were beds: little single day-beds which were found everywhere; double marriage-beds for bedrooms; and dining-beds for three people (*triclinia*). The finest were made of sculptured bronze or rare woods, for example thuya inlaid with shell and ivory; and on them and round them was scattered a profusion of covers and carpets and quilts and cushions and hangings and screens of a kind that can be reconstructed from the finds at Herculaneum.

The table-services were magnificent. Even lesser men would have been ashamed not to eat off silver, and the rich had their plate parcel-gilt or set with precious stones. Poor men made do with pottery and truckle beds in the miserable attics for which they paid 500 *denarii* a year, a twentieth or thirtieth part of the rent of the *piano nobile*.

*

All the same the poor men of Antonine Rome grumbled less about their lot than do their successors in England or France today. For one thing, a depressing lodging is more easily borne in a sunny country, in which the tenant passes the brightest hours out of doors; for another, the fourteen districts of the *urbs* did not offer that sharp contrast between working-class and wealthy districts which may be seen in modern capitals, and there was the same kind of accidental egalitarianism in the Rome of the Caesars as there was later to be in the Rome of the Popes, with wretched apartment houses and magnificent palaces built next door to each other, and millionaires and men of modest means living on different floors under the same roof. Furthermore, and more significantly, the poor men of Antonine Rome endured a poverty less harsh than that of today, for the very poorest could always escape into the aristocratic peace of parks and gardens, or to the Roman countryside.

Though Roman houses equalled those of our own day in height and size, they were set without formal alignment along streets as narrow and winding as those of the Middle Ages. Under an edict of Julius Caesar that was still in force, carriages were forbidden to use these streets by day, since it was found that there was not room in them both for wheeled vehicles and pedestrians. Even the disastrous fire of A.D. 64 had not given the town-planners space enough to provide their metropolis with the regularity and ease of communications which Hippodamos of Miletus had been able to bestow on Piraeus and Thurii as early as the fifth century B.C. The planners succeeded in imposing their plans only on such limited sites as Ostia, where it seems that Apollodorus of Damascus, or at least one of his imitators, was at work at the time when Hadrian decided to build it anew.

The Roman planners were therefore reduced to dealing indirectly with their problem; but they succeeded, if not in solving it, at least in making it less acute. They prevented the increase of winding streets and bottle-necked lanes, the dark entanglement of *viae* and *vici*, though they could not altogether transform them. They devoted their ingenuity to seeing that they did not spread their tentacles over empty spaces, they surrounded them with open esplanades, and intersected them by wide avenues of light and air. They beautified the *Campus Martius*, from which dwellings were excluded. They maintained the gardens with which great men had surrounded their private houses, and which, one after another, had been incorporated into the imperial demesne and opened to the public. Thus it was that Antonine Rome offered at first sight the contrast between the red of tiles and bricks, the white of marble, and the greenery which dotted and surrounded the built-up areas. The occurrence of these "green belts" was indeed most striking. On the Esquiline the gardens of Maecenas were continued in those of Aelius Lamia, of Statilius Taurus, of Pallas, and of Epaphroditus. In Trastevere the gardens of Julius Caesar lay beside those of Mark Antony. On the Vatican the gardens of Nero adjoined those of Domitia. On the Pincian there was no boundary between those of the Pincii, the Anicii, the Acilii, which the financial administration had taken over together with the *horti* of Lucullus, and—perhaps the most beautiful of all— the *horti Sallustiani*. The presence of these gardens at the centre as at the periphery of the *urbs* gave it a double aspect. There were two Romes in one: a Rome that was still involved in its ancient past, archaic and inchoate, stifled and twisted, deafened at night by the rattle of chariots, besieged during the day by an army of busy walkers, casual Praetorians, and rough muleteers and by haughty and aristocratic litters borne on the shoulders of eight porters—a Rome of which the hubbub and colour and stench and crowds and hurly-burly can only now be seen in some Eastern souk or in the Medina of Fez; and another Rome, which the emperors had tried to purge and modernize, which encroached upon and surrounded the first with its *horti*—airy, peaceful and verdurous as the squares and parks of London.

Nor was this all. The Romans of the second century were the proud possessors of sanitary arrangements of which the inconvenience and the rudimentary efficiency would make us, now, smile or groan; but to them they seemed new and wonderful.

To escape from the constriction of their alleys, they multiplied the many kinds of balconies that projected from their long façades, and pierced their walls with windows of which the size astonishes the modern visitor to Ostia. The spectator forgets that, in default of transparent glass, the Romans covered these wide openings with curtains or shutters which not only protected the rooms from curiosity, rain, and cold, but also shut out daylight. At night oil-lamps (*lucernae*), candelabra, and wax candles (*cerei*) were equally inefficient in lighting town houses.

Those who went out after dark lighted their path with the lanterns they carried, like villagers going to a midnight Mass; and this black-out encouraged highwaymen and gangsters of every sort and kind. The imperial administration did its best to suppress them, and redoubled the activity of the police. Thus Hadrian enforced the beats walked by the watchmen—*vigiles*—with unexpected inspections by his secret police.

The Caesars of the second century occupied themselves not only with the security of their capital, but also with its sanitation. They kept up the magnificent network of sewers that Agrippa had established under the city, first on the line of the ancient *cloaca maxima* from the Capitol to the Velabrum, then on the cross-line from the Circus Maximus, and finally from the Pincian to the Pons Fabricius. Since their engineers could only apply their sewage system to the ground floors of the houses it served, they supplemented it for those who lived in the upper floors by the construction of numerous public conveniences, promiscuous enough, but furnished with marble seats, and—to judge by the remains of those near the *forum Julium*—with suitable heating systems.

Moreover they completed the provision of spring water to a Rome that still enchants us by the melodious murmur of her innumerable fountains. Trajan alone raised the daily output of the *Anio Novus* to 177,000 cubic metres, and built the aqueduct for Trastevere that still bears his name and feeds the roaring cascades of the Aqua Paola on the Janiculum. This cool, pure water, which spouted in the public squares and at the cross-roads, was not carried to the upper floors of the houses, and the benefit of running water—like that of main drainage and central heating—was economically reserved for the inhabitants of the ground-floor apartments. The Romans of the second century tried to counter the cold not by building chimneys (which came into use later, and only in the northern provinces of their empire) but by installing under their floors the heating system which C. Sergius Orata had invented fifty years before Christ. A furnace was built, to take a fire of faggots and dry weeds,

PLATE 5

THE ARCH OF TITUS AND THE COLOSSEUM
Erected A.D. 81 and 70–82 respectively

PLATE 6

PROCESSION IN HONOUR OF ISIS
Relief from a marble Sarcophagus, 170 A.D.

SOLDIERS RECEIVING RELEASE
Marble relief, middle of 1st century B.C.

ROMAN DRAPERS SHOP : SELLING CUSHIONS AND STOLES
Marble relief, middle of 1st century B.C.

which sent its heat, smoke, and soot between the piers of brick
on which the pavement rested and up the conduits made in the
lower walls. This rudimentary central heating, however, was
confined to the basement and to the rooms immediately above
it. The ordinary Roman who lived in a flat on the upper floors
not only had to go into the street to use the nearest public
latrine and to buy his drinking water from the water sellers
under his window (as indeed the citizens of Paris did under
Louis-Philippe and Napoleon), but had also to face a cold
(which, it must be admitted, was rarely severe) with the sole
aid of smoky and unhealthy braziers, and to cook his stew over
a chafing-dish. He could console himself for these incon-
veniences, to which centuries of habit had inured him, by the
good smell of the excellent food with which he was provided by
the foresight and generosity of his emperor.

*

Never, indeed, had so many people been comfortably off in
a city in which even poverty had lost its sting. Peace, of which
the atmosphere is as necessary to a healthy economy as fresh air
is to healthy breathing, seemed eternally assured. Trajan's last
great conquest, that of Dacia in 107, had enabled him to divert
to Rome a stream of Pactolus in the form of gold from Transylvania and treasure from the vanquished. At one blow the
emperor found himself master of milliards of sesterces, which
permitted him to rain down plenty on a world that had never
before known such abundance. A series of measures, easily
financed by a treasury that commanded what seemed an in-
exhaustible source of wealth, benefited every part of the empire
and especially its mistress, Rome. Trajan was able to diminish
taxation and to increase the national income. By recoining the
aurei, making them of a fixed weight, and establishing a constant
relation between the respective values of gold, silver, and copper
coins, he was able to cut out large monetary inflation for two
generations, and to arm the Romans with the monetary stability,

5

at least of silver, that is the best weapon against speculation and rising costs of living. Then, since he had an enormous quantity of cash at his command, he could, disinterestedly but without sacrifice, provisionally renounce those dues of which the temporary suspension would attract labourers to the parts of his domains that were lying fallow or neglected, who would exploit them and ultimately give back to him a part of their harvest. Further, he invested large sums in loans which he granted to the landed proprietors of Italy who were short of capital: loans which were in fact hidden subsidies of agriculture. Finally, he dedicated yet larger sums to great undertakings likely to stimulate production because they offered producers an easy market for their goods.

New roads were constructed in Italy, Asia, and Africa, with a view to facilitating the intercontinental trade, which the restrictive conditions of the traditional way of harnessing draught horses limited to an average of 500 kilograms a cartload. New harbours were built, for instance at Ancona and Centumcellae (Cività Vecchia), or repaired, as at Brindisi and Terracina, or deepened and enlarged, as at Ostia, to encourage on all the sea routes of the Mediterranean a trade of which the speed and tonnage may fairly be compared with those of seventeen centuries later, before the invention of steamships. Hadrian brought back into use the warehouses or *horrea* in the suburbs of Rome and outside Ostia, where foodstuffs were stored on the banks of the Tiber; and in the very heart of Rome, at the junction of Quirinal and Capitol, beside his forum and his basilica, Trajan erected his five-storied central markets for the sale and distribution of food. The excavations of 1932 have shown how impressive was their lay-out and how harmonious their proportion.

One would have said that the imperial machine was geared only to soften the material conditions of life and that the emperor had no other duty than the amelioration of the human lot. So, indeed, declared the ministers of Hadrian, with rather pompous flattery, in a resolution of which I discovered the text in Tunisia forty-six years ago: "*Caesar pro infatigabili sua cura, per quam adsidue humanis utilitatibus excubat.*" Thus the interests of the masters of the world were identified with those of their subjects. The provinces furnished Rome with the fruit of their earth and their labours; and Rome, by giving them riches in return, linked them to the general prosperity. The "Corporation Square" at Ostia, of which the plan and decoration date from this time, bears witness to this wonderful collaboration. In the middle rise the ruins of the temple of Annona Auguste, the *Annona Sancta* of the Roman people: that is, the deified provision of the people of Rome with food. The terrace that surrounds it is closed to the south by the back wall of the stage of the theatre and on the other three sides by sixty-one rooms each about sixteen metres square, with a portico before each and a mosaic floor which shows by its figures and inscriptions to which corporation the room belonged. Each one of these professional associations had a direct part to play in the service of Annona: ship-builders of Carthage, Alexandria, Cagliari, Narbonne, and Mauretania; fullers of cloth, ropemakers, skinners, timber merchants, inspectors of weights and measures, and the rest. As one treads the pavement used by these merchants and sailors and craftsmen, one seems to see them sailing and rowing in from all the shores of the Mediterranean to meet the needs of the mother city and to shower upon her the products of their countries; and looking at the mosaics on which their corporations have proudly set their canting badges, one realizes that their burdens were lightened by their fidelity to Annona Auguste, and that the satisfaction they felt in serving the needs of Rome partook of a religious enthusiasm.

It was thanks to such corporations as these that Rome enjoyed regular imports of corn from Africa and Egypt, of wine from the Greek Islands, of oil from Spain, of hams from Gaul, of peaches from Persia, lemons from Media, plums from Damascus, dates from the oases, silphium from Cyrene; of spices from the Far East that reached her from India by the caravan route through newly-conquered Arabia and vassal

Palmyra, or directly by sea from the depths of the Persian Gulf by the Ptolemaic ports of the Red Sea, Myos Hormos and Berenike, each now with its garrison of legionaries. There was so much trade in ginger and cinnamon and pepper at this time, when the armies of Trajan had reached as far as the Shatt el Arab, that a whole floor of Trajan's market was assigned to it. Long afterwards, when the market had been given up and its halls used for other purposes, the medieval tenements of the street still bore the name of Via Biberatica, a clear deformation of Via Piperatica, the Pepper Street of ancient Rome.

Archaeological and literary evidence combine to indicate the delicacies that the ingenuity of gourmets invented at this time, and the junketings which the masses were every day invited to enjoy. No citizen of Rome need then die of hunger. As M. Denis Van Berchem has recently shown, the entire urban proletariat—that is to say all Romans who were neither senators nor knights—were listed on the rolls of the Public Assistance Board, which gave them the right not only to draw every month a free ration of five pecks or *modii* of corn, but also permitted them on festival occasions, in which the emperor wished his people to share, to draw cash gratuities—75 *denarii* in 99 and 102; 500 *denarii* in 107; 800 under Antoninus Pius, 850 under Marcus Aurelius—which were so many windfalls and gave them some of the feelings of the workman who has won the big prize in the pools. On the other hand the emperor, whose immense fortune spread its tentacles everywhere, and whose tithes from provincial taxpayers filled the warehouses, could at any moment control current prices by his monopolies and effectively oppose any increase in the price of food. The lofts and cellars of Rome overflowed with provisions and wine was cheap.

This fact, far more than the presence of impressive police forces—Praetorian Guards, *vigiles*, city cohorts—explains the civic order which in the second century reigned in the overcrowded city, and the maintenance of untroubled peace in spite of devastating social inequalities. At the bottom of the ladder were the slaves whom their masters had fallen into the habit of paying, and who saved, *sestertius* by *sestertius*, the money to purchase their freedom. Then came the *plebs*, citizens with little or no capital, living from hand to mouth, but with no cause to take thought for the morrow, since victuals were cheap and each and all could count on the free issue of rations and on the uncovenanted mercies of gratuitous *congiaria*. Above the *plebs* came the two orders of chivalry: first the *bourgeoisie* of the Equestrian Order, and above them the nobility of the Senatorial Order. The burgess rights of the knight could only be obtained by those who owned at least 400,000 *sesterces*. Promotion to the nobility presupposed an annual income of a million *sesterces*; but this was merely an administrative minimum and senators thought themselves only moderately well off if, like the younger Pliny, they left only twenty millions. Finally, far above even the most fortunate nobles, there sat in superhuman glory the golden majesty of the emperor, the multi-millionaire on whom the revenues of the treasury, his immense properties—farms, mines, quarries, brickworks, factories scattered through Italy and the provinces—not to mention his overlordship of the land of Egypt, conferred the prestige of an incomparable way of living and an almost unlimited sphere of action.

It is frightening to see the vast social perspective that stretched between him and the poor men of the *plebs* and the domestic slaves; and as if there were not classes enough for him to dominate, in the first half of the second century the emperor introduced yet more divisions into society. While the *honestiores*, who owned at least a clerkship or else a property, came to be distinguished more and more clearly among the plebeians from the *humiliores* who had not so much, Hadrian detached from the bulk of the knightly class—who were content to call themselves men of distinction, *viri egregii*—an *élite* of men eligible for the prefecture to whom he granted the title of *viri perfectissimi*; and a yet higher class, from which he drew the commanders of his guard, the highest officers of his general staff, who received the title of eminence, *viri eminentissimi*: a title that passed from them to the cardinals of the Roman Church.

Yet in spite of these social divisions which divided them more drastically into classes than before, the citizens of Rome lived together on an admirably friendly footing. There was no sedition among the proletariat, there were no revolts among the slaves. The slaves, indeed, were treated more humanely than they had been in the past. Both Hadrian and Antoninus forbade their masters, under severe penalties, from prostituting or mutilating them or from putting them to death; and Arrian, a senator who was governor of Cappadocia between 131 and 137, had no hesitation in publishing his conversations with Epictetus, a former slave from Phrygia, who had made himself the greatest teacher of his time of Stoic asceticism. The emperors commonly allowed freedmen entry to public careers and the right to wear the gold ring that marked them as knights. Slaves and freedmen could elbow free men as brothers in the sanctuaries where social distinctions were forgotten, at the Corporate feasts, in the religious and funeral guilds, as in the college of Diana and Antoninus at Lanuvium in 133.

It was a happy time, indeed, when it was possible to create more class divisions without giving rise to class conflict; when the inequalities among men became more and more apparent, and yet seemed to offend their victims less and less. The egalitarianism of the masses found satisfaction in the fact that all classes were equally subject to the benevolent despotism of the emperor, and that he had driven real misery away even from the humblest homes. When every man's larder is full, there is little reason to become cannibal. The American workman in his car does not worry because he has not a collection of Old Masters, and the Romans of the second century were released from envy and hatred by their sense of well-being. Their daily bread was assured by the free monthly ration; their pocket money by the hope of the next *congiarium*; they had no grievances; they could, if they were ambitious, hope to escape from their happy mediocrity by effort and thrift, yet they were not overburdened by the necessity of hard work; and the generosity of their ruler provided ample amusement for their leisure hours.

*

It would be a great mistake, in my opinion, to take too seriously Rostovstev's epigram that imperial Rome was a city of *rentiers* since she held within her walls 400,000 people who received the free issue of corn. It would be as true to assume that the millions of people covered by Health and Unemployment Insurance in London and New York and Paris spent their lives with their arms idly folded. Rome, in fact, in the second century was a city humming with activity, with the business of her merchants, the trade of her shops, and the work of her craftsmen. The vastness of her population ensured constant activity in victualling, clothing, and housing them. In a classic book Waltzing has listed all the corporations necessary to her life: guilds of those who had to build or repair the houses; of the bakers, pastrycooks, confectioners, butchers, fishmongers, vintners, and wine merchants; of those who dressed and shod and washed and scented the citizens; of boatmen, hauliers, drivers, vanmen, and porters. Moreover her pre-eminent position as mistress of the world brought within her walls the offices of the central government, the Bullion Exchange that regulated the money market, and the supreme courts that judged the most important or the most delicate cases. In consequence there were vast numbers of civil servants, bankers, money-changers, lawyers, law-clerks, and scribes. Finally, her wonted luxury, which set a standard for all other great cities, was maintained by a host of decorative industries, in textiles, fine woods, ivory, and jewels. The Romans were thus far from idle; and with a little energy and *savoir-vivre* a man could save enough for the slave to purchase his emancipation, the freedman to push his clever sons into the knightly order or the civil service, the knight to gain senatorial rank. The time was as yet distant when military reverses would affect the recruitment of slaves, and first slow and then stop this social climbing. The sky was still clear, and seemed to promise a future even more brilliant than a present that was already eminently satisfactory for anyone willing to work.

Industry was already organized in such a way that although very different from that of our own day, it made even the hardest kind of labour bearable. While our own aim is to give equal opportunities to both sexes, the Romans permitted women only exceptionally to enter professions other than those indicated for them by decency or aptitude—as that of dress-maker (*sarcinatrix*), hairdresser (*ornatrix*), midwife (*obstetrix*) and wet-nurse (*nutrix*). Apart from these, women in second-century Rome were seldom admitted to any profession. They did not go out to market; they stayed at home and occupied themselves with the ordering of their households and the comfort of their husbands—unless great riches, by freeing them of every material care, left them with nothing to do but to dress fashionably and amuse themselves.

Most modern nations have limited by law the number of working hours and working days in a week. The forty- or forty-eight-hour week, the week-end, and bank holiday, have become a part of our everyday life by enactment. By force of habit the Romans of the second century had achieved the same result. Apart from the Senate, whose members might be called upon to sit without respite from dawn to dusk, and apart from certain trades, such as those of the barbers, keepers of eating houses, warders of exhibitions, sports ground attendants, and the staff of the public baths, who were busiest when other men were at leisure, one may say that normally they worked every day; but that they only worked from dawn until about mid-day. After the fifth hour—which ended at ten-forty-five a.m. at the winter solstice and at eleven-fifteen a.m. at midsummer —the more easy-going employers let their workmen go. One of the parasites whom Martial satirizes comes to his host a little before he is asked; the sixth hour is not over, and it is not yet midday, but he has already on his way met a troop of slaves

whose master had let them go and who were heading for the
baths. In any case, after one o'clock in the afternoon there was
not a shopman that did not make ready to close his shutters,
nor a manufacturer that did not shut his gates. Martial, again,
is our informant: "Rome prolongs her activities until the fifth
hour; the sixth hour brings rest to the weary; the seventh is the
end for all."

In quintam varios extendit Roma labores
Sexta quies lassos septima finis erit.

Thus at a quarter-to-one in winter, and a quarter-past in
summer, work was over until the next morning in every section
of the city's economy. If one considers, as one should, the Roman
winter hour as equal to forty-five minutes, that implies that in
Martial's day, in the second century, the working day was seven
astronomical hours long in summer and less than six in winter.
The forty-hour week was ordinarily only worked in winter, but
in every season the twenty-four-hour day included seventeen or
eighteen of complete liberty. Indeed citizens enjoyed so many
hours of leisure that they would not have known what to do
with them if the injunctions of the calendar and the generosities
of the ruling powers had not helped to fill the void. The calendar still transmitted the traditions of an older paganism, at
least in its feasts, and lengthened as their list was by the addition
of new festivals in honour of the imperial cult, it ended by
indicating a festival every two days.

The government, through the munificence of the emperors
and the highest officers of state, met the greater part of the cost
that these endless holidays entailed. There were religious feasts
for every taste. Some recalled the peasant origins of the great
city, like the fishing competition of the 8 June that was linked
with the ancient cults of Vulcan and the Tiber; others of the
kind were the sack races of the *Robigalia* on 25 August, the foot
races and mule races of the *Consualia* on 21 August and 15
December; the horse races of the *equus october* on 15 October,
and the *ludi martiales* on 1 August. Since the end of the first

century the gaieties of Saturnalia, when slaves might joke
with their masters if not against them, and eat at their table
and even make them wait upon their own servants, had
been extended over a whole week, from the 17 to the 25
December.

There were two series of *ludi*—the official games, pageants
and chariot races, which had been established by the devotion
of the pious in the last centuries of the Caesars in honour of the
imperial divinity or to commemorate their victories; they now
lasted for six, seven, thirteen, or fifteen consecutive days. Furthermore there were the sporadic and frequent *munera*, combats
between gladiators which horrify us now but which were then
shockingly popular. Under Trajan they once lasted un-
interruptedly for a hundred and seventeen days, from 7 July
to 1 November 109; in these three months four thousand nine
hundred and twelve pairs of gladiators spilt their blood to
satisfy the cruel frenzy of pitiless crowds of spectators.

On the days when there were no state-supported spectacles,
the Romans could find other pastimes: guild meetings, ward
festivals held round the shrines of the Lares at cross-roads; and
a host of more individual amusements. Connoisseurs could
dawdle round the exhibitions of works of art in the Campus
Martius; the intelligentsia could attend public lectures, or
ensconce themselves in one of the two libraries, one Greek and
one Latin, that Trajan had established by his triumphal
column; the pleasure seekers could haunt the *cauponae* of more
or less dubious reputation or pub-crawl round the bars of the
thermopolia; the lazy could loiter under the porticoes and in the
basilicas whose pavements still show the wear from their tread,
and the marks of draught-boards and shuffle-boards that they
traced upon them. Finally men of every social class could meet
and every taste be satisfied in the monumental baths which the
emperors designed as real people's palaces. Entry to them was
free or nominal (the quarter of a brass *as*) and every pastime
and recreation was to be found under their roof: swimming
pools and Turkish baths, gymnasia, walks under covered

porticoes, bars and restaurants in their annexes, and even libraries and a museum of works of art.

It is noteworthy that the use of leisure was governed by the Roman working day, in which a free afternoon followed on a morning's labour. Two examples will suffice to show this. If the *munera* sometimes lasted all day, the programme was planned as if their organizers were anxious to hide the more shameful exhibitions from the great crowds. The most horrible items, when naked men and women and girls were thrown to the wild beasts, or men fought a fight that was no fight but simply the massacre of an unarmed man by a gladiator armed to the teeth, who in the next round was the unarmed man, were of set purpose staged in the morning hours when ordinary men were at work. They were played to empty benches, or rather to benches that held only a few sadists and psychotics drawn from their *dolce far niente* by the scent of blood, as the dregs of our population used to be drawn to a place of execution. The *munus* itself only began after midday, and comprised equally matched combats between gladiators in which victory, and life with it, went to the strongest and bravest. It might end with the *venatio* that, to judge by Roman inscriptions, crowned the proceedings not only in Rome but also at Alba Fucens in the Abruzzi, at Pisaurum on the Adriatic, and at Pompeii: a lively battle in which gladiators with lassos, boar-spears, and swords, fought with bulls and wild beasts and re-enacted for the spectators the excitement and noble traditions of the chase. Thus the majority of the onlookers saw only the sporting half of the *munus*; the shameless and abject turns were unseen by the multitude.

This tendency to adapt the times of amusements to the leisure hours of workers is still more evident in the police regulations established by Hadrian for the public baths. For the first time, to translate literally the phrase of his biographer, he divided the baths according to sex: "*lavacra, pro sexibus, separavit*". The division was made not by any partition of space, but by a separation of time. At Rome the sixth and seventh hours were reserved for women, who, having little employment outside their homes, could come at any hour. The eighth and subsequent hours were kept for men, of whom the busiest would only be free after the seventh hour.

The emperors were in a particularly strong position to regulate their subjects' employment of leisure, since they met the cost. To have some idea of their prodigality in this respect, it is enough to consider some of the most impressive ruins in Rome. Of the Circus Maximus, where a hundred and fifty thousand spectators could view the chariot races, nothing remains but the outline of its immense ellipse; it was rebuilt after the fire of 64, and was only finished forty years later, under Trajan. The theatre of Marcellus, however, restored at the end of the first century, still stands in the imposing symmetry of its travertine arches and the monumental variety of the three orders of its columns. If we can forget the nature of the spectacles that it witnessed, the Colosseum itself must fill us with admiration for its size, the honest solidity of its building, and the perfection of its plan. Finally, though the colossal mass of the baths of Caracalla (211–217) did not rise between the Appian Way and the Aventine until after the second century had elapsed, the reign of Trajan yet saw the erection of the baths that bore his name on the site of the Domus Aurea—baths adorned with such sculptures as the *Laocoön*—and of those called after his most intimate friend, the vice-emperor, Licinius Sura. The baths of Agrippa, which had been destroyed in the fire of 80, were rebuilt, enlarged, and beautified, under Hadrian.

These varied constructions, destined only for the pastimes of the people, cost many millions, and their magnificence sheds a significant light on the importance attached to leisure by imperial policy. Juvenal might well grow indignant that his contemporaries no longer felt strongly about anything but bread and circuses:

> . . . *duas tantum res anxius optet*
> *panem et circenses.*

Less than a century later, the senator, Dio Cassius, far from

sharing in the poet's indignation, was to honour the memory of
Trajan for the skill which he had shown in exploiting the strongest forces at the emperor's disposal. "The wisdom of Trajan",
he declared, "never failed to pay attention to the stars of stage,
circus, and arena. He well knew that the excellence of a government is shown as clearly in its anxious watch over amusements
as in its dealings with serious matters, and that even if the distribution of coin and money satisfy the individual, there must
also be spectacles to satisfy the people as a whole." Dictators,
indeed, whatever the ideology of their absolutism, are bound to
come to the demagogic view that, after bread, amusement is a
people's first need. The French revolutionary, Danton, was to
declare that it was education; and it was because they had not
given enough heed to this salutary truth, because they had been
too timid in fulfilling the educative mission that under their
system of government was incumbent on the ruler, that the
Caesars of the second century allowed an intellectual rust to
spread over their age of gold, which was ultimately to cause its
decay.

*

We must not, however, exaggerate. Without question the
tensions of a mixed population, the inequality of fortunes, the
rapidity with which some men became rich, the insolence of a
luxury that was on the way to becoming dissolute, the temptations to idleness, debauchery, and wastefulness which were
inherent in the distribution of *congiaria*, the baseness and
savagery of some of the spectacles enjoyed by crowded
audiences, created conditions that were favourable to a
negligent *laisser-aller*, to selfishness and the propagation of vice
rather than to the virtues in which had lain the strength of
Rome: virtues which should have endured to justify Roman
supremacy for a long time to come. Yet, in spite of these causes
of internal decline, the greater part of the population remained
healthy-minded, and even if the Caesars of the second century
did not effect the drastic reforms which the changing climate of

society and the implications of their conquests demanded, they none the less tried to prevent by legislation and example the lowering of the standards of feeling and thinking which, if it was not checked, might bring about the collapse of the empire.

The Antonines—the brute Commodus alone excepted—were better men than their predecessors. With a slight modification of Albertini's striking phrase, I would say that they brought into being the best world which was possible in antiquity. Coming of provincial stock—Gaulish in Antoninus, Spanish in the others—they brought to their accession a wider political vision, extending to the farthest limits of the *orbis romanus*, and a fresher energy, derived from a family unspoilt by the hereditary enjoyment of supreme power. They had a high conception of their functions, the higher because none of them had been born to the purple; and all of them, even those who were in later generations predestined to the throne by birth, seemed to attain sovereignty by their merit alone. Antoninus, surnamed Pius, was a man of wisdom; Marcus Aurelius, who was called Antoninus the Philosopher, was a saint. Trajan was granted by popular acclaim the title of *Optimus*, "the Best", and the surname was voted to him by the Senate. Trajan, Hadrian, Marcus Aurelius—the first two with cheerful optimism, the third with serene resignation—all endured without flinching the rough life of the camp, sleeping in tents, eating the same stew and fat bacon, drinking the same sour wine as their soldiers, indifferent to danger, which in time of peace they sought in the chase. People might whisper that Trajan drank too much, but it must be admitted that he hid his weakness remarkably well, and that he used to astonish the guests whom he liked to invite to his castle of Centumcellae by the frugality of his table and the general dignity of his manners. As to Hadrian, his biographer accuses him of many adulteries, and he was cynic enough to try to transfer the empire to his favourite bastard; but to mask his intention, he never called his son anything but *Verus*, "the True"; he did not reveal his purpose until his wife, Sabina, was dead, and he did not fail in her lifetime to shower upon her the outward marks of the deepest respect, whether at court or on the journeys they undertook together; punishing remorselessly any allusion to their domestic differences, and brutally disgracing his official historian, Suetonius, for a want of consideration to the empress. Even when they did not practise it, the Antonines always preached virtue.

Moreover they tried to make their subjects virtuous. So far as lay in their power, they tried to purify the use of the leisure accorded by their princely generosity. The regulations for the baths made by Hadrian re-established decency, their enlargement helped to develop sports and physical culture. If the *ludi scaenici* had degenerated to a point when tragedy and comedy were the exception and the usual level of programme was that of the music-hall, Trajan, although he himself enjoyed variety turns, none the less tried to restrain indecency, especially in the actors' gestures, by forbidding certain sorts of pantomime. Inscriptions scattered as far afield as Leptis Magna show that there existed at Rome an imperial *Conservatoire* for the training of mimes: one might almost say an imperial School of Ballet. As to gladiatorial combats, Marcus Aurelius had the courage to discourage their shameful popularity, and not only set a ceiling cost to municipal *munera*, but also wished to substitute harmless representations, *lusiones*, for the homicidal duels fashionable in Rome.

These various reforms prove that the Antonines, even if they did not find the solution of the problem, had at least given attention to the education of the masses.

With them the Roman state for the first time came to the aid of unfortunate children. Ever since the principate of Nerva (96–98), in spite of the financial difficulties of a treasury exhausted by the wild extravagances of Domitian, grants— *alimenta*—had been made towards the maintenance of young children, boys and girls, legitimate and illegitimate. By an ingenious system of compensatory transfers Trajan collected the money from the interest on the loans he had made to landowners to help them to clear land and increase its production.

In their turn Hadrian and Marcus Aurelius increased the amount of the *alimenta*. If none of these emperors went so far as to proscribe the abandonment of babies, an ineffaceable stain on the societies of antiquity, at least they tried to mitigate its results. One of them, Hadrian, became an enthusiast for the kind of enlightenment that the eighteenth century called "*la diffusion des lumières*". A skilled man of letters, himself an occasional poet in Greek as well as Latin, with a tireless curiosity, this remarkable emperor, who enjoyed the pleasures of learned controversy with grammarians, geometers, rhetoricians, and philosophers such as Favorinus—his favourite companion in argument—organized in Rome a system of higher education. It was based on the rudimentary beginnings that Vespasian had instituted forty-five years before, for the benefit of Quintilian. Hadrian showered benefits on the professors, whose lectures he supervised in person; if he judged them not to be up to their work he sent them home, laden with riches and honour. Although his biographer is silent on the subject, he was no less interested in elementary schools. We have a decisive proof of this interest in the fact that when his procurators had to draw up regulations for the various professions to be allowed to settle in a mining district of Lusitania that belonged to him, the only person they exempted from tax in the town of Vipasca was the schoolmaster: "*ludi magistros immunis esse placet*". Elementary education might not yet be compulsory and free, but it was already general even in the depths of the remoter provinces because of its cheapness and the encouragement given to teachers.

There is thus no cause for surprise in the fact that in the second century education was more widespread than ever before. For a long time illiteracy had been identified with barbarism in Rome and the Italian cities, and those who could not read or write were an insignificant minority. At the end of the second century such men were only to be found in backward provinces. Quintilian only came across them among the village boors: "*rusticus illitteratusque*". In a fashionable town like Pompeii every

PLATE 7

TRAJAN
Roman Emperor, A.D. 98–117

HADRIAN
Roman Emperor, A.D. 117–138

ANTONINUS PIUS
Roman Emperor, A.D. 138–161

MARCUS AURELIUS
Roman Emperor, A.D. 161–180

PLATE 8

MARCUS AURELIUS OFFERING A SACRIFICE IN A MILITARY CAMP
Relief of the first century A.D. Later transferred to the Arch of Constantine

one could read and write, which is the reason why its walls are covered with a rash of electoral posters and *graffiti*. In the second century even slaves were literate; those of Lanuvium were able to collaborate in the drawing up of the statutes of their guild. It was not rare to discover humble servants in the households of great men, who had pursued their studies beyond the level of the elementary school: men such as the freedman mentioned in a conceit of the younger Pliny's, who not only knew his letters but was even literate: "*libertus est mihi non illiteratus*". Most men of some standing, engaged in the civil service of either half of a bilingual empire, knew Greek as well as Latin, and prided themselves on their knowledge to a point when out of intellectual snobbery they would choose to listen at Rome to the lecture of a man speaking in Greek. Favorinus, a Gallo-Roman born at Arles, was in the habit of lecturing in Greek; and Lucian, a Greek of Samosate, collected a fortune on his lecture tours in the west. May not this progressive hellenization even have been one of the causes of the decline of Latin literature? Who would wish to cultivate the mother tongue when even the emperor disdained the language of his ancestors, and Marcus Aurelius drew up the spiritual testament which he bequeathed to posterity in Greek?

In the first half of the second century Greek had not yet won this pre-eminence. Already, however, the literary inflation that derives from a passion for public lectures was visible. Soon the seeking after effect and applause, inseparable from these performances before a *cénacle*, of which every member is familiar with the author's personality, corrupted the general taste with preciosity and artifice, and an avalanche of petty and conventional talent overwhelmed the spontaneous creative power of the greater men. In about the year A.D. 120, however, there was a happy change for the better, and the glory of Rome was uplifted in poetry by the epic furies of Juvenal and in prose by the genius—the most pictorial and the most modern of antiquity—of Tacitus.

In the sphere of morals it would be a mistake to take the

6

epigrams and satires of the time literally. They show us the wrong side of the tapestry in a distorting mirror. The structure of society still held firm, and the level of morals was such that their bitterest censors were best-sellers. Naturally there were in Rome gangsters and spivs, gluttons and drunkards, pimps and debauchees, pederasts and lesbians. But the Romans of the old school tried to believe that these unfortunate specimens of humanity were usually of exotic origin, and the indignation they directed against them testifies as much to their innate decency as to their xenophobia. In fact, Stoic austerity had never more adherents than at this time. Not so long before, under the Flavians, it had been persecuted; now it was admitted both privately and publicly in court. The opposition had been converted into its supporters. Trajan used the homilies of Dio of Prusa both to oppose sedition among his legions and to support his own bold agrarian policy. According to the *Historia Augusta*, Hadrian enjoyed the conversations of Epictetus. Finally Marcus Aurelius, himself an adept, preached the Stoic doctrine; and the alliance with his dynasty of a school of philosophy of which he had become the propagandist explains both the ascendancy of the Antonines over their contemporaries and their prestige in history.

At the same time as this lofty philosophy was fashionable a new religious fervour did much to uplift men's hearts and minds. The devout were no longer satisfied with abstract deities, mechanically performed rituals, and fossilized creeds. They tried to introduce into the state religion the aspirations of their spiritual life, the spontaneity of their private prayers, and the force of their hopes of an after-life; and when their attempts failed they turned away from the dry formalism of the official cults and sought spiritual food elsewhere. Most of them were initiated into the oriental mysteries which, for all their irregular and orgiastic side, were not lacking in spirituality; they became the devotees of gods who were not local and impassive, but divinities of universal power, undergoing suffering and rebirth, jealous and protecting, capable of balancing the merits of

a man in this world against the rewards due to him in the world
to come. Already a few of them lent ear to the evangel that
reached them, in Greek, from Aramaic Palestine: the gospel
that had circulated freely in Rome ever since Trajan, initiating
a rule of religious toleration that was to survive until the end
of the century, had forbidden the persecution of the followers
of Christ and declared he wished only to punish those who
offered them provocation. The Church of Christ the Saviour,
the Son of the Only God, was thenceforward established in the
city. The catacombs where the Christians honoured their dead,
the halls in private houses where they celebrated their
Eucharists, were filled with unheard-of promises of peace and
love; and a Christianity hardly yet born illumined the golden
age of Rome with its dayspring.

Only a century later the Romans saw their property ravaged,
their creations ruined, and the evils which they had thought to
have suppressed for ever once more coming to life: *coups
d'état*, insurrections, secessions, plagues, famines, defeats in the
east, invasions in the west. Their material advantages were born
of effort, and they had allowed themselves to relax. The moral
progress that at first had accompanied these advantages had
lost its highest inspiration, that spirit of abnegation and that
collective will to action, without which societies, numbed into
an insidious inaction, and states, undermined by widespread
selfishness, are disarmed by the fear of making sacrifices, and
are soon, for all their brilliant appearance, no more than
majestic idols with feet of clay.

Christian Constantinople

10TH–11TH CENTURY

STEVEN RUNCIMAN

As the Roman empire passed into decadence, harassed by barbarian invaders from over the frontiers and worried by constitutional and economic problems beyond the understanding of its government, the city of Rome became unsuited to be the imperial capital. It was far from the border-lands where the emperors now spent most of their days; it was placed in an impoverished province, away from the sea, and all its food had to be imported; it was the home of the senatorial families, with their traditional dislike of the autocracy, and of the Praetorian Guard, with its ambition to make and unmake emperors. Few of the third-century emperors had resided there for long; and at the end of the century Diocletian planned definitely to move the seat of government to the east, nearer to the Asiatic frontier, where the rival power of Persia provided a perpetual menace, and the Danube frontier, along which the threat of barbarian invasion seemed most urgent. His choice of Nicomedia, at the eastern extremity of the Sea of Marmora, was ephemeral; but the greatest of his successors, Constantine, revived the plan. Constantine is one of the most important statesmen in history. It is due to his work that the Roman empire was able to survive the collapse of the west. He reformed the administration. His monetary policy gave the empire a currency that kept its value for more than seven centuries. His conversion and his recognition of Christianity provided a spiritual binding-force for the Roman world. And he founded

PLATE 9

THE EMPEROR JUSTINIAN, A.D. 527—565
Byzantine mosaic, 6th century

PLATE 10

CHRIST ENTHRONED, MARY, THE ARCHANGEL GABRIEL AND THE
KNEELING EMPEROR LEO VI (886—912)
Mosaic tympanum over the main entrance of the Hagia Sophia

THE CISTERNA BASILICA
The most important of the covered cisterns in Constantinople built by
the Emperor Justinian

a great city to be the capital of the new Christian empire, the city still commonly called after him: Constantinople.

The site was chosen with care. Constantine had considered the sentimental claims of his birthplace, Nish, and the romantic claims of Troy before his choice fell upon the old Greek colony of Byzantium. Byzantium was set at the end of a small peninsula on the European coast, where the narrow strait of the Bosphorus comes out into the Sea of Marmora. The peninsula was triangular, with curved sides. The twelfth-century French chronicler, Odo of Déols, compared it to a three-cornered sail bellying in the wind. At the eastern end its apex curved northwards, looking up the Bosphorus towards the Black Sea. The southern shore, along the Marmora, was convex at first, then slanted south-west. The concave northern shore ran along a splendid bay known to the Greeks and their Turkish successors from its shape as the Horn, and to the west from its riches as the Golden Horn. Along the peninsula there were, as at Rome, seven hills; and on these seven hills Constantine built the city that he named New Rome.

It was a superb situation, quite apart from its natural beauty. It commanded the easiest land-route from Europe into Asia and the sea-passage between the Black Sea and the Mediterranean. The huge land-locked harbour of the Golden Horn could accommodate a vast armada; and if sailing ships had difficulty in rounding the point into the harbour against the prevalent north wind and the currents of the Bosphorus, there were snug little anchorages along the southern shore. The wooded hills outside the city were well endowed with springs, and the neighbouring provinces, Thrace in Europe and Bithynia across in Asia, were rich in corn-fields and pasture-lands. The site was easy to defend, with its two longer sides protected by the sea. Only on the third were strong fortifications required.

The town of Byzantium was swallowed up in the new capital. Constantine's land-wall that was to limit the city left the Golden Horn about a mile and a half west of the apex of the

city and curved in a generous arc to reach the Marmora nearly
a mile farther west. At the apex, on the old Acropolis of
Byzantium, he built a citadel to be the main arsenal of the
empire. Just to the south, on the site of the chief pagan temples
of the old town, he laid the foundations of a church dedicated
to Hagia Sophia, the Holy Wisdom of God. Sloping down from
Hagia Sophia to the Marmora was the area reserved for the
imperial palace, the residence of the emperors and the seat of
the government. It was bounded on the west by the Hippodrome, enlarged from the old Hippodrome of Byzantium,
built by the Emperor Severus, to suit the needs of a capital.
From the palace gate the main street of the city, the Mese or
Middle Street, ran westward, through the Forum of Constantine, where his statue looked down from a tall column on
his city, and the later Forum of Theodosius. Just before it
reached Constantine's land-wall it passed the second great
Christian shrine founded by Constantine, the Church of the
Holy Apostles, which was to be the mausoleum of the Christian
emperors.

To fill his city, Constantine encouraged immigration from all
parts of the empire. Before his death large numbers of noblemen, merchants, and artisans, had gathered there, to be near to
the imperial court. Constantine's immediate successors seldom
lived at the new capital, but the immigration continued; and
when the emperors of the Theodosian dynasty definitely
established themselves there, it became apparent that the
founder had miscalculated. Early in the fifth century, during
the minority of the Emperor Theodosius II, the regent, the
Prefect Anthemius, built a new line of land-walls, about a mile
to the west of the walls of Constantine, so as to include within
the city an area over half as large as Constantine's original area,
in order to provide room for the growing population. Apart
from a slight extension at the northern end, these walls marked
the official limits of the city throughout the Byzantine period.

History soon justified the foundation of the new capital. After
the death of Theodosius I in 395 the empire was divided into

two halves; and not many decades passed before the western half disintegrated. There were various reasons for its collapse and the survival of the eastern half, but one of the most useful assets of the east was this prosperous and impregnable administrative centre. There was nothing to compare with it in the west.

During the reign of Justinian, in the mid-sixth century, the population of Constantinople rose to be about a million. Plague later in the century may have caused a temporary reduction; but it never fell far below the million-mark till the Frankish capture of the city in 1204. Justinian himself greatly embellished his capital, especially after the great fire that accompanied the riots of 532. To his builders we owe the present structure of Hagia Sophia, as well as the Church of the Holy Apostles that survived till the Ottoman conquest and served as a model for St. Mark's at Venice. The disasters of the seventh century, the long Persian war and the subsequent loss of Syria and Egypt to the Arabs, helped rather than hindered the growth of the city, in spite of anxious moments during its siege first by the Persians then twice by the Arabs. The great rival metropoles of Alexandria and Antioch passed into infidel hands and declined in prosperity; while refugees from the lost provinces crowded to seek safety in the capital. There was a certain economic depression till the middle of the ninth century, when both political security returned and foreign trade improved. Thenceforward for three and a half centuries Constantinople was without doubt the greatest city in Christendom and probably the richest city in the world.

It was her riches, even more than her size, that impressed the medieval traveller, whether he came from the east or from the west. Indeed, the Christian westerner found the civilization of Constantinople, the civilization known in history as Byzantine, stranger to him than did the Moslem from the east; for the Arabs, like the Byzantines, had retained the urban civilization of the Roman empire and were accustomed to great cities, whereas western Europe in the early Middle Ages followed a

self-sufficient rural economy, and its cities were small provincial market-towns. The accounts that survive of western
travellers who visited the great capital all show a regard that is
sometimes envious, sometimes frankly hostile, but always awe-
struck. During the late tenth and early eleventh centuries,
when Byzantine civilization was at its zenith, there were many
such travellers; for the pilgrimage to Jerusalem was now
highly popular, and Constantinople lay on the route.

During the tenth century the wealthy pilgrim from the west
usually went to Venice and there took a ship; for by the end
of the century Venetian ships had the monopoly of the mail
services from west to east and were regularly used to convey
official visitors. But travel by land was cheaper, and many
pilgrims rode or walked to southern Italy, to Naples or Amalfi,
or, to shorten the sea-passage, to Bari, the capital of the
Byzantine province. From all these ports there were frequent
sailings to Constantinople. It was cheaper still to cross the
Adriatic from Bari to Durazzo and thence to follow the Via
Egnatia, the great Roman road that ran across Macedonia to
Thessalonica and on through Thrace to the capital. But this
journey necessitated a passage through Bulgarian territory and
was impracticable if the empire and Bulgaria were at war.
It was only after Basil II, the Bulgar-Slayer, had reconquered
the whole Balkan peninsula, in the second decade of the eleventh
century, that roads in the Balkans were safe. Thenceforward it
was possible to travel by land for the whole journey, through
Croatia or Hungary to the imperial frontier at Belgrade and
on by an excellent road through Sofia, Philippopolis, and
Adrianople to the Bosphorus. Whether he came from Durazzo
or Belgrade, the land-traveller followed the coast of the Marmora for the last lap of his journey. From Rhegium onwards,
some fifteen miles from the city, he passed through a succession
of suburbs, mostly fishing-villages, smartened by villas and
hunting-boxes belonging to the aristocracy. At last the huge
walls of the city appeared, first a foss that could be flooded in
times of siege, then a lower wall, and behind it the high wall of

Anthemius with its crenellations and its regularly-spaced towers. The road led straight up to the Golden Gate, the ceremonial entrance to the city, made of honey-coloured marble and ornamented with sculpture and with plaques of bronze. After entering through the gate the traveller followed the Triumphal Way of the Emperors, which passed through the busy quarters by the Marmora to join the Middle Street about a mile from the imperial palace.

The traveller by sea, unless he were a crowned head and could disembark at the private harbour of the palace, did not make such an impressive entry into the city; but he was compensated by the superb view of Constantinople rising out of the sea. The skyline was not, as now, interrupted by tapering minarets; it was lower, but more congruous. It was dominated on the right by the great dome of Hagia Sophia, with the walls of the citadel behind and in front the varied domes and roofs of the imperial palace. To the left the high curved end of the Hippodrome towered over the Church of St. Sergius and St. Bacchus, and beyond there were other domes on the skyline, and houses covering the slopes down to the walls that ran along the sea-front. Trees and patches of garden appeared in between the buildings, which stretched away for nearly four miles south-westward to the towers of the land-walls and to the suburbs beyond. Across the Bosphorus on the right were the large suburbs of Chrysopolis and Chalcedon, and a series of villages, with churches and monasteries and palaces, and the lighthouse at Hierum jutting out in front of them. The Princes' Islands rose on the starboard beam, and behind in the distance were the snow-peaks of Bithynian Olympus, famed in Byzantine days for its many holy monks. The ship had already been stopped at Abydos, on the Hellespont, to be cleared by the imperial customs. Now she could sail freely up the Sea of Marmora. If the wind were kindly or if she had sufficient rowers on board, she would move on round the eastern tip of the city, under the Acropolis, and turn the corner into the Golden Horn, through the narrows where the suburb of Galata on the north bank comes closest to the city. It was here that in times of siege a great chain was stretched across the entrance into the harbour. The ship would fetch up eventually opposite one of the quays that lay with their warehouses on the foreshore between the water and the city wall. If a northerly gale was blowing—and the chief disadvantage of the Constantinopolitan climate is the prevalence of a bitter north wind, blowing down the funnel of the Bosphorus from the Black Sea and the steppes of Russia— then the ship would not attempt to round the point, but would use one of the anchorages on the southern shore, probably in the harbour of Eleutherius, where the valley of the Lycus debouched into the sea.

When he had entered the city the pilgrim had to find himself accommodation in one of the hostels reserved for the use of foreigners. To facilitate police control, the Byzantine authorities liked a visitor to inhabit quarters definitely assigned to people of his same provenance. Russian merchants, for instance, were lodged in specially reserved houses in the suburb of Saint Mamas, just outside the walls; and if they were registered traders they did not have to pay for their lodging and were in addition allowed one bath a week free of charge. In the eleventh century pilgrims from the west usually stayed in a great inn known as the Hospice of Samson, in the heart of the city, not far from the site still occupied by the Great Bazaar. The management of the hostelry apparently had to report the visitor's arrival to the police; but, so long as he behaved himself, he was otherwise left unmolested during his visit.

To the Christian pilgrim the main attraction of Constantinople lay in its tremendous collections of Christian relics. The most famous were kept in the chapels attached to the imperial palace; and piety as well as a natural curiosity would make a visit to the palace the chief objective of the pilgrimage. If he made a friend amongst the palace officials such a visit was easily achieved; but it seems that there were also occasional escorted tours for humbler pilgrims. To reach the palace the pilgrim passed down the Middle Street through the arcade of the

Golden Milestone into the great square of the Augusteum. Opposite him, on the east side of the square, was the low but dignified building of the Senate House. On the north towered Hagia Sophia. In the centre of the square was a great column surmounted by an equestrian statue of the Emperor Justinian and other statues stood round the sides of the open space. On the south the main entrance to the Hippodrome abutted on to the Golden Milestone, while on the square itself was the Great Gate of the Palace, with a huge icon of Christ set amongst polychrome marbles over the entrance.

The palace area was surrounded by a strong wall and carefully guarded. For whoever held the palace held Constantinople and the empire. Within this area there was not one large single building, like a royal palace of today, but a series of halls and pavilions, dwelling-houses and baths, churches and libraries, offices and barracks, a prison and a textile factory, all set amongst gardens and orchards, with shady streams and lakelets, and terraces skilfully laid out to catch the sunshine and the view. The palace was not only the residence of the emperors; it was the seat of the imperial secretariat and the chief ministries of state. The treasure of the empire was kept in its vaults, from which was extracted the salary of every imperial official. Down on the eastern slopes was the factory where women operatives wove the famous imperial brocades destined for the ceremonial wear of the court and occasionally as gifts to specially favoured foreign potentates. The visitor passed first through the vestibule of the Chalce, built by Justinian. Long arcades permitted him to go on under shelter to the other ceremonial halls. There was the Chrysotriclinium, a throne-room lined with gold mosaic, built by the Emperor Justin II. There was the later throne-room of the Triconchus, built in the ninth century by Theophilus and modelled on the fashionable architecture of Baghdad. It was here, now, that foreign envoys were received in audience, with all the fantastic accompaniments that Byzantine ingenuity could devise. While the ambassador bowed down before the Presence, his forehead touching the ground, the

throne would slowly rise, and he would lift his eyes again to
find the emperor seated high above him; and at the same
moment the golden lions that flanked the throne would roar
and wave their tails, and the jewelled birds that sat on the gold
and silver trees round the chamber would open their beaks and
sing. Round the Triconchus, set in formal gardens, were some
elegant pavilions where the emperor could receive his friends
informally. Official banquets took place usually in the halls of
the Caenurgium, the palace built by Basil I close to the
Thrysotriclinium. For their actual residence the emperors preferred buildings farther down the slope towards the Marmora,
where their official suites were grouped round a series of courts.
There, too, was the Gynaeceum, the buildings reserved for the
empress and her ladies. There the empress was complete
mistress, and no man, except eunuchs, could enter without her
express permission. But neither she nor the ladies of the court
led the secluded lives of Moslem women. They emerged as
frequently as they wished, to take part in the court ceremonies or
to pay visits to the outside world. But the emperor and empress
usually preferred to inhabit some quieter villa within the palace
precincts. In the later tenth century Nicephorus Phocas refitted
the small but magnificently decorated palace which is sometimes called the House of Justinian, on the edge of the sea,
for the use of himself and his empress, Theophano; and there
it was, on a December night in 969, that she brought in her
lover to murder him. Beside this palace was the imperial
harbour of Bucoleon, so named from the statue of a bull
fighting a lion that stood on the harbour wall. Here the
emperor and empress would land when they crossed the straits
from Asia, and here a few favoured foreign potentates were
allowed to disembark. There were many chapels and oratories
dotted about within the palace area. The largest and most
recent was the New Basilica, built by Basil I, according to the
latest principles of Byzantine architecture; but the chapel that
attracted most attention stood on a hill behind the Bucoleon
next to a lighthouse that served to guide shipping round the

PLATE II

IVORY CONSULAR DIPTYCH, BYZANTINE 10th CENTURY
Carved on both leaves with the figure of Rufinus Gennadius Probus
Orestes, Consul of the East. He is seated on a curule, holding in one hand
the mappa circensis, in the other a sceptre. On either side of him stand
figures representing Rome and Constantinople. Above are busts of an
emperor and empress, thought to be Justinian and Theodora

PLATE 12

THE LID OF THE VEROLI CASKET, BYZANTINE 10th CENTURY
Ivory and bone carving showing the rape of Europa, Orpheus, centaurs
and a Bacchanalian dance. Alternate medallions of the border show
busts of a Byzantine empress

CASKET OF WOOD, BYZANTINE 10th CENTURY
Covered with bone and ivory plaques, representing huntsman with
trophies of the chase, and above, heads of emperors and empresses

point into the Bosphorus. In this shrine of Our Lady of the Lighthouse were kept the holiest relics of Christendom, the objects connected with the Passion of Our Lord. You could see the Crown of Thorns, the Lance, the Seamless Coat as well as the chief portion of the Wood of the Cross and a phial of the Holy Blood. Every pilgrim sought to pay worship here.

After emerging from the palace the visitor might cross the square into the Church of Hagia Sophia. This was the Cathedral of Constantinople, where the patriarch conducted the service on feast-days and where the emperor traditionally was crowned. This huge edifice, built for Justinian by Anthemius of Tralles and Isidore of Miletus, enclosing an open floor space, unrivalled for size till modern times, under a dome so delicately poised that, as Procopius said, you would think it suspended by golden chains from heaven, with splendid side-aisles and galleries, has never failed to impress all that see it. Now it has the chill of a museum; but the visitor of the late tenth century could see it at the height of its living glory. The columns were of porphyry and verde antique; the lower walls were covered with plaques of many-coloured marble. Above them was gold mosaic, patterned with grey and blue. Great figure-mosaics shone in the apse and on the pendentives of the dome. The altar-screen was of marble and of gold, and the thrones of the emperor and the patriarch blazed with jewels. An earthquake in 989 caused a crack to appear in the dome. After its immediate repair, by an Armenian specialist, further figure-mosaics were added to increase the richness of the upper walls. It was all dazzling enough if you visited the shrine by day; but during the great services that took place after dark the effect was still more dazzling. In the bright, tremulous light of a thousand lamps and candles, with clouds of incense floating upwards, the mosaics glowed with a rhythm that was almost hypnotic. It was small wonder that the ambassadors of Vladimir of Russia believed that they had seen angels descending from the dome.

There were magnificent buildings round the cathedral. Its Baptistery shone with mosaics showing the life of John the Forerunner. The Patriarchal Palace was a splendid edifice, and behind were the rich churches of Saint Irene and the Virgin Chalcoprateia, the latter containing Our Lady's own girdle. Entrance to the Acropolis was doubtless forbidden to foreigners; but they might visit the Church of St. George nearby, to see the relics of the saint.

No visitor of enterprise would fail to attend a spectacle at the Hippodrome, to watch the chariot-races that were the chief entertainment of the people of the city. Forty thousand spectators could be contained within its walls; and on special holidays the emperor and empress in person witnessed the scene from the imperial box, where they were received with a tremendous formal ritual. The passionate quarrels between the circus-factions of the Blues and Greens, that in earlier centuries had often led to riot and bloodshed, had now been stilled; the factions only kept a formal entity for ceremonial purposes. The Hippodrome was also used after a triumphant war, to parade the prisoners that had been taken.

Starting from the Golden Milestone, the Middle Street led straight into the chief commercial quarters of the city. It followed the central ridge of the city, in a slight curve; for the Byzantines preferred to avoid straight streets that served as funnels for the wind; and it was lined with arcades, on to which opened the more important shops, arranged in groups according to their wares. Nearest to the palace were the goldsmiths and the silversmiths, and behind them, towards the Great Bazaar of modern times, was the building known as the House of Lights because its windows were lit up by night. This was the silk bazaar. After passing the imperial law-courts and the offices of the Prefect of the City you came to the Forum of Constantine and on to the clothiers' and the furniture-makers' shops. The bakers' market lay behind to the north; and the whole area down to the Golden Horn was mainly given over to commerce. The Middle Street led on to the huge Forum of

Theodosius and the Church of the Holy Apostles, where the bodies of past emperors and empresses lay in sarcophagi of porphyry and of basalt. As you moved farther towards the land-walls and the Charisian Gate, or down the Triumphal Way to the Golden Gate, the districts became less specialized and the city became, rather, a conglomeration of townships, each complete in itself and joined to its neighbours by orchards and gardens. In the valley of the little river Lycus, which flowed down from beyond the walls into the Sea of Marmora, there were even a few small corn-fields. But on the whole the gaps between the built-up areas were very small, till after the thirteenth century when the population began rapidly to decline.

There was no smart residential district. In every quarter palaces and monasteries, shops and slums had grown up side by side. The older houses of the rich were built in the Roman manner, two stories high, presenting a blank exterior and facing inward round a courtyard which was often roofed over and was usually adorned with a fountain. Later, three-storied palaces were built, to look outward over a terrace commanding one of the splendid views for which the city was renowned. Sometimes monasteries would be converted into palaces, or palaces into monasteries. The houses of the middle classes were built with their upper story jutting out over the street or else with balconies. They had almost all been built by private enterprise; but a law of the fifth century attempted to introduce some control. Where thoroughfares already in existence were less than twenty-two feet wide new buildings were not allowed windows for prospect but only gratings for ventilation. Side streets must be at least twelve feet wide, and balconies must not extend to within ten feet of the opposite wall. Outside stair-cases on the street were forbidden. This law remained in force throughout the history of the empire; but it was impossible to control the wooden shacks in which many of the poor were living. Drainage was carefully regulated. All the drains led into the sea; and no one but an imperial personage might be buried within the city. Water was brought to the city by magnificent aqueducts, of which most foreign visitors spoke with admiration; and it was stored in innumerable cisterns. There were big underground cisterns near the palace and the Acropolis and still larger open cisterns nearer to the walls. In addition, most monasteries and private houses had their own cisterns, which, it seems, could be filled in winter from the aqueducts. Even in times of siege the city was never short of water. There were many public baths, kept up by the munici- pality; and there were hospitals and orphanages attached to many of the monasteries. Such charters dealing with their foundation as survive show that careful attention was paid to hygiene. There was only one authorized brothel in the city, in the Zeugma quarter by the Golden Horn. It was marked by a statue of the pagan goddess Aphrodite.

In spite of all these regulations many of the poorer quarters, especially by the Golden Horn and in the districts towards the walls, were horribly filthy. In the tanners' quarter the stench was notorious, for the water used for tanning would be thrown out afterwards carelessly on to the street. Constantinople was a city of contrasts. The main streets, with their handsome build- ings and their arcades, the squares ornamented by memorial columns and many of the finest statues of antiquity, the well- kept public gardens and all the splendid public edifices gave little hint of the squalor of the poorer alleys behind. Even amongst the slums you would find some famous church. The pious pilgrim would certainly wish to visit the ancient monastery of Studium, in Psamathia towards the Golden Gate, to admire the Church of Saint John. Still more, he would hurry to see the Church of Our Lady of Blachernae, where was housed the por- trait of the Virgin painted by Saint Luke himself. It lay at the extremity of the city, where the land-walls came down to the Golden Horn; and nearby, right up against the wall, which they reconstructed for the purpose, the emperors of the twelfth century made themselves a new palace, smaller than the Great Palace but less diffuse and even richer in its decoration. The whole history of the empire was said to be depicted in its mosaics and frescoes. They were great huntsmen; and it suited them to be able, when the pressure of business was relaxed, to slip out through the walls to the countryside. To the earlier emperors, obliged to ride through four miles of city streets or else to take a boat to a suburban harbour, this recreation was impossible unless they moved with their household to some country seat; and it was seldom that they could take so long a holiday.

Even the various suburbs of the city were each of them comparable with a great town of the west. A bridge led across the Golden Horn near Blachernae to Pegae and Galata on the northern bank. Fishing-villages and market-gardens alternated with palaces and monasteries along both shores of the Bosphorus. The sheltered Asiatic coast of the Marmora was a favourite resort of the wealthy; and there, too, were grown early fruits and vegetables for the city markets. Small boats plied incessantly across the straits to bring passengers and goods to and fro. Though Baghdad and Cairo may each at times have held a larger population than Constantinople itself, there was nowhere in the medieval world so large a conglomeration of people as in the area round the imperial capital.

The interior of the houses was equally surprising to the pilgrim from the west. Furniture was finely carved and often encrusted with metal or mother-of-pearl, very different from the crude carpentry to which he was used. Instead of rushes on the floor he saw patterned marble or exquisitely-woven carpets; there were rugs even in the poorer houses. He was unused to window-panes of glass or of thinly-cut alabaster, or to curtains of brocade. Table and toilet utensils were mostly of metalware, though there were many factories making pottery.

Next to the size of the city and the splendour of its public buildings the visitor was struck by the diversity of human types that he saw in the streets. Its commercial activity made Constantinople a cosmopolitan centre. There were always foreign

7

merchants in the city. As you passed through the bazaars you
might meet a company of Russian traders, come to sell furs
and wax and slaves, wandering with a police escort—for one
could not trust such barbarians' behaviour—or you might see
Arab merchants treated with the deference that members of a
sister-civilization deserved; or slick Italians, from Venice or
Amalfi, fraternizing with the citizens but viewed always with a
certain suspicion. Occasionally you might come across a group
of Persians or slant-eyed men from Central Asia, or might
watch members of the small Jewish colony welcome co-
religionists from the Caspian or from Spain. In the main
streets you might at any moment be pushed aside to allow the
passage of some foreign ambassador and his train, come from
Egypt or from Germany to present his credentials to the
emperor; or it might be a vassal-prince from the Caucasus
riding by in state. And in his hostelry or at the sacred shrines
the pilgrim would almost always find some of his own com-
patriots.

To a traveller coming from lands where strangers were
seldom seen this international activity was particularly impressive; it was the aspect of Constantinopolitan life with which
he naturally came into contact and one which he could easily
appreciate. It was not so easy for him to understand the lives
of the citizens themselves. The wearisome and squalid lives of
the poor have always been much the same all the world over;
but to the medieval westerner, unused to the sight of urban
slums, the poverty that he could see in Constantinople seemed
more alien and shocking than it would appear to us. But the
lives of the bourgeoisie and the nobility were quite incomprehensible to him. At his home everyone wore woollen garments;
and the ladies and gentlemen of Constantinople in their silks
and linens seemed to him decadent and immoral. It was
distressingly effeminate, too, to eat your food with knives and
forks instead of the fingers given you by God for that purpose.
He could not sympathize on the one hand with the taste
for personal cleanliness or for intellectual discussions that

characterized the Byzantines, nor, on the other hand, with their deplorable delight in intrigue and in sharp business dealings. Even the magnificent Byzantine army did not display the qualities that he admired. Individual knightly prowess was discouraged there; for Byzantine strategists, like the best generals of today, believed in discipline and in only risking a battle when victory was assured. The various military disasters that had befallen the empire had almost all been due to some rash hero neglecting proper caution. Nor was the Church that the westerner found in Constantinople familiar to him. It used a language and a ritual different from his own. Priests, monks and nuns all wore strange clothes. To the more ignorant pilgrim it sometimes seemed questionable whether they were really Christians, and he resented their guardianship of so many sacred relics.

The Byzantines returned his contempt, and with better cause. They had inherited the old Greek arrogance towards the barbarian. But it was a cultural and not a racial feeling. The Byzantines themselves were of very diverse origins. Greek and Roman blood had long since been mixed with the blood of the indigenous stock of Asia Minor and the Balkans and was constantly enriched by the immigration of Armenians, Syrians and Slavs, Arabs and Turks, and even Franks from the west. Spaniards, Syrians, and Armenians had all reigned as emperors, and there had been empresses of Slav and Frankish and even Turkish descent. The bond was supplied by membership of the Orthodox Church and by the belief that every citizen belonged to the one true Christian empire, whose emperor was God's viceroy on earth. Had you asked a Byzantine what was his nationality he would have answered "Roman"; for he considered his empire to be the direct continuation of the supranational empire of Rome, hallowed by the adoption of the Christian faith. He even called the Greek language, which was now the official language of the empire, by the name of Roman or Romanic. Anyone who would conform to the Orthodox Church and admit the sovereignty of the emperor was welcomed within the empire, whatever his origin. The barbarians were the ignorant folk who would not conform; and for them the Byzantine felt no real friendship nor much regard, merely a certain curiosity. Of such foreigners he preferred the Moslem to the Frank; for Moslem civilization, despite its heterodox religion, had some resemblance to his own. He felt far more at home in Cairo or Baghdad than in the primitive little towns of the west. Yet for all his exclusiveness the Byzantine was very ready to adopt foreign fashions, so long as they could be moulded, like foreign immigrants, to fit into his way of life.

Byzantine life pivoted round the emperor. He was the autocrat, the source of law and the head of the Church. But he was not an irresponsible despot. Though he might make and amend laws, the Law was considered to be above him; he could not go against its principles. He might appoint the Patriarch; but the Patriarch represented a moral force that he could not defy with impunity. He was the crowned emperor; yet if he lost the favour of his subjects they had no hesitation in rioting to secure his fall. Tradition and public opinion alike limited his power. His job was no sinecure. He was in charge of the government; and much of his day was spent in administrative routine. On every feast-day there was some ceremony in which he played the leading rôle as representative of the Christian Commonwealth. He was commander-in-chief of the armed forces; and many emperors spent long months campaigning on the frontiers, governing the empire from their tents. At such times everything depended on the presence of loyal and efficient ministers at Constantinople; and it says much for the Byzantine civil service that there was so seldom trouble at home when the emperor was away at the wars. Other emperors, like the tenth-century Constantine VII, spent their spare time in literary activities, no doubt with the help of a host of secretaries. But an emperor bent on a life of pleasure seldom held the throne for long. There was no hereditary succession to the empire. Nominally the army, the Senate, and the People elected their ruler; but an emperor could co-opt a junior colleague, who on his death succeeded to the full power and who in the meantime could take over some of the ceremonial duties. A visitor to Constantinople about the year 1000 would probably never have seen the great warrior-Emperor Basil II in person. During his many absences, on the Bulgarian or the Armenian front, his place in the court ritual was taken by his younger brother, the co-Emperor Constantine VIII.

The empress led almost as busy a life. Part of the palace was under her control. She had large estates and revenues to manage, and innumerable ceremonies to perform. There were several highly efficient empresses-regent in Byzantine history, in complete control of the government. There had been already an empress-regnant, Irene, who fell from power more from her own ill-health than from incompetence or from any dislike of her sex. For a few months in the eleventh century the visitor would have seen the remarkable spectacle of two old ladies sitting side by side on the throne of the Caesars; and one of them died some years later as the sole depository of the imperial power. The empress was not necessarily the emperor's wife. She had to be specially crowned; and it was part of her imperial right that in the absence of a crowned emperor she could nominate a successor.

Round the emperor and empress were grouped the officials of the court, arranged in strict precedence. No title was acquired by birth, except that of Porphyrogennete, reserved for children of the empress born in the Purple Chamber of the Palace. Other members of the imperial family had specially to be appointed to their rank. Many of the titles were purely honorary but commanded a salary. They could be bought, and thus represented a form of gilt-edged security, very useful in the days before banking. The offices of state all had their traditional names. But the conception of the Byzantine civil hierarchy as a rigid, inelastic affair is wholly misleading. As in England old titles survived but were given new functions to suit the needs of the day. It provided an efficient machinery; and particular regard was paid to finance. The imperial treasury was in ultimate control. Except in certain unruly districts where the governors lived on the taxes that they managed to collect, the provincial administration was paid from Constantinople, though the governors were given wide administrative and military powers. But they were continually visited by inspectors from the capital.

The nobility was not, as in the feudal west, necessarily a hereditary affair. There were great families in Byzantium, though few arose before the late ninth century when at last it became safe to invest money in land. But throughout Byzantine history, as in eighteenth-century England, a successful financier or general, often of humble origin, might buy or be granted estates, and henceforward would take his place amongst the aristocracy. He might himself be despised if his accent was rough or his education deficient; but his sons and daughters, if they conformed in culture and manners, could mix and intermarry with the oldest families. It was not an idle aristocracy. Its members went into the army or the court or the civil service; they were not above commercial affairs. But almost all of them loved pomp and luxury and modelled their palaces on the emperor's. By the middle of the tenth century they were beginning to grow ominously powerful, particularly in the provinces.

The Church was drawn from all ranks of society. The parish priest was then, as now in Orthodox countries, a simple villager, only a little better educated than his parishioners; and he had to be a married man. But the regular clergy, from whom the ranks of the hierarchy were drawn, contained peasants' sons as well as noblemen's and merchants'. An imperial prince might be succeeded by the child of an artisan on the Patriarchal throne. The episcopate was open to all-comers, though influence certainly might be useful; and nearly all the great hierarchs of Byzantine history were men of character and high intellectual gifts. Their influence was tremendous; and though the emperor had the last word in any quarrel with the Patriarch, for he could convene and put pressure on the synod of Bishops, yet he would seldom go to such lengths unless he had a considerable backing from public opinion. Even more powerful than the Church hierarchy were the monasteries, who by gifts and legacies and good management had acquired enormous estates throughout the empire. Many emperors tried vainly to curb their power; for they represented a force of opinion that was not always helpful to the government, while the growing numbers of monks deprived it of many potential soldiers and cultivators. Yet the monasteries performed many useful tasks. They ran hospitals and orphanages, and they acted as alms-houses and homes for the aged. Thousands of men and women, rich and poor alike, would, when their active lives were over, retire to some monastic establishment where they could prepare themselves in peace for the hereafter, thus ridding their families or the state charities of the burden of their upkeep. The eastern monk's life is given more to prayer and less to work than the western; but the monasteries indulged in several useful intellectual labours. There were learned monastic authors, historians and biographers as well as theologians; and many manuscripts were copied and stored in their libraries.

The visitor would be struck by the high general level of education. Only the poorest classes were illiterate. The mother of the historian, Psellus, who belonged to the lower bourgeoisie, considered it a grievance that she had not been taught her letters adequately. She educated herself in later life in order to direct the studies of her brilliant young son. At that time—the very beginning of the eleventh century—illiteracy was rare in her class. In the wealthier classes boys and girls alike were given a sound general education, based on the *Trivium* and *Quadrivium* of Roman times, which included grammar, rhetoric and philosophy, arithmetic, geometry, music and astronomy. This education was given either by private tutors or in schools run by the Church. At this time, about the year 1000, the State University was in abeyance. The Emperor Basil II was an austere man who did not have much faith in the value of higher education. He would have agreed with the old soldier, Cecaumenus, who had served under him and who held that a study of the Scriptures and a little training in theoretical reasoning was all that anyone required. But the average Byzantine felt otherwise. He admired a cultured mind; he would be ashamed not to recognize a quotation from Homer or a reference to Plato's Dialogues. It was a matter of general satisfaction when the Emperor Constantine IX reopened the university in 1045, chiefly because the lack of authorized law-schools was damaging the quality of work in the law-courts. In particular the study of Latin had been neglected.

Soldiers were not much in evidence in the streets of the city. The visitor might notice the tall, magnificent Scandinavians who formed the Varangian Guard, attached to the emperor's person. But the main army was kept away from the capital, in barracks along the high roads of Thrace or Bithynia. The men could thence be more easily moved to the front; and meanwhile they were beyond the reach of scheming politicians in Constantinople. Each province also had its own local regiment. But the imperial fleet might be seen anchored in the Golden Horn, or, more usually, in one of the nearby Asiatic harbours.

The western visitor was sometimes surprised by the position of women in Byzantium. The women in the poorer and middle classes led much the same lives as their sisters in other lands, running their houses, bringing up their children, sewing for their families, and gossiping in the market-place. But the high-born lady of Constantinople seemed strange to him. She seldom emerged without a train of servants, and was probably carried in a litter. She wore a veil to protect her complexion, which anyhow was protected by a shockingly thick layer of cosmetics. Her clothes were usually of silk; her hair was braided with jewels. She had her own exclusive quarters in her house. She seemed at first sight as restricted as any Moslem lady and certainly quite incapable of supporting the hard, robust life led by a western noblewoman. But in fact, though fashion and convention required her to appear fragile and retiring, the

Byzantine lady moved freely in society and made her influence felt. She might never, like a western châtelaine, be called upon to defend her castle, unless, perhaps, she lived close to the frontier. War never came near her; and it was anyhow to the Byzantine an unpleasant job which was left to professional soldiers. Instead, she expended her energy on passionate political intrigue; and if her plots failed, her sex did not protect her from punishment. She was the heiress of the Roman empresses and the Hellenistic princesses, not a passive ornament in a harem. Or she might be a lady of letters; a poetess like Casia, whose pert repartee lost her an imperial husband, or a historian like Anna Comnena, herself an incorrigible intriguer. Or she might run a great business concern, like the widow, Danelis, who owned most of the western Peloponnese and would occasionally visit Constantinople with all the pomp due to a millionairess who had once befriended an emperor. There were women doctors to attend ladies who were too modest to endure attention from a man. There were even women saints; but they were rather rare. Yet, despite the luxury with which Byzantine ladies surrounded themselves, their private lives were not markedly immoral. They were so seldom left unattended that adultery could not pass unnoticed.

There were two aspects of life in Constantinople that the average westerner found definitely repugnant. First was the presence everywhere of eunuchs. Eunuchs had been introduced into Roman life by the Emperor Diocletian, in his desire to copy the ritual of the Persian court. Soon every great household had its eunuchs as servants who could wait upon the ladies without scandal. Eunuch secretaries and eunuch medical attendants appeared, and were equally appreciated by the ladies that they served. Before long the emperor began to find amongst the eunuchs his most faithful and useful ministers; for eunuchs had no children whom they sought to enrich, and a rigid convention kept them from aspiring to the imperial throne. There were eminent eunuch soldiers, like Justinian's great general, Narses; there were eunuch patriarchs, and innumerable

eunuchs amongst the high officers of state. In the tenth-century
tables of precedence the eunuchs figured at the head of each
titular category. Parents considered it no disgrace to castrate
one of their sons and so help him to advancement in the Household or in the civil service. But to western eyes these strange
creatures were unnatural and rather horrible; and later in
Byzantine history, when Occidental fashions grew more
popular, the eunuch became far rarer, to be reintroduced into
Constantinople by the Ottoman Turk.

The second repellent sight was the number of mutilated men
to be seen in the streets. Byzantine justice was on the whole
fair, but the punishment given to convicted criminals was
severe. The Byzantines disliked the death penalty. Though
murders were not infrequent, and though when the temper of
the crowd was roused human life was of little account, in their
calmer moments the Byzantines felt that it was wrong to kill.
Their strictest theologians even held that to slay an enemy in
battle was canonically murder, however patriotically desirable.
For political crimes such as treason the punishment was often
nothing worse than relegation to a monastery, where the
criminal could repent and save his soul far removed from the
temptations of active life. But, though there were prisons in
Constantinople, the authorities found it cheaper and simpler to
punish offenders by extracting fines or confiscating property;
and for the many criminals whose possessions were too few for
such punishment a rough system of mutilation was evolved.
Serious crimes were punished by the loss of sight or of the right
arm, lesser offences by the loss of an ear or by branding. The
maimed beggars that resulted from this method were not a
pleasant spectacle.

It is possible that these horrors merely threw greater emphasis on the splendour of the city. For its glory and magnificence were always the main theme of every traveller's tale. Its
conquest had long been the aim of every Moslem chieftain.
Every Slav potentate dreamed of reigning in Tsarigrad, the
city of the emperors. Merchants from west and east brought

home stories of its luxury and beauty. Warrior princes set sail from Norway and Iceland to have the honour of serving in the Emperor's Guard at Micklegarth; and thither, to join them, came Anglo-Saxon adventurers dispossessed by William the Conqueror. Pilgrims, too, could not withhold their admiration, though many, from jealousy or from genuine disapproval, murmured of Babylon and the burden of cities whose pride is an offence to God. We may question whether all this luxury was in fact so tremendous as visitors made out. In the old Roman empire there had been cities quite as wealthy, Alexandria or Antioch or Rome herself; and the coming Renaissance was to bring an equal splendour to the cities of Italy, though not perhaps on so large a scale. The extraordinary impression made by Constantinople on its foreign contemporaries was much of it due to their own comparative poverty and simplicity of life.

Byzantium was at the height of its power in the first years of the eleventh century. Before the century was over disasters had befallen it. Its internal organization, perfected as an instrument of defence against a hostile world, broke down in the face of prosperity. Its hegemony over the Mediterranean Sea was lost with the Norman conquest of southern Italy and the simultaneous growth of the Italian merchant-cities. Worse still, the plains of Asia Minor, its main source of man-power and of food, were irretrievably lost to the Turks. During the twelfth century the splendour of Constantinople seemed still undiminished. The imperial army, with its scientific armaments, its well-run commissariat and medical services, was still a formidable factor in world-politics. But the emperors were living on accumulated reserves. Many wealthy provinces had been lost; and trade was passing into Italian hands. When disaster struck again and the great army perished in a ghastly and unnecessary battle against the Turks, there was no chance of recovery. The horrors of the Fourth Crusade, when western adventurers, pledged to fight against the infidel, joined the Venetians in an attack on the great Christian city, which they

captured and sacked and burnt, left Constantinople a desolation. During the half century of the so-called Latin empire its
population went down by some two-thirds. Large areas fell
into ruin; the Great Palace became uninhabitable and was
deserted. The great relic-collections were dispersed. The return
of the Byzantine emperors brought an ephemeral return to
prosperity; but money was scarce, and commerce had crossed
the Golden Horn to the Italian colony at Galata. Travellers to
the city in the thirteenth and early fourteenth centuries told of
vast areas within the walls where you saw the remains of former
houses lying in open fields. The city seemed to have become a
series of disconnected villages. Yet they still all admired the
gracious lives led by the court and the nobility. They still saw
Hagia Sophia in all its glory; and though many older churches
were in decay, others had arisen, such as the monastery-church
of the Chora with its gay mosaic decoration. But an element of
sadness hung over it all. Christian Constantinople was doomed.
The end came on 23 May 1453, when the last of the emperors
fell fighting at the breach in the walls, and the Turkish soldiery
passed in over his body. The centre of Christian civilization
had moved long since to the west; and though Constantinople
was soon again one of the world's great cities, it was the capital
not of Christendom but of Islam.

It was as the Byzantines always had foreseen. In the melancholy climate of the Bosphorus, with its sudden changes from
heat to chill, with its bitter north wind and its sultry south
wind, its constant rain and the mist from the sea, the Greek
temperament lost much of its natural gaiety. For all its wealth,
for all its wise statesmen and efficient institutions, the empire
was haunted by insecurity and fear. Countless prophecies
warned the citizens that their glory would come to a finish, that
the number of emperors was fixed and that their heritage would
in the end pass to the infidel. The emperor might be God's
viceroy on earth, and the splendour of his court a reflection of
the splendour of the Courts of Heaven. But, with the barbarians growing in strength around them, his subjects had no

faith in human progress, no confidence that their empire would endure. They knew that the pomps and pleasures of this world are transitory things, and that the eleven centuries of their imperial destiny were as nothing in the eyes of God, whose Kingdom alone is eternal.

Medieval Paris

12TH–13TH CENTURY

DAVID DOUGLAS

THERE are men who in their time seem so to bestride their generation as almost to stand outside it. So also is it with cities which likewise possess their own inherent life. Yet in the one case as in the other, it is often the pre-eminent which best represents the generality, and no town has ever better reflected the civilization of which it formed a part than did medieval Paris. Its early growth was intimately connected with that of the medieval social order; the transformations which later came upon it exhibited the changes which were in due course to disrupt the medieval world; and in the resplendent interval of its medieval maturity, Paris between 1150 and 1300 took its place, as of right, as the most characteristic city of western Europe. It was, in this sense, the heir after a long interval of Antonine Rome. It was also in some respects the heir of that newer Rome on the banks of the Bosphorus which had helped to preserve the legacy of Mediterranean culture for the benefit of western men. In so far as the cultural achievement of the Middle Ages was based upon a classical tradition modified by the teaching of the Church, to this extent may medieval Paris be said to have represented that civilization at the climax of its development.

If, therefore, medieval Paris is best to be surveyed as it was in the thirteenth century, it was none the less the product of a long growth which itself accurately reflected some seven hundred years of European history. Certainly, no visitor to Paris in the time of St. Louis could fail to be conscious of an intimate blend therein between the past and the present. At his first impression, for instance, he would have perceived the town to be dominated by the Christian Cathedral of Notre Dame set on the island of the *Cité*, which is the heart of Paris and which had been the seat of the first Roman administration. To the south, on the hill of Sainte-Geneviève—which is even now the Latin Quarter—he would have found the most famous University of Europe, and there he would have discovered men concerned above all with questions of divinity, but speaking Latin as the language of learning, and studying Aristotle as a guide to Christian theology. In such ways were the ancient sources of medieval civilization displayed in thirteenth-century Paris, and its very streets might have served yet further to impress the traveller with the continuity of western culture. It was a Roman road (now the Rue Saint-Jacques) which could lead him from the Christian cathedral through the academic home of secular and ecclesiastical learning. It was likewise a Roman road (now represented in the Rue Saint-Martin) which could take him from the same essential starting-point north-ward through the merchant quarter of the Halles. Even today there is perhaps no spot in all northern Europe better suited than the *Parvis* in front of Notre Dame to impress the modern observer with that subtle medieval achievement whereby the long pathway of the Latin genius was merged almost imperceptibly into the Via Sacra of the Cross.

Yet during the twelfth and thirteenth centuries Paris might also have been regarded as a new city pregnant with the impulses of a new life. Our visitor would have found established there the greatest of the new monarchies which were giving secular order to Europe, a monarchy which had its first home in the *Cité*, and which had but recently created the fortress of the Louvre outside the walls. The merchants of the Halles would have told him of new privileges recently won, and new economic ventures recently undertaken. Passing to the Left Bank, he would have met a multitudinous student body which had but lately been set all afire with a new curiosity. A fine wind of hopeful endeavour was in fact already blowing through the narrow alleys of this thirteenth-century city whose stench impelled Philip Augustus to his plan of paving the Paris streets. Men were living adventurously in the present, although so conscious of the past, and the urgent quality of their immediate enterprise was plentifully exhibited in their town. Most clearly of all was it to be discerned in the new ecclesiastical architecture that was everywhere arising. Massive Romanesque arches, redolent with age, could still be seen in the abbey of Saint-Germain-des-Près, but it was a fresh "Gothic" impulse that was now giving expression to the most lively inspiration of the age. Notre Dame was still in this sense new, but newer still was the lovely shrine which Louis IX had just erected. The Sainte-Chapelle remains today almost as it was when it was completed in 1258 after three years' labour, and it typifies the resurgent energy of medieval Paris at the height of its constructive endeavour.

This city was at once intensely individual and widely representative, and if today every instructed traveller can find in Paris a cosmopolitan as well as a French town, and is conscious that here the two qualities are in harmony, that is due in large measure to a legacy from the Middle Ages. The golden age of medieval Paris lasted for little more than a century, but it enshrined, between 1150 and 1300, very much of the European past, and it held much of the European future in its keeping. So active, however, was its own contemporary life that this may be studied for itself: in the men who then dominated the city, in the buildings they erected, and in the labours they undertook. This was the Paris of Philip Augustus and Louis the Saint, the greatest of the medieval kings of France. This was also the Paris of the great churches, of the earliest Halles, of the first Louvre, and of the first walls. This was, finally, the Paris of Abelard and the rising university. Nor is the bare recital of these famous names itself without significance to an explanation of the greatness of medieval Paris, or of its influence upon Europe.

PLATE 13

PETER ABELARD
Illumination from a French Manuscript, late 14th century

PLATE 14

A VIEW OF PARIS
Illumination from a French Manuscript, c. 1309

Medieval Paris was royal; it was ecclesiastical; it was (though to a lesser extent) mercantile; and it was above all the centre of European learning. By combining together these essential characteristics Paris became in the thirteenth century a unique city, and only thus was she then enabled to mirror the civilization of the age.

*

It was the royal house of Capet which was primarily responsible for the rise of medieval Paris, but the kings of that dynasty none the less here built upon foundations which were already old. The importance of the site of Paris was in fact clearly indicated by geography. The three islands in the Seine, chief of which is the present *Cité*, commanded the most important reach of the greatest waterway of northern France, and dominated the plain that controlled the confluence of the Seine with the Oise and Marne, the one leading to Picardy and the other making an avenue from the east. With their strong sense of actuality, the Romans had, therefore, recognized the importance of this site, making *Lutetia* (as it was then called) the centre of a road system. They erected a temple on the *Cité* and also administrative buildings, whilst on the hill to the south, which they termed *Mons Lucotitius*, an urban settlement grew up. There was a forum near the present Luxembourg gardens and an amphitheatre where now runs the Rue Monge. With the breakdown of the Roman administration, however, this flourishing settlement slowly declined; and continuity was, here as elsewhere, only maintained through the permanence of the ecclesiastical organization which inherited so much of the Roman political system. St. Denis, bishop of Paris in the fourth century, had his successors, and it was these men and their followers who were enabled, albeit with difficulty, to preserve the Parisian identity. From the fifth century to the eighth the chief persons in the history of Paris are thus the saints who were in due course to give their names to Parisian churches: Marcellus and Germanus the bishops, and Geneviève, from Mont

8

Valerien. All else save the Church was in decay. The Roman buildings crumbled; over the baths and edifices of *Mons Lucotitius* vegetation spread; the *Cité* remained intact but deserted; and no secular ruler came to revive the splendour of the Roman past. Paris was but one—and not the most important —of the seats of Merovingian government; Charlemagne looked rather to Rome and Aachen; and his successors in Gaul reigned not from Paris but from Laon. Not until the last quarter of the ninth century did the fundamental importance of medieval Paris begin to be foreshadowed in connection with a new dynasty.

Western civilization was in greater danger between 850 and 950 than ever it was in the sixth century, and it was in the work of preserving this civilization in its darkest hour that Paris emerged into the European consciousness as in a true sense a capital of the west. The wave of Scandinavian expansion which formed Normandy, and transformed England, all but submerged western Christendom under a pagan tide. That it did not do so was due largely to the work of the West Saxon monarchy in England, and also to the achievement of a family of magnates in northern France whose home was by the Seine, and who took the title of Counts of Paris. The successful defence of Paris against the pagan "Northmen" between 885 and 887 was one of the turning-points in the history of Europe, and neither the city nor its secular rulers ever lost the prestige which they then won. Later when a successor of these early Counts of Paris, by name Hugh Capet, in 987 established a new royalty in France he centred this in his own town by the Seine. From henceforth every advance in Capetian power was reflected in the city, and it was from these beginnings that the royal Paris of the Middle Ages arose.

It is well to observe, however, how much these early Capetians had here to do. The ancient town which Hugh Capet chose for his royal seat had shrunk to scarcely more than the *Cité* with some few buildings on each of the adjoining banks of the river. Grass grew where the Roman forum had stood on *Mons Lucotitius*, and there were still marshes between the river and Saint-Paul. Around the central settlement there was thus the desolation of ancient decay, but farther out (though still by modern standards very close) there remained the great monasteries which during the long centuries of decline had stood like rocks in a receding tide: Saint-Germain-des-Près and Saint-Germain-L'Auxerrois faced each other across the river; Sainte-Geneviève was on the southern hill; Saint-Marcel stood near the modern boulevard of that name; and towards the north there was Saint-Merry near the present Halles. These great churches, all situated in what is now the midst of Paris, had in the past been each the centre of a small hamlet, and at the beginning of the eleventh century these hamlets still remained distinct from the central Paris of the *Cité*. The first growth of medieval Paris under royal tutelage was, so to speak, to enclose them. Slowly did the new monarchy grow under the first four Capetian kings (987–1108): equally slow was the concurrent growth of their capital. Nor were the two movements ever unconnected. There is an account of Philip Augustus at a later date sitting in the palace that had been built on Roman foundations at the western extremity of the *Cité*; he is described as gazing at the turbid waters of the river and brooding over the town which lay around him; and that picture is symptomatic of the origins and early growth of medieval Paris.

Thus did the eleventh century come and pass, and before its close there was everywhere the stirring of a new life. The Normans set out on their triumphant career of conquest. The Crusades were about to start. Hildebrand at Rome was presiding over an ecclesiastical revival. The "Twelfth Century Renaissance" was at hand. In all this Paris and its kings shared, and all this likewise they helped to promote. In the early twelfth century there were in Paris, at one and the same time, Abelard representing the revival of learning, and Suger, the great minister, developing the royal government. If they ever met they would have had much to say to each other about their related, though distinct, interests, and about the city in which they dwelt. For Paris was responding to such stimulus more rapidly than ever before. It is reported to have doubled its size during the reign of Louis VI (1108–1138). The "suburb" of Saint-Merry was already absorbed, and there were now scattered dwellings where stands today the Church of Saint-Eustache. Eager students were beginning to move southward from the *Cité* into the Latin Quarter. The *Mons Lucotitius* had become the famous "Mount" of Sainte-Geneviève. Paris was still small but it contained within itself all the germs of a great expansion. Already, too, it had become the special home of most of what was most productive in medieval civilization.

With Philip Augustus, who succeeded in 1180, the profitable results of this close connection between the Capetians and their capital reached their climax. This king became, more truly than any of his predecessors, king of "France", and his reign was marked, as if inevitably, by something of a transformation of the royal city. He began to pave the streets with stone, and he built the first walls, so that medieval Paris was for the first time circumscribed and can be watched as an entity. The walls of Philip Augustus have only survived in fragments but their course was reconstructed by the careful scholarship of M. Halphen, and they are worth contemplating in that they girdled what had become the most important city of transalpine Europe. Perhaps, however, it is the smallness of the area which they marked out which may be of most surprise to the modern observer. For the Paris thus walled by its great king did not stretch so far as the Louvre on the west, or east beyond the present Rue Saint-Paul. The northern circuit of the walls did not extend beyond the streets north of Saint-Eustache, and the southern circuit which started on the east at the Quai de Tournelles did not go farther than to include the site of the modern Pantheon, and then swept back along the line of the Rue des Fossés Saint-Jacques, past the present École de Médicine, to regain the river at a spot near the present Institut de France. In this restricted area so much of primary importance to Europe was already enclosed! Not until the middle of the fourteenth century were the northern ramparts of Paris to be constructed along the line now made familiar by the Grands Boulevards.

The Paris of Philip Augustus and Louis the Saint was, however, far larger than any town which had previously existed on this site, and it possessed a unity which it had not exhibited since Roman times. Of ancient lineage it had, moreover, been so transformed that physically it must then have appeared white and new. For this was not only the capital of a rising monarchy, it was also an ecclesiastical capital whose importance was reflected in the number and character of its churches. To this phase in the history of Paris must for instance be assigned the familiar outline of Notre Dame which in its present form was begun by Maurice de Sully, bishop of Paris from 1160 to 1196, and continued by his successors until its virtual completion in 1235. What was later to be added, was, so to speak, in the nature of an elaboration of a design which had been conceived and brought to perfection during the most brilliant years in the history of medieval Paris. Elsewhere, too, similar, if smaller, churches were arising, sometimes freshly built, though more often created by an adaptation of older Romanesque edifices. By the middle of the thirteenth century Paris was in fact studded with churches, some old and some new, but all giving an impression of recent construction, and all testifying to the ecclesiastical influence which pulsated through the royal city.

*

The Church had preserved the continuous life of Paris through the Dark Ages. The kings of the house of Capet gave it a new life. But neither the Church nor the Monarchy could of themselves have provided for Paris its unique position in the medieval social order. Alone among the great capital cities of medieval Europe, Paris possessed a university, and the University of Paris was in turn to serve as the prototype of nearly all the universities of northern Europe. Moreover, although the University of Paris was at different times to be styled "the eldest daughter of the King of France", and also "the first school of the Church", it possessed always its own inherent life. It sprang in some sense from the two chief forces which combined to make Paris great, but if it derived from Paris it gave to that city as much as it received. Like Paris itself, of which during the Middle Ages it was the mind, and in part the soul, this University was a force of European significance. Perhaps more than any other institution in the west it reflected the special quality of medieval culture. The *University* as an instrument of learning was, it should be remembered, a creation of the Middle Ages. The University of Paris was the greatest of all the European universities and is the parent of most of them. Its uprising in the city of Louis the Saint was, therefore, an event of European importance, and one which of itself would have made medieval Paris the worthy representative of a golden age in European culture.

The beginning of the University of Paris—and indeed the prime cause of its activity—must be found in that great stirring of the European mind which is often termed "The Twelfth-Century Renaissance"—a revival which in its manifold products must be reckoned as one of the most important factors in the growth of western civilization. The pervasive manifestations of this movement could be watched in many directions. It was marked, for instance, by a revival of legal studies which in due course were to find their special home in Bologna. It was marked also by the fine humanistic learning which spread over the west from centres such as Chartres. It found expression, again, in the new developments in ecclesiastical architecture which were characteristic of that age. Best of all perhaps might it be detected in the spread among humble people of an ever-extending curiosity. There has been much sentimental eulogy about the wandering scholars of this period, but it is none the less a phenomenon of great significance to the historian of European culture that at this time the roads of western Europe became alive with the figures of men and boys constantly travelling, eager to learn, to inquire, to argue, and to teach.

They moved from place to place to sit at the feet of the master of their choice. They were often shabby, frequently disrespectful, sometimes unworthy of their high profession. But they formed, so to speak, the seed-bed from which sprang the flowering scholarship of the age. And where they came, and where they most settled, there were to arise the great universities of medieval Europe.

That Paris was to become the chief of such centres is now a commonplace of knowledge. But at the beginning of the twelfth century there was as yet little to indicate that such a development would take place. There were, however, in Paris at that time schools established at the monasteries of Sainte-Geneviève, Saint-Victor, and Saint-Germain-des-Près, and at the Cathedral of Notre Dame; and these, though not specifically distinguished, were made to serve as the basis of the new movement. One of the great educational changes of the period was to be a transference of general teaching from the monks to the secular clergy, so that in one sense the rise to predominance within Paris of the cathedral school of Notre Dame might be regarded as the first movement towards the later formation of the university. But by itself this would have meant little, for as yet even the school of Notre Dame had not begun to rival the more notable schools established elsewhere, as at Chartres and Rheims. It was, in short, not through any administrative action but owing to an astonishing wave of popular enthusiasm that the schools of Paris rose to leadership in Europe. The University of Paris was not to be created. It grew. And the beginning of its growth is to be dated from the coming to the *Cité* of one of the most famous teachers of his age. It was from the presence of Abelard in Paris in the middle of the twelfth century, from the disputes he stimulated, and above all from the crowds of pupils he attracted that the University of Paris took its origin, in spirit, if not in form.

To estimate the place of Abelard in the history of European thought is no part of the purpose of this essay, but he is certainly to be regarded as one of the makers of medieval Paris.

For it was he who first gave to the Capetian capital its position as a centre of European learning. As an exponent of a new Nominalism he brought into opposition against himself many of the most notable scholars of the age, and the debates between them attracted an ever-increasing audience. The neighbourhood of Notre Dame began to swarm with an ardent, tumultuous and disrespectful student body, and Abelard's own conflicts with the ecclesiastical authorities led him and his followers to desire a position of greater independence from the officials of the cathedral. The abbot of Sainte-Geneviève on the Mount was thought by some to offer a suitable counterpoise to these, and partly for this reason Abelard migrated for a time from the *Cité*, and his followers began to establish themselves in what has ever since been known as the Latin Quarter—a district which has from that time remained unique in the world. This community, which was rapidly becoming self-conscious, was still, however, completely unorganized, and not until after Abelard's stormy and unhappy life did any university exist in Paris in the modern sense of the term. The intellectual and social ferment which had been engendered, can, none the less, be regarded as the true mainspring of the University of Paris which at a later date was to achieve a distinct and independent existence.

The evolution by the University of Paris of a constitution proper to itself is, none the less, itself of considerable interest, because it concerns the formal establishment of what has ever since been regarded as the best medium for the higher education of Europe, and because university organization everywhere still tends to reproduce with suitable modifications the forms which were first crystallized in Paris during the twelfth and thirteenth centuries. The original schools at Paris were (like those of Chartres and elsewhere) under the control of the bishop's chancellor, and as has been seen it was from these schools that the university grew. The chancellor therefore always remained an extremely important figure in the government of the university. But the beginnings of a more distinct type of organization can be seen in the development of a guild of teaching masters which was gradually to become self-conscious and to vindicate its right to a considerable measure of independence. A charter of Philip Augustus suggests that this Guild was already of importance in 1170, but for a long time after this the Masters' Guild had still to struggle for its autonomy against the bishop and his chancellor. The claim of the teaching masters could in fact best be watched in relation to what was called "Inception"—that is to say the ceremony through which the Masters of Paris insisted that a newcomer should pass before he was admitted to their fellowship. And so far were they successful in this that before the end of the twelfth century, two things had become necessary before a man was permitted to teach in Paris: firstly he must have obtained the permission of the bishop's chancellor, and secondly he must have been made free of the Masters' Guild by the ceremony of "Inception". And the authority of the Guild became predominant when after a long struggle it was recognized that the chancellor's licence must be given gratuitously to anyone who had formally been made a member of the Masters' Guild. Soon, too, the corporate character of this Guild was to be more formally recognized when it was allowed to plead by means of a proctor, to elect common officers, and to use a common seal. By these steps medieval Paris was brought to give to the world the idea of the university as a learned corporation possessed of its own independence and informed with its own individual life.

The Guild of Masters was thus in Paris the core of the nascent university, but in respect of the control of teaching it had to contend with a formidable rival. From the first the two great Orders of Friars had been closely connected with the learned movement in medieval Paris. In 1221 the Dominicans established themselves by the banks of the Seine, and speedily developed what has been described as a separate and exclusive school of orthodox theology. Within the next few years the Franciscans followed, and even before the death of St. Francis the learned Franciscan, Alexander of Hales, was lecturing on the Mount. From this time forward, throughout the Middle Ages, many of the greatest scholars in the university were to be friars, and a mention of even a few of their names would indicate the magnitude of their achievement. Bonaventura the theologian, and Roger Bacon the scientist, were both Franciscans, whilst in the work of the Dominican Thomas Aquinas, who likewise studied and taught on the Mount, the medieval theological system achieved its formal perfection. Such men, and many more like them, gave to the University of Paris a distinction it would never otherwise have possessed, but the coming of the friars none the less created a difficult institutional problem. The friars wished to occupy University Chairs without submitting to the discipline of the Masters' Guild, whilst the Guild strove to exclude them altogether from the university. After a long struggle, which culminated between 1251 and 1257, a compromise was reached. The Guild was compelled to recognize the claims of Mendicant teachers of theology, though the Masters of Arts managed to exclude them from their faculty. On the other hand the friars undertook to observe the oath of teaching masters and to abide by the university statutes.

As a result of these conflicts, the medieval University of Paris perfected its organization—an organization which was to be followed in whole or in part by nearly all the universities of northern Europe, and to give us the academic terms with which we are familiar today. For by the end of the thirteenth century the Masters' Guild had itself become elaborately organized. It was divided into four "faculties"—Theology; Law; Medicine; and Arts. And the Faculty of Arts was divided into four "Nations": France; Normandy; Picardy; and England. The faculties other than Arts were each presided over by a "Dean"; and each of the "Nations" in the Faculty of Arts by a "Proctor". The whole Guild was under the rule of its "Rector".

This organization, with its elaborate regulations as to membership and duties, on the whole worked well since it provided at least one of the most vital necessities of university life: the free interchange of thought among an independent and qualified professoriate. But it carried within it certain defects which needed remedy. In the first place it made no pecuniary provision for teaching, since there were no salaries, and since every doctor, master, or professor (the terms in the thirteenth century were almost synonymous) had the right to teach for whatever fees he could extract from such students as he could persuade to come to his lectures. Secondly, the Guild of Masters tended to be out of touch with the student body as a whole, which was frequently undisciplined and could itself provide no assistance to its poorer members. It was largely to meet these two needs that a college system early came into existence in medieval Paris. The colleges were at first only unofficial lodging-houses for students, but they later came to be officially recognized, and became more and more a part of the university organization, making themselves responsible both for the teaching and for the good conduct of those they housed. The earliest of these Paris colleges was a small house for poor students set up in the *Cité* in 1180 and known as the Collège des Dix-Huit, but during the next century more important colleges were established on the Mount. It was in 1257 that the Collège de la Sorbonne was founded, and some twenty-five years later the Collège d'Harcourt. Even more lavish in their early endowments were the Collège du Cardinal Lemoine, and the Collège de Navarre founded respectively in 1301 and 1304. Many of these medieval colleges were to have a long and distinguished history, and that of the Sorbonne was finally to give its name to the University of Paris itself. They have left abundant traces in the street names of the Latin Quarter today.

The developing form of the University of Paris supplied the whole of north-western Europe with a pattern of academic organization. Thus before the twelfth century had closed, Oxford had started its career as a university modelled upon Paris, and during the thirteenth century the movement spread throughout the west. Its amazingly rapid growth is not, however, to be explained solely, or even chiefly, by reference either to administrative skill or to lavish endowments. The beginnings of the movement in Paris derived directly from an awakened curiosity stimulated by the presence of great teachers filled with ardour, and from the enthusiasm of a multitudinous student body eager to learn. It was this tradition carried out without interruption from the time of Abelard which gave to medieval Paris an undisputed hegemony in the republic of European learning. To write the history of the University of Paris would in fact necessitate a survey of almost the whole of medieval scholarship. Law might find a special home in Bologna. Some of the older humane studies characteristic of twelfth-century Chartres may have been lost. But philosophy and theology, and later law also and medicine, were prosecuted at Paris to an extent unparalleled elsewhere. Between 1150 and 1350 there was hardly a single notable scholar in western Europe who did not at some time in his career either study or teach in Paris. To such an extent did the pervasive influence of the Parisian university inform the mind of western Europe in the Middle Ages.

The great masters in the University of Paris during this period were not only notable scholars themselves: they were also great teachers developing the older educational system of the *Trivium* and *Quadrivium* to impart an instruction to their pupils which might stand comparison with that of any age. And the student body which surrounded them was equally remarkable. Constantly changing, it can seldom during the thirteenth century have numbered less than six thousand persons at any one time. And it was cosmopolitan in character. The teachers at Paris were not invariably or even usually Frenchmen, and their pupils came from all over Europe. They thus gave to the Parisian population a special quality. They were, moreover, the future clerics in an ecumenical Church, and having been welcomed on the banks of the Seine, they carried the influence of Paris throughout the west. It was not only through the medium of professed scholars, but also at the hands of popes and prelates, that the teaching learnt at Paris became the affair of all Europe. Indeed, it is doubtful whether the independence of the University of Paris could ever have been achieved apart from the support given to the Masters' Guild by popes such as

Innocent III, who could recall the years of their youth spent on the Mount. The teachers and students of Paris in the thirteenth century were conscious of forming an intellectual *élite*: a scholarly leaven in European society.

It is hardly surprising, therefore, that the dominance exercised by this cosmopolitan society should have conferred a unique prestige on the city in which it was established. There seem indeed to have been hardly any limits to the respect and affection which Paris could excite in those who had passed through its university. "Paris!" exclaimed one of these— "Paris! Queen among cities! Moon among stars! On that island Philosophy has her ancient seat, who with Study her sole comrade, holds the eternal citadel of light!" "Happy city!" declared another, "where the students are so numerous that their multitude almost surpasses that of the lay inhabitants!" No scholar could feel a foreigner in Paris, remarked John of Salisbury, the great English humanist of the twelfth century; and in the fourteenth century, Richard of Bury, Bishop of Durham, could still enlarge on the "mighty stream of pleasure which made glad his heart" whenever he had leisure to revisit the city. Such declarations are constant, and their significance to the position occupied by Paris in the medieval world can well be seen in the contemporary description given by a thirteenth-century chronicler:

"In that time—he says—letters flourished in Paris. Never before at any time, or in any part of the world, whether in Athens or Egypt, had there been such a multitude of students. The reason for this must be sought not only in the beauty of Paris itself, but also in the special privileges which King Philip and his father before him had conferred upon the scholars. In this great city the study of the trivium and the quadrivium, of canon and civil law, as also of medicine, was held in high esteem. But the crowd pressed with a special zeal around the professorial Chairs where Holy Scripture was taught or where problems of theology were resolved."

Such sentiments are not to be dismissed as empty phrases. They are among the important factors of history. Certainly, they go far to explain the special function discharged by medieval Paris in the history of Europe. Christian in its scholarship, ecumenical in its interests and membership, the University of Paris in the thirteenth century reflected all that was best and most characteristic in the culture of the age.

*

Medieval Paris achieved its pre-eminence in Europe as a royal city, and as the home of the greatest university in western Christendom. It thus owed its position to political and cultural causes, and no view of the historical process which is based upon an exclusively economic interpretation of the past will suffice to explain the importance of Paris in the medieval world, or the influence it then exercised over the minds and imaginations of European men. Its commercial development was also notable, but always secondary in significance, for medieval Paris developed no "heavy industries", and if its crafts were distinguished they were not peculiar to itself. The Parisian bourgeoisie, vigorous and active as it was, had its counterpart in most of the great cities of the west. Nevertheless, no sketch of medieval Paris, even as it reflected to a special degree the civilization of the age, can omit to mention, however briefly, the merchants and traders who served this great capital, who met the needs of the court and the aristocracy gathered in it, and who ministered to the crowd of scholars who lived and wrangled on the Mount. For the city, which had acquired such prestige, steadily grew in size. By the middle of the fourteenth century it had come to comprise a population of not less than 150,000 persons. Even the latest walls to the north, running along the line of the Grands Boulevards, were now insufficient to contain it.

This population needed to be fed and clothed. In its midst therefore were a multitude engaged in retail trade, and within it great mercantile houses arose. The small traders of medieval

Paris have formed an attractive subject for detailed study, and they are worthy of it. Among them were the dealers in meat, fish, and wine, and of a wider importance the *marchands à l'eau* developing the ancient river trade, and carrying their enterprise up and down the Seine from Burgundy to Rouen. The drapers and merchants in cloth already famous in the thirteenth century formed early connections with the wool merchants in England, and with the cloth manufacturers of the Flemish towns. The mercers, who were among the richest of the Paris merchants, dealt not only in ordinary apparel, but also in silks from the Levant and in furs from the north. All these had their place in the teeming mercantile life of medieval Paris, and luxury trades also developed and in their turn administered to the arts. Gold and silver ornaments were made and the decoration of manuscripts played such a large part in Parisian commerce that Dante was constrained to give it a special mention in his *Divine Comedy*. Banking in its turn developed, attracting to Paris the Lombard manipulators of the money market, and a large Jewish community which had its first home in the *Cité*, but which later moved, under compulsion, to the *Rive Droite*. Here in truth was the reproduction on a large scale of the economic life of any great medieval town.

Typical also was the organization of that life. The thirteenth century was the golden age of the craft guilds, and those of Paris were notable and distinguished. All the familiar features of that system were developed, for each craft in Paris as elsewhere had its separate organization which fostered the welfare of its members, regulated its production, and supervised its relations with the world outside. These guilds controlled their several crafts, forbidding participation in them to those who were not members of the guild, insisting on a high standard of professional competence by means of the apprenticeship system, regulating wages, and to a certain extent attempting also to regulate prices. Such a system of corporations was in fact characteristic of the age of St. Louis, and only after his time did it begin everywhere to break down, with the rise of a new class of capitalist traders who obtained an ever-increasing control of industry, and with the consequent creation of a proletariat of workers who could themselves never hope to become masters. There was, of course, in this tendency towards oligarchy nothing that was peculiar to Paris, but it helps to explain why the municipal history of Paris in the later Middle Ages was to be a stormy one. For a more perfect social equilibrium among the trading classes in Paris it is necessary to turn rather to the condition of the earlier thirteenth century. Never after that time was there the same balance between a large body of independent craftsmen organized in their guilds, and on the other hand a smaller body of wealthier merchants whose activities stretched throughout Europe and beyond. Such an harmony could hardly be expected to endure when trade became less local in its scope. But so long as it lasted it provided a life of self-respect for a large class of small traders, while at the same time it gave to the wealthier members of the mercantile community a political opportunity to impart a sense of communal self-consciousness to the city they aspired to rule.

The special interest attaching to the Parisian bourgeoisie at this period derived, however, not so much from its share in an economic activity that was common to western Europe, but rather from its close association with the monarchy. Paris was the royal town, and as the power of the Capets grew, so also did the importance of the citizens of the capital. From the first, there can be seen a connection between the two interests. Very early royal charters protected the "Lendit Fair" on the road to Saint-Denis, and established the Halles on the site that the modern building now occupies. Soon, too, an even more remarkable association was to be disclosed. In 1190, when the king was about to depart on the Crusade, among those whom he appointed as regents during his absence were six burgesses of Paris who were entrusted with the custody of the royal seal, and given a key to the royal treasure in the Temple. Subsequently, (after the king's return), the names of Parisian burgesses are frequently to be found as witnesses to the royal charters, and

PLATE 15

SCENES FROM THE LIFE OF SCHOLARS AT THE SCHOOL OF NOTRE-DAME
Relief from Notre-Dame, middle of the 13th century

ST. LOUIS WITH ST. JOHN
In the background the Seine, the Tour de Nesle and the Louvre
French painting, 15th century

PLATE 16

The Upper Chapel

The Lower Chapel

SAINTE-CHAPELLE IN PARIS

Built in 1243—1248

when in 1226 the young Louis IX entered Paris against some opposition, he put himself under the protection of a guard of the citizens. From this time, indeed, dates the notion that the citizens of Paris had their own special part to play in the government of France. This claim was to be voiced again and again in French history, and to find its most spectacular expression through the mouth of Danton during the French Revolution.

*

The primary factor in promoting the greatness of Paris during the period of its finest medieval achievement was, in fact, the close harmony which then prevailed among the dominant forces which were there displayed in exceptional strength. The four cardinal institutions which contributed to the making of this city—the Monarchy, the Church, the University, the Bourgeoisie—seemed here for a brief period to be able to co-operate with a wholly remarkable felicity. Philip Augustus may have constructed his fortress of the Louvre outside his walls in order to be able if necessary to dominate the city, but he never needed to use the stronghold for this purpose, and he is to be remembered rather as the friend of the citizens, the first paver of the Paris streets, and the first man to girdle the capital with ramparts. Similarly, both he, and his greater son, consistently stood friends to the rising university; and the debt was repaid with affection and support as when men out of all countries sallied forth from the Mount in 1213 to acclaim the king on his return from Bouvines, victor over his conquered enemies. In its turn, the influence of the Church impregnated every Parisian activity at this time. The Church fostered the craft guilds which were religious as well as trading organizations. It supported from Rome the Masters' Guild in the university. It inspired the scholarship and art of the town and it gave a special sanction to the Monarchy. Thus were the multifarious activities of this city united in relation to a common purpose. Could the spirit of medieval Paris in its golden age be better

9

discerned in the university where theology was the Queen of Sciences, or in the Sainte-Chapelle which St. Louis, as king, constructed as a casket of stone to receive the Crown of Thorns?

The Church, Secular Government, and the University—*Sacerdotium, Imperium, Studium*—these, according to a medieval writer, were the three powers which guarded the health of Christendom, and it was precisely these three which by their combined action on a single favoured city made medieval Paris the capital of European civilization. When these powers weakened in their influence, and ceased in this place to work in harmony, the unique position of Paris in the medieval world at once began to be less assured. Set like a jewel in Parisian history, is, therefore, the brief period which elapsed between the accession of Philip Augustus in 1180 and the death of Louis IX in 1270. Afterwards, there was to be much notable achievement but never again such confident equilibrium. It is not to be forgotten that the fourteenth century in Paris began with the mysterious scandal of the Templars, or that the suppression of this ecclesiastical Order was effected by a French king by means of the most savage brutality. It was a grandson of St. Louis who brought the papacy to humiliation at Anagni, and during the same century the activities of Parisian citizens were usually associated with revolt or disorder. The harmonious balance of cultural forces which in the early thirteenth century had made Paris so representative of medieval civilization was itself coming to an end.

Each of the dominant powers within the medieval social order seemed now to be entering upon a period of strain, and the results were speedily to be seen within Paris. The French monarchy was never stronger than under Philippe IV, but it was already displaying a tyrannical lack of moderation. Soon the disasters of the Hundred Years War would fall upon it, and the long Valois tragedy would begin, with calamitous results for Paris. The University of Paris grew in size during the fourteenth century, but its pristine vigour waned, and the philosophical studies which were its pride, though never without importance, seemed often to be degenerating into a war of words. The bourgeoisie increased in wealth, but became more sundered between rich and poor. Étienne Marcel might rouse for a time a municipal patriotism which found expression in the first Hôtel de Ville, but he brought violence to Paris, and he died murdered; and when at the beginning of the fifteenth century the early democratic movement of the "Cabochins" gave Paris for a time into the hands of the butchers, tripe-sellers, and skinners of the Halles, the atrocities of their rule shocked the conscience even of a brutal age. Finally, the Church, whose influence was pervasive through every institution in medieval Paris, itself entered upon an epoch of difficulty. It continued of course to produce great scholars and great saints; and notable artists were still devoted to its service. But in the increasing ornamentation of the Parisian buildings, and in the growing subtleties of Scholastic theology may perhaps be detected the curse of cleverness which is the symptom of fatigue. The papacy underwent its schism. There were scandals and revolts.

It is, of course, misleading to compare the dominant figures of one century with the lesser men of another, and it is easy to over-emphasize a general tendency to which there were plentiful exceptions. But concentrating the gaze more exclusively upon Paris, it is difficult not to make the contrast between the king whom Joinville praised, and the men whom Villon knew. Nor (if the comparison be held unfair) would it be difficult to press it elsewhere. Between 1350 and 1450 Paris suffered many disasters which were not of her making, but within the city itself there were none the less signs of an inherent *malaise* that was exhibited alike in the growing isolation of the rich, in the breakdown of secular order, and in the degeneration of learning from a hard discipline into a soft diversion. Even in the more strictly political sphere something of the same transformation might be watched. Paris shared to the full in the French misfortunes during the Hundred Years War, but perhaps she reacted to them with less than the former vigour which had once for three hard years held the *Cité* against the pagans.

Henry V from England might ride in triumph out of a flaming
countryside to pass down the ancient Rue Saint-Martin, pausing
only to kiss the relics which were successively offered for his
veneration, but, in the full waning of the Middle Ages, it was
not the men of Paris, but a girl from Lorraine, who saved
France.

The golden age of medieval Paris had passed. Men were
beginning to listen to new voices—voices which came from over
the Alps and which would soon be heard with especial clarity in
Medicean Florence and Borgian Rome. They spoke of a
renaissance very different from that of the twelfth century, though
perhaps no greater. Soon in Paris would be seen in Louis XI
a king spinning over Europe a web of other texture than that
woven by Louis the Saint, and in the boisterous scorn of
Rabelais would in due course be found the solvent of former
enthusiasms which had at last grown cold. Yet the earlier
achievement was none the less to endure, and it left its abiding
mark upon Europe. Medieval Paris may be seen today in many
edifices, and more particularly in adapted buildings which still
stand on the sites originally chosen for them in the twelfth
century. It survives also in the tradition of secular government
there propounded, and sometimes put into practice, by the
greatest of the French kings. Most particularly does it survive
in the spirit which still broods over the university hill of Sainte-
Geneviève. These things are all a legacy from the Middle
Ages, but separately they represent only part of the inheritance.
Medieval Paris represented Europe by being itself, and it
bequeathed to the future its own intense personality. It was the
microcosm of western Christendom which ever since has been
a reality, though often, as today, in mortal danger. And for that
reason, no one conscious of being part of western civilization,
has, since the Middle Ages, ever been able to enter Paris wholly
as a stranger. He comes conscious of a fundamental debt, and
confident of recapturing an ancient inspiration. Even as a man
in age may revisit a lover of his youth, or an exile after long
wandering return to a second home.

Medicean Florence

15TH CENTURY

HAROLD ACTON

CLIMB the hill of Etruscan Fiesole north of the river, or the height of San Miniato to the south, and look down over the valley. Let your gaze be leisurely, for this panorama exhales a spirit of civilized leisure. It has an infinite deal to communicate, of human culture, of powerful personalities, and a strong unbroken tradition. Even if you know but little of history, a sense of the past must sweep over you, a past which is polished and alive, not dusty and dead.

All Florence is spread beneath you, cupolas, towers, multitudinous roofs. Without swarming, the city calmly covers the plain. From Fiesole the view is bird's eye, topographical; San Miniato provides a man's eye view, more intimate but equally impressive. Does distance lend further enchantment to what is enchanting? There is no doubt that it accentuates the grandeur of Brunelleschi's Duomo, the bristling height of the battlemented Palazzo Vecchio where the gonfalonier and priors used to preside over the republic, the shimmer of the broad Arno winding westward between stone embankments and the walls of mellowed houses. There is no doubt that it often reveals what may be lost in the labyrinth at closer range. The eye may select jewel after jewel, the octagonal casket of the Baptistery and the Campanile of Giotto; it may linger on the venerable Ponte Vecchio, only saved from the general holocaust of bridges because Hitler was said to have admired it; then it may wander to the background of hills, to the nearer slopes meticulously cultivated, chiselled and terraced with sun-steeped villas, almost invariably flanked by slim cypresses and silvery olive-groves, to the remoter Apennines whose summits are often inseparable from cloud. But nothing seems very remote, if the weather be fine, in this crystalline Tuscan air. Every ridge and rill has the sharp outline of a miniature.

You need not be psychic to be aware of the presence of the great dead Florentines. They amble beside you and merge with the throng in the middle of the street or piazza which is all their own. How the Tuscan type persists! The strongly-marked bone-structure of faces; the broad cheeks, level brows, square jaws, firm muscles of mouth and chin, are just as Donatello sculpted them. How like Dante's that lean profile peering into the bookshop; and there's Machiavelli scrutinizing the *Corriere!* The hatless young women along the Via Tornabuoni have all the poise of their forebears in Ghirlandaio's frescoes.

Here the past does not have to be excavated: by sunlight or moonshine it is alive and omnipresent. Under a full moon, especially, does its physical impact grow powerful. Many a palace, reticent, as if holding its breath by day, breathes more freely when caressed by lunar light and shadow. Exquisite details surge into sudden prominence, street corner shrines, stone shields with carved escutcheons over doorways. Among the latter the Medicean balls are ubiquitous. Some maintain that these were originally pills and that the Medici were descended from a doctor (*medico*); while mythomaniacs, who claim that they were descended from Perseus, would persuade us that the balls represent the golden apples of Hesperides. Others have offered more scurrilous explanations. . . .

It is easy to visualize the city as it was in the fifteenth century. Except that it was then encircled by walls with fifteen gates, protected by forts and bastions, the salient features of Florence have changed little, with due allowance for growth. And the fifteenth was an essentially Florentine century, when Florence was the centre of human culture, second only to Athens in its influence on European civilization. Since the greatest of the

Medici then rose to power, it might equally be called the Medicean Age.

Even in the previous century the intellectual leadership of Florence was acknowledged throughout Italy. The Italian language itself had come to be known as the "Tuscan idiom" or the "Florentine vernacular". At the Jubilee of 1300 Pope Boniface VIII had observed that all the ambassadors of the Christian powers assembled in Rome were citizens of Florence, and his remark that the Florentines were a "fifth element" has become proverbial.

This leadership was all the more striking because Florence was no great city by material standards. The boundaries of her state fell between some sixty miles of length and ninety miles of breadth. She owed much to her strategic position on the high road which led from the north to Rome and passed over the Arno bridge.

One by one the thriving cities of Tuscany, Colle di Val d'Elsa, San Gimignano, Prato, Pistoia, Volterra, San Miniato dei Tedeschi, had fallen under her sway, some, like Pisa and Arezzo, after bitter and protracted struggles, until, in the thirteenth century, Florence had become the predominant power in Central Italy. In 1421 Leghorn was sold to Florence by the Genoese, thus opening the sea to her merchandise.

Her trade guilds (*Arti*), already well established in the twelfth century, were close-knit microcosms of the republic, each with their own statutes and a similar constitution. Originally there were twelve guilds: seven major, which were engaged in wholesale commerce, and five minor, engaged in retail traffic and internal trade; the latter were eventually increased with variations in number and constitution. The *Signoria* was composed of "priors of the arts" chosen from the major guilds, who became the chief magistrates of the state under the leadership of a gonfalonier or standard-bearer of justice, who held office for two months only.

For a long period the guild of wool dressers and dyers, to which the Albizzi belonged, was the wealthiest and most

influential. When the supply of local wool ran short the merchants imported it from France, Flanders, Holland, and
England. After opening cloth factories abroad they sent the
material to Florence to be dressed and dyed. Nowhere else had
this process been refined to such a degree; consequently the
Florentine product commanded a high price all over Europe,
and French or English cloth could be sold again at a profit in
the land of its origin. When the manufacture improved in
England and Flanders, the Wool Guild continued to make
handsome profits by exporting to the East. The Silk Guild
waxed when the Wool Guild waned: towards the end of the
fifteenth century there were at least eighty-three silk factories
in Florence, and Florentine satins, velvets, and gold brocades
had an unrivalled reputation in Europe.

In all the chief centres of commerce Florentine merchants
established agencies which became local clearing-houses,
whence the origin of our present system of banking. An
extensive system of correspondence was begun, enabling the
merchants to make payments on receipt of written orders. The
Florentine florin was a harder currency than the dollar is
today, and Florentine bankers had a world-wide reputation in
the fourteenth and the fifteenth centuries. They made colossal
loans to foreign princes, and even when the Bardi and Peruzzi
lost the sum of 1,365,000 gold florins to England in 1338 they
managed to recover. Philippe de Commines asserted that
Edward IV of England owed his crown to the financial support
of Florentine bankers, and later French enterprise depended
upon the support of the Strozzi bank in particular, which had
branches in Lyons, Venice, and Rome.

Apart from promoting prosperity, the trade guilds had an
educational effect which was of considerable political value.
The government of each was representative, and as many
took part in its administration a great number of citizens
were qualified for public life. This helps to explain the
advanced political insight and varied forms of human development for which Burckhardt said that Florence "in

this sense deserves the name of the first modern State in the world".

Constant political reforms had confirmed the democratic character of the government, and every change was described and criticized by its pioneer historians, from Giovanni Villani in 1300 to his more mature and illustrious successors, Machiavelli, Guicciardini, Segni, Varchi, and others. "Rome is sinking", wrote Villani, "my native city is rising, and ready to achieve great things. Therefore I wish to relate its past history, and hope to continue the story to the present time, and as long as my life shall last." Already we may note that new sense of historical continuity for which, as H. A. L. Fisher observed, the great school of Florentine historians and publicists was distinguished. Trade and commerce had stimulated economical and political science as well as the fine arts.

The Visconti of Milan had been inveterate enemies of Florence, but after the death of Filippo Maria in 1447 Cosimo de' Medici shrewdly allied himself with the *condottiere*, Francesco Sforza, whose claims to the duchy of Milan he supported financially. This was a new departure in Florentine foreign policy, and the alliance, though unpopular in Florence, became one of the chief factors in the balance of power in Italy when Naples joined it. Except for the war with the nepotistic Pope Sixtus IV which was forced upon Florence by the Pazzi Conspiracy, Lorenzo de' Medici succeeded in maintaining this balance of power, which for the time being offered a united front against alien incursions.

The crossing of the Arno at Florence offered unique advantages, as Mr. Edward Hutton has pointed out: "The whole traffic of the peninsula lay north and south and had to cross the Arno immediately before or immediately after crossing the mountains. The traffic lay north and south partly because of the shape and formation of Italy and partly because the south needed the farm produce of the Lombard plain, as the north needed the wool of Latium. Those who held Tuscany were perforce middlemen, traders; and those who held the passage of the Arno were the pre-ordained masters of Tuscany, of Central Italy that is." But this mastery could not have been maintained without a rare combination of characteristics.

Merchants, bankers, lawyers, artisans, business-men who understood the manipulation of money, the hard-headed Florentines were eminently realistic. An exceptional genius might revolt, but however high he soared some part of him clung to Mother Earth and retained her solidity. Boundless curiosity was combined with a talent for exact observation, and the visual arts flowered from a passionate awareness of the tangible, visible world. Like the Greeks, the Florentines were "guided by some peculiar instinct toward temperance and beauty". In painting they preferred form to colour, in architecture the most delicate simplicity, in literature the purest narrative. Thus it was to the Greeks that they turned, as to long-lost parents, as soon as they emerged from the muddled Middle Ages. They had never been Gothicized. The rediscovery of Greek culture in the beginning of the fifteenth century became known as humanism, and Florence under the early Medici was the busiest hive of the strenuous humanists: a minority of talented and creative men working in a sensitive and intelligent society.

From a distance the spectacle of the Renaissance may strike one as if the marble statues of antiquity had sprung from the Italian soil and wakened to a new lease of life after centuries of sleep beneath the olives and cypresses. Actually, the transition from the medieval to the modern world was gradual, though in Florence its pace was somewhat accelerated. The contrast between medieval and modern society, however, between an atmosphere hostile to free inquiry and one in which science could thrive, is clearly perceptible.

During the Middle Ages the Church and all culture were one. Latin was the universal language of the educated, and knowledge had reached a blind alley of theological commentaries. Man was only half-conscious of himself apart from his clan or corporation. Most of his achievements in the fine arts were anonymous. Roger Bacon, Chaucer, Villon and, above all, Petrarch, were sporadic flashes of a more enlightened future. In Florence the tradition of humane learning had never been wholly interrupted since the time of Dante, Petrarch, and Boccaccio. Conditions had long been favourable to that growth of individual character of which the fifteenth-century humanist was the quintessence. Trade and commerce had boomed during the Crusades, creating a middle class united against feudal disorder. The new humanist who replaced the medieval monk could thus live in an atmosphere of leisure and freedom. Instead of remaining a provincial recluse, he became a citizen of the world.

Rich merchants hoped to win immortality from scholars and artists, who shared the same ardent desire. Vespasiano da Bisticci has left vivid brief biographies of these fifteenth-century scholars, some of whom served as secretaries of the republic or held chairs in the university. Leonardo Bruni, Carlo Marsuppini, Poggio Bracciolini, and Giannozzo Manetti enjoyed immense contemporary fame, and it was largely due to them and to collectors of rare manuscripts, like Niccolò Niccoli, that Florence became an intellectual capital. To us they would seem pedantic, perhaps, with their cold imitations of Cicero, but their contribution to European culture was inestimable. They were orators, poets, scholars, and teachers; and their audiences were responsive and eager to learn. They prepared for the Renaissance by insisting on the individuality of man; by encouraging the adoption of the mother-tongue in literature, an interest in the life and letters of antiquity, and a close interrogation of nature. The artist went straight to flesh and blood essentials; the human body cast off its cloistral cocoon and leapt into the Arcadian sunlight.

In the meantime France was convalescing from the disastrous English wars, and in England the Wars of the Roses were preparing for the reign of Henry Tudor. Compared with Italy, both countries were in a state of barbarism. It was not until the sixteenth century that the Renaissance gained a firm foothold outside Italy, and such buildings as Fontainebleau, Hatfield, and Knole announced its happy arrival in France and England. In the days of Queen Elizabeth it became the fashion for English noblemen to travel in Italy and frequent its universities. The Italianate Englishman would return from Florence steeped in the theories of Machiavelli and Castiglione, in the "power-politics" of *The Prince* and in the politeness of *The Courtier*, which Sir Thomas Hoby translated in 1561.

It was under the subtle guidance of a single family that Florence achieved her fame as pilot of the Renaissance. Hysterical historians have attacked the Medici without looking fore or aft. The majority accuse them of crushing republican liberty. But the Florentine republic had never enjoyed much liberty in a modern sense, since both the nobility and the labouring masses had been excluded from the administration. Its early history had been a monotonous tug of war between Guelphs and Ghibellines, between city merchants of Italian stock and feudal barons of Teutonic origin, who pillaged them or levied tolls on their wares. Eventually the merchants won, and their highly organized guilds (*Arti*) monopolized the government. The feudal minority was assimilated or banished, and a new aristocracy cropped up from the trading classes. Towards the fifteenth century a syndicate of wealthy families ruled, and the wealthiest and most ambitious of these were the Medici.

The early Medici were typical Florentines with an extra dose of sagacity and foresight. Their habits of thought, their mode of life, were similar to those of their fellow-citizens, and their interests were identical with those of the dominant merchant class, which they understood thoroughly. They also understood the advantages of a democratic attitude. Though the richest members of the Guild of Bankers and Moneychangers, they became the leaders of the opposition. As gonfalonier, or chief magistrate of the republic, Salvestro de' Medici had supported the "little people" during the revolt of the *Ciompi* in 1378 against the oppressive Wool Guild and the extremists of the Guelph oligarchy. The revolt was suppressed and Salvestro was banished, but the influence of his clan continued to increase. The Albizzi family swayed the republic, a fact conveniently forgotten by detractors of the Medici. Maso and Rinaldo degli Albizzi were ruthless in the persecution of political adversaries, and they incurred much hatred by their heavy taxation of the people. Consequently the opposition gathered strength. While the Medici were kept out of office they extended their banking ramifications and gained more partisans by their discreet liberality. Finally the Albizzi were caught napping and Giovanni de' Medici was elected gonfalonier in 1421.

The gonfalonier was changed every two months, and Giovanni saw that there was little to be gained from his post under actual conditions. The executive was weakened by perpetual interference. Disliking the violent methods of other Italian states, Giovanni decided that the best way to safe predominance was to organize a party strong enough to guarantee the highest offices of the republic to its own adherents over a prolonged period. This became the chief article of his family's political creed. He was credited—some say wrongly— with advocating a new system of taxation known as the *Catasto*, by which every Florentine citizen was required to make a declaration of his property for the regulation of income tax. This proved a boon to the majority and put a stop to the unjust levying of forced loans. Thus, while he secured the financial supremacy of his family in Italian and European markets, he soared steadily on the pinions of democracy, paving the way for his eldest son, Cosimo, who succeeded him in 1429.

Amongst other parting precepts, the dying Giovanni had recommended Cosimo to avoid attracting attention. Cosimo was never to forget this advice. Envy, as he said, is a plant one should never water; and there was plenty of envy in Florence. Frugal in his personal habits, living as a homely citizen among citizens ultra-sensitive to the semblance of equality, he was content with the realities of power: others, like Luca Pitti, could keep the trappings. Instead of showing himself off in the Palace of the Signory, he quietly pulled the strings of government from his private mansion, now Palazzo Riccardi. Instead of building himself a vast edifice like that of the Pitti, he built one of more modest dimensions—modest, that is to say, for one far richer than any contemporary king.

Vasari tells us that Brunelleschi had first designed a palace for Cosimo, but this seemed "too sumptuous and magnificent, and would attract the envy of his fellow-citizens," so he chose the simpler and less costly design of Michelozzo Michelozzi, the loyal companion of his exile. The building was begun in about 1444, and Vasari said truly that it was "the first palace built in Florence in the modern style". It remains a complete example of the Florentine palace in the fifteenth century: that of the Strozzi, which was derived from it, is another. In Rome there are palaces more grand and extensive, but those are less intimate. Cosimo's mansion, as Hawthorne wrote, "gives the visitor a stately notion of the life of a commercial man in the days when merchants were princes". The salient features of its façade are the bold projection of the heavy cornice, the irregular rough-hewn blocks of the ground floor, solid as a ledge of granite, the modified relief of the first floor, and the smooth surface of the top storey. Its character is severe and substantial: the building becomes more refined as it approaches the crowning cornice.

The ground floor consists of two courtyards, the first surrounded with a pillared arcade of that cool grey *pietra serena* which is peculiarly Tuscan. Halls, drawing-rooms, waiting-rooms, studies, bakeries, kitchens, and staircases opened on to these courtyards. One of the darkest and smallest rooms is the most sumptuous: this is the chapel covered with frescoes by Benozzo Gozzoli, who must have painted them by lamplight. Here the pageantry of the Medici has been perpetuated in a courtly cavalcade of the Three Kings to Bethlehem. The kings and their attendants are identifiable portraits, and the landscape is that of Tuscany. The Florentines, so frugal in private life, had always been noted for the splendour of their public entertainments, which increased under the Medici. Besides the Adoration of the Magi, the event so gracefully illuminated by

Benozzo was the General Council for the union of the Greek and Latin Churches, which had been transferred from Ferrara to Florence in 1439. The Greek Patriarch and the Emperor John Palaeologus, who attended the Council, are depicted as the first two kings of the fresco.

The Council of Florence did more to revive the study of Greek than to unite the Churches: it was one of the three events, as Lord Acton wrote, "which determined the triumph of the Renaissance". (The others were the fall of Constantinople and the election of Parentucelli as Pope Nicholas V.) Among the Greek dialecticians present was Gemistos Plethon who devoted his long life—he died a centenarian—to the study of Plato. So captivated was Cosimo by the novelty and force of his arguments that he decided then and there to cultivate this "new philosophy", with far-reaching effects throughout Europe. Plato was set up in the place of Aristotle, and the Platonic Academy was founded to propagate his doctrines.

With uncommon perspicacity Cosimo selected Marsilio Ficino, the eighteen-year-old son of a doctor from Figline, to become the high priest of Platonism in Florence. "Thy son", he told the doctor, "is born to minister to minds, not bodies"; and he took him to live in his palace, as his grandson, Lorenzo, was to take Poliziano and Michelangelo. Henceforward Ficino devoted himself entirely to Plato and the Neo-Platonists, translating their works and writing copious commentaries. One of Cosimo's last letters to Ficino is an eloquent proof that his enthusiasm for Plato was no passing fad: "Yesterday I came to the villa of Careggi, not to cultivate my fields but my soul. Come to us, Marsilio, as soon as possible. Bring with thee our Plato's book *De Summo Bono*. This, I suppose, you have already translated from the Greek language into Latin as you promised. I desire nothing so much as to know the best road to happiness. Farewell, and do not come without the Orphean lyre."

While other countries were plunged in feudal barbarism, here in Florence was an intellectual atmosphere akin to our own. Here are men we may understand, whose ideas to a certain extent resemble ours, though we may not have time to follow a Ficino through the maze of his metaphysical and theological doctrines. "The Renaissance of the fifteenth century", wrote Pater, "was, in many things, greater rather by what it designed than by what it achieved." Ficino summed up the aspirations of his age. He wished to reconcile Christianity with Platonism, to prove that the one was the consequence of the other. Though a sincere Christian who eventually took orders, he burned a lamp before the bust of Plato and revered him as a saint. His influence on the culture of the age was immense: it permeated Florentine society, inspiring the highest achievements of Florentine art and freeing the human intellect from the last fetters of the Middle Ages. Little wonder that students came from all over Europe to attend his lectures.

Thus Cosimo de' Medici was directly responsible for the growth of Italian Hellenism and stood in the vanguard of the spiritual tendencies of the day. Though many of his recorded sayings sound cynical, such as, "a government cannot be maintained by paternosters", this seeming cynicism is a Florentine veneer not incompatible with piety. He spent many an hour of retreat in the Convent of San Marco, which he had caused to be rebuilt by Michelozzo after his return from exile in 1434. Here the Blessed Fra Angelico began the great work of his life, the decoration of the convent walls; here the prior, Savonarola, was to play his disastrous rôle at the end of the century. When the insatiable collector of manuscripts, Niccolò Niccoli, died bankrupt in 1437, Cosimo paid all his debts and placed four hundred of his *codices* in the library of San Marco for public use. These were later increased at his own expense, and formed the first public library in Europe. Tommaso Parentucelli, who catalogued this library for Cosimo and noted the books that were necessary to complete it, was to become Pope Nicholas V, and repaid past services by making Cosimo his banker.

Cosimo's power was felt beyond Italy, for he had branch banks or agents in France, England, the Netherlands, and the

PLATE 17

PIERO DE' MEDICI
From a painting by Piero di Cosimo

LORENZO DE' MEDICI
As one of the three wise men in the painting by Benozzo Gozzoli

PLATE 18

GIULIANO DE' MEDICI
From the tomb by Michelangelo in the New Sacristy,
San Lorenzo, Florence

A TOURNAMENT IN FLORENCE
From a Florentine cassone of the 15th century

Levant. He had extended Florentine commerce until "a blow aimed at the Medici gave a shock to every European market, and hence it was the interest of foreign princes to protect their credit". Besides his financial acumen, which was prodigious, he was quick to recognize talent, and he was probably at his best with artists and men of letters. Giovanni Rucellai expressed the feelings of many of his fellow-citizens when he thanked God that he was a native of Florence, "reputed the noblest and most beautiful city in the world", and that he lived in the age of Cosimo de' Medici.

With the exception of one painter of genius, Masaccio, who died young, humanism bore its earliest fruit in sculpture and architecture. The precursors, Ghiberti, Brunelleschi, and Dona-tello, had appeared at the beginning of the century, but their influence continued far beyond it. These gave visible form to the ideals of the newly-awakened intellect. Ghiberti had won the competition for the bronze doors of the Baptistery at the age of twenty, in 1401, a convenient point of departure for the development of Renaissance art. Brunelleschi won the second place in this competition, which was fortunate for architecture. In 1403 he set out for Rome with his friend, Donatello, then aged sixteen. Their interest in the ruins, then infinitely less ruined than today, was incomprehensible to the Romans, who imagined they were digging for treasure, as indeed they were in a spiritual sense. They devoted the next four years to a study of the classical style, a course which was then quite novel. No doubt the completion of the Florentine Cathedral was at the back of Brunelleschi's mind. In 1420 his opportunity came: he was appointed to execute the work. His study of the Pantheon helped him to raise the Duomo, on which Michelangelo was to base his design of St. Peter's.

The various suggestions at the meeting of master-builders in 1420 explain why Brunelleschi's project—a free dome built with the aid of scaffolding at relatively small cost—seemed incredible to his contemporaries. The most extravagant was that the dome be raised over a huge mound of earth piled on the floor of the

10

cathedral; silver coins were to be mixed with it to encourage
the workmen to hasten its removal. In the meantime Brunelleschi had the jealousy of Ghiberti to contend with, and he was
often exasperated to the point of resigning. The cupola was not
finished till 1436, and it was then the largest in existence, the
diameter 138½ feet, and the altitude of the dome itself 133 feet,
measured from the cornice of the drum to the eye of the dome.
It was the first great achievement of Renaissance architecture,
though the smaller buildings which Brunelleschi completed
while the dome was in progress had an influence quite as
fruitful. The Pazzi Chapel, built between 1420 and 1430,
was in every serene and balanced detail distinctive of the new
age; few would disagree with Anderson that it "was probably
the very first ecclesiastical building in Renaissance style, unmatched by any previous building that we know of". The
interior and old sacristy of San Lorenzo, the Badia of Fiesole,
Santo Spirito, the loggia of the Spedale degli Innocenti, or
Foundling Hospital, the original design of the Pitti Palace—all
these masterpieces were due to Brunelleschi, who died in 1446.

Most of Ghiberti's life was dedicated to modelling, casting,
and gilding the north and east doors of the Baptistery. They are
triumphs of artistic workmanship, and since Michelangelo
remarked that they were worthy to be the gates of Paradise
there is nothing new to be said in their praise. They have to be
seen in all their golden glory. Panel by panel, niche by niche,
their influence on painting as well as sculpture has been
tremendous. Ghiberti and Donatello did not imitate the antique;
they studied it to learn its secrets and apply them to modern
sculpture. It was Donatello who persuaded Cosimo to collect
antique statues for public exhibition, and these were arranged in
the garden of San Marco so as to form an open-air museum
and art academy combined. Many a broken statue was
repaired by Donatello himself, and the study of the antique
was made easier for his successors. With due respect for
Ghiberti's doors, Donatello towered above contemporary
sculptors. He embodied in sculpture, as his junior Masaccio did

in painting, the beauty and dignity of the individual with his peculiarities, of outward life, of physical power, and self-reliance. Both selected forms which realized their conception of physical and intellectual ability. Their true interests were those of the humanist.

In his commentary on Dante's *Divine Comedy* the humanist Landino, writing in 1481, mentions Masaccio, Fra Angelico, Fra Filippo, Paolo Uccello, and Andrea del Castagno as the names of the great painters of the fifteenth century no longer living, Brunelleschi, Ghiberti, Donatello, and Desiderio as the great sculptors. Already the Florentines were conscious of the glory bestowed upon their city by the works of art within its walls. Masaccio's few frescoes were long the chief model and inspiration of the whole Florentine school. A naturalism was evolved which had little to do with realism, since it was always tempered by a pervading sense of the decorative. The human form, anatomy, physiognomy, relief, linear and aerial perspective, these became the essential objects of study. Uccello would sit up half the night working out rules of perspective, and when his wife urged him to go to bed, he would merely exclaim: "Oh, how sweet a thing is perspective!" Few of his works survive, but these have achieved a clamorous popularity after centuries of neglect. His three heraldic battle-scenes of the *Rout of San Romano*, which were commissioned by Cosimo and hung in the bedroom of Lorenzo the Magnificent, give us a clearer insight into the poetic chivalry of the period, through his mastery of colour and design, than of the perspective upon which he plumed himself. Castagno came closer to realism; his aim, as Mr. Berenson observed, was to communicate at any cost a feeling of power. His single figures were plainly influenced by Donatello; the full-length portraits of famous Florentines which he painted for the hall of Villa Pandolfini at Legnaia, are admirable illustrations of the forceful qualities then generally admired: thus would these Tuscans have wanted to be portrayed. The works of the saintly Dominican Fra Angelico and the sensual Carmelite Fra Filippo Lippi are more numerous;

and both won immediate plaudits from all Florentine connoisseurs.

The last year of Cosimo's life was clouded by the loss of his son, Giovanni, and his grandson, Cosimino, and he sighed that his palace was now too large for so small a family. His eldest son, Piero, was crippled by gout. However, till the end Cosimo found solace in philosophy. Talking to Ficino, he lamented the misery of humanity and looked forward to the happier prospect he felt opening ahead of him. Ficino cited similar ideas from Greek authors, especially from Xenocrates, whereupon Cosimo begged Ficino, as a last service, to translate his treatise on death into Latin. Cosimo died at his villa of Careggi in 1464, at the age of seventy-five, and was buried without pomp in San Lorenzo, at his own request. To commemorate the death of the real head of the state, his fellow-citizens awarded him the posthumous title of *Pater Patriae*.

Cosimo was succeeded by his son, Piero "the Gouty", aged forty-eight. In spite of chronic ill health Piero continued to control foreign policy, and his correspondence reveals a stoical strength of character. He was also a discriminating art collector and the true organizer of the Medici museum, but his reputation has been overshadowed by his dazzling son, Lorenzo.

Born in 1449, Lorenzo was only fifteen when Cosimo died, but he was already qualified to step into the public arena. According to Plato, the foundation of government is the education of youth, and Lorenzo had been educated by accomplished Platonists. Gentile Becchi of Urbino, the Greek Argyropoulos, Ficino, and Landino were his tutors; he had associated freely with his father's and grandfather's guests, including statesmen, financiers, and ambassadors, at an age when modern children are more concerned with bicycles. He enjoyed riding and open-air sports, and he had a zest for country life which was to give a spontaneous vitality to his poems. Paolo Uccello's romantic *Hunt*, in the Ashmolean Museum at Oxford, may represent Lorenzo hunting near Pisa: it is a superb evocation of the thrill and rhythmic elegance of horsemen and hounds converging upon their quarry in a dark-green forest.

Owing to Piero's gout, Lorenzo and his younger brother, Giuliano, became the social pivots of the Medici party. They shared their youth with the whole of Florence, and the sweet spirit of this fleeting festive season is still vibrant in Lorenzo's Carnival Songs and in the *Primavera* of Botticelli, whose painting was in perfect harmony with Lorenzo's aesthetic aspirations. Lorenzo was always a poet, and this is what has baffled the historians, who are unaccustomed to the poetic temperament. His complex personality, so sensuous, subtle, and impressionable, was a tissue of amazing contradictions. Ficino said that he possessed the three endowments called graces by Orpheus: splendour of intellect, light-heartedness in resolution, and the gift of renewing his youth. He was the new type of Renaissance gentleman, whose portrait was to be idealized by Castiglione in the *Cortegiano*.

Lorenzo inherited little of his parents' caution and sobriety. He had an almost morbid cult of springtime, and he delighted in beautifying the popular festivals which Florence had celebrated since time immemorial, transforming them into splendid spectacles. He personally supervised the pageants for St. John the Baptist's day (24 June), the patron saint of the city, choosing the most original artists to design triumphal chariots, and composing special hymns.

"You must study to be old beyond your years, for the times require it", wrote his ailing father, who described himself as a man without hands apart from Lorenzo. So Lorenzo was sent in his teens on missions to Milan and Rome, where he gained precocious experience of the world. These missions were more complicated than they appeared: during his visit to Rome in 1466 he had to negotiate a concession of valuable alum mines and try to gain papal support for the Sforza of Milan. The death of Francesco Sforza caused a political crisis in the meantime; uncommon tact was required to deal with such problems. Piero's foreign policy, like Cosimo's, was based on the triple alliance of Naples, Milan, and Florence, and his letters to Lorenzo prove that he could confide in him as in an adult, though Lorenzo was only seventeen.

But business was always combined with pleasure. The tournaments which Lorenzo organized in the square of St. Croce have been described minutely in verse. They appear to have been more decorative than dangerous. Each knight entered the lists preceded by an equerry bearing his standard. Some suitable allegory, or the portrait of the lady whose colours he wore, was painted on the latter. For the joust Lorenzo held in honour of his mistress, Lucrezia Donati, on 7 February 1469, no less an artist than Verrocchio painted his standard. Lorenzo rode into the square in a surcoat with a red and white silk cape, and a scarf embroidered with roses, some fresh and some withered, surrounding his motto, *Le Tems Revient*, picked out in pearls. A plume of gold filigree set with diamonds and rubies stood from his black velvet cap, to display a pearl of exceptional value. For the combat he wore a velvet doublet embroidered with golden lilies, and a helmet with three blue feathers replaced the jewelled cap. His shield was emblazoned with the three gold lilies of France, the privilege for bearing which had been granted to his father in 1465, and in the centre shone the great Medici diamond. Naturally Lorenzo won the prize, although, as he modestly wrote, "I was not a very vigorous warrior, nor a hard hitter."

Six years later a tournament was held by Giuliano in the same square, in honour of his mistress, Simonetta Vespucci. Verrocchio painted another standard and designed a gala helmet for this occasion. Giuliano's connection with the beautiful Simonetta, like Lorenzo's with Lucrezia Donati, was too widely advertised to be other than platonic. Both young ladies were married and highly respectable, and were regarded in the light of Dante's Beatrice or Petrarch's Laura by the poetical brothers. One hears little of their husbands: Simonetta's was cousin to the navigator, Amerigo Vespucci, who was to bequeath his name to the New World. To the artists who knew her,

Simonetta was a feminine personification of the Renaissance. She was reputed to have been the "distinct and peculiar type" so frequently painted by Botticelli, who was haunted all his life by her exquisite blend of Christian and pagan charm; and Poliziano wrote of her that "among her other excellent gifts, she has such sweet and attractive manners that all those who enjoy her intimacy ever so slightly, or on whom she bestows the lightest attention, believe themselves to be the sole objects of her affection. And at the same time no woman is jealous of her and all praise her without reserve. It seems extraordinary that so many men love her to distraction without arousing jealousy."

There is a tragic poignancy about the fate of Simonetta and Giuliano, whose lives were like symbols of a too brief, too happy spring. Simonetta died of consumption just a year after she had crowned Giuliano victor of the joust he had held in her honour, and precisely two years later, at the age of twenty-three, Giuliano was stabbed to death in the cathedral. After hearing of Simonetta's decease, Lorenzo wandered out into the night with a friend. Suddenly he stopped: a brilliant star was shining overhead. "Look," he exclaimed, "it must be the soul of that lovely lady! Either she has been transformed into this new star, or she has gone up to join it." Another night, while walking in the garden of one of his villas, "he observed a sunflower, which at eventide turns towards that western horizon which has stolen the sun away, until in the morning the sun reappears in the east . . . and he beheld therein an image of our destiny when we lose a being we love, for thus we remain with all our thoughts turned towards the vanished vision".

Piero waived family tradition in finding a bride for Lorenzo outside Florence. A marriage was arranged with Clarice Orsini, of the noble Roman clan whose vast influence and possessions extended from Rome to Naples. Lorenzo's mother, Lucrezia, went to Rome to inspect the bride. Her brother, Giovanni Tornabuoni, was papal treasurer and head of the Medici bank there, but she could only trust her own eyes.

Lucrezia was the perfect Florentine matriarch, dignified, intelligent, and cultured: old Cosimo had called her "the man of the family". From Rome Lucrezia wrote to her husband describing the bride to be: "On the whole the girl seems to be far above the average, but she cannot compare with Maria, Lucrezia, and Bianca (her own daughters). Lorenzo has seen her and you should find out whether she pleases him. Whatever you and he determine will be well done, and I shall be content. Let us leave the issue to God."

Lorenzo discriminated between passion and policy, and he was satisfied with the choice. His marriage gave further opportunities for celebration, though the festivities did not differ considerably from those of other great Florentine houses. Many a dowry chest of the period was depicted with similar scenes, the wedding procession advancing to the sound of trumpets and fifes under a long striped awning. The dishes were copious but simple, and the arrangements were in good taste without flamboyant luxury. The veal, poultry, fish, including trout, and the confectionery washed down with local wines, would also figure on a modern bill of fare, except for the pullets garnished with sugar and rose-water, and the caramels made of pine kernel. At Lorenzo's wedding the guests were entertained in the palace now called Riccardi, where Donatello's *David* in the courtyard and *Judith* in the garden formed centres for the various tables "laid with the finest white damask according to our fashion". Outside the palace a stage had been erected for dancing, which was decorated with tapestries and draped with large curtains of purple, green, and white, embroidered with the arms of the Medici and the Orsini. Lorenzo himself refers to the event rather laconically in his diary. But the bride soon won his affection and became a devoted housewife.

On 2 December 1469, Piero died of rheumatic gout at the age of fifty-three. "The second day after his death," wrote Lorenzo in his diary, "although I was very young, being twenty-one years of age, the principal men of the City and of the State came to our house to condole with us, and to persuade me to take charge of the City and the State, as my father and grand-father had done. I consented to do so, but unwillingly, as con-sidering my youth the responsibility and danger were great, in order to protect our friends and property, since at Florence life is insecure for the wealthy without control of the government."

This candid statement was not hypocritical. The drudgery of administration must have been wearisome to a youth of Lorenzo's temperament, but having inherited the tiger he had to mount it. He rode that wild animal with such skill that it is often forgotten he was much more than a great statesman. His historical importance and, to paraphrase Burckhardt, the spell which he cast over Florence and all his contemporaries, was due less to his political capacity than to his leadership in the culture of the age.

One of Lorenzo's first acts on succeeding to power was to restore the University of Pisa, which had decayed since Florence conquered Pisa early in the century. The university soon be-came famous throughout Italy, and a Pisan degree was made obligatory for Florentine practitioners of law. In Florence a bevy of distinguished Byzantine exiles taught Greek—Argyro-poulos, Lascaris, Chalcondilas, Andronicos of Thessalonica among them—so that Poliziano, who translated Homer into Latin, could write truthfully: "Greek learning, long extinct even in Greece itself, has come to life and lives again in Florence. There Greek literature is taught and studied, so that Athens, root and branch, has been transported to make her abode—not Athens in ruins and in the hands of barbarians, but Athens as she was, with her breathing spirit and her very soul."

Early in the century the humanists had been mainly pre-occupied with recovering and interpreting the long-forgotten classics of Greek and Latin literature, and Ghiberti had written of the discovery of antique marbles as rare and wonderful events. Whatever added to knowledge of the ancient world, and thereby to deeper knowledge of themselves, was eagerly collected. At first the admiration for all things classical had been indiscriminate, but the Platonic Academy led to the formation of critical standards. In literature, however, this was not a creative period. Philology and rhetoric had smothered originality, and the growth of vernacular literature was interrupted until the advent of Lorenzo the Magnificent.

Cristoforo Landino, who is best known for his *editio princeps* of Dante's *Divine Comedy* (1481), must have inspired his pupil Lorenzo with that enthusiasm for the Tuscan language which was to revitalize Italian literature. In 1466 Lorenzo wrote to Federigo of Naples his eloquent plea for the vernacular, which he elaborated in a long prose commentary on his own sonnets. This reveals Lorenzo as a critic comparable to Joachim du Bellay. Muratori selected four of his sonnets as worthy to rank with the best of Dante and Petrarch. More recent pundits prefer his longer poems, such as *Corinto*, *L'Ambra*, *L'Altercazione* (a Platonic dialogue in verse), and the *Canti Carnascialeschi*, or carnival songs, of which "Bacchus and Ariadne", with its dancing chorus, is so deservedly famous:

> *Quant' è bella giovinezza*
> *Che si fugge tuttavia:*
> *Chi vuol' esser lieto, sia,*
> *Di doman non c'è certezza.*

Certain it is that a new master of lyric verse had arisen. The lightness of the rhythms, the spontaneity of the images, the purity of the colouring, these were entirely his own. He reached maturity early, but considering his strenuous life of forty-three years his poetic achievement is wonderful in its variety of subject, metre, and mood. In his poems it is easier to recapture the effervescence of the Renaissance than in the more polished writings of Poliziano. *Nencia da Barberino* is no longer attributed to him, but there is no question of his authorship of *Ambra*, an allegory of his favourite villa of Poggio a Caiano. The story is artificial, and parts of it happen to be precociously baroque, but what Lorenzo has made of the whole was something quite fresh at the time. Instead of the usual flashing knights and twittering spring, for instance, he describes Tuscan peasants and the winter flood. Image by image the cold landscape is stippled, from the flight of screaming cranes above to the fish under the ice below. Gradually he leads up to a symphony of winds and waters let loose, with a swelling grandeur far in advance of the limited poetic vision of that age.

The carnival songs were melodious trifles especially composed for that festival, when Lorenzo would mingle with the populace and join in their merrymaking. He has been accused of pandering to the lower instincts for political ends; in fact he sublimated them with imaginative processions and masquerades. These represented episodes of ancient history or legend, or some topical allegory. Such fanciful artists as Piero di Cosimo were engaged to decorate them.

These picturesque entertainments were enjoyed by rich and poor alike, and Lorenzo acted as their impresario. Imagine one who combined the functions of a Prime Minister, a banker and business magnate, a Lord Mayor, a director of national galleries and museums, a president of the national academy, and a chancellor of two universities: such was Lorenzo when, without ever losing his dignity, he went out into the streets of Florence and led a masquerade. Far from diminishing his prestige, this proof of his versatility enhanced it.

Il Lasca, who compiled and published Lorenzo's carnival songs in 1559, tells us that some were composed for the olive-oil makers, for the young wives and old husbands, for the gold thread makers, the pastry-cooks, and so forth. The Magnificent Lorenzo's sense of humour was typically Tuscan, and it found literary vent in his rollicking burlesque of *The Divine Comedy*, the *Simposio* or *Beoni*, a forerunner of the satires of Berni and Ariosto. His humour also found expression in outrageous practical jokes, like the hoax on Doctor Manente recounted by Lasca. The sort of conversation he relished on a higher plane has been recorded in Landino's *Disputationes Camaldulenses*, dialogues supposed to have been held by members of the Platonic Academy in the beech woods near the convent of Camaldoli on four summer days in 1468. Virgil was discussed amid Virgilian scenery, and Plato's doctrine of the contemplative life. Leon Battista Alberti argued that the rulers of men should occasionally retire from the world and devote themselves to meditation, for how could anyone reach perfection when he was distracted by material things from developing his spiritual faculties? Lorenzo objected, for what would happen if all the best men withdrew from the duties of government? Would not worse men promptly step into their shoes?

In practice Lorenzo succeeded admirably in leading both the active and the contemplative life. His sonnets and sacred poems show to what a mystical extent this man of the senses could be contemplative, and his *Altercazione* proves that he was steeped in the new Platonism. He was as indefatigable as Cosimo in the collection of *codices*. Lascaris even searched Mount Athos on his behalf. Though Florence was rich in manuscripts, printing was not introduced there until 1471. Conservative collectors despised the printed volume mainly on aesthetic grounds. Lorenzo's library was available to scholars, and he employed a troop of copyists to enrich it and copy manuscripts for brother collectors like Federigo of Urbino and Matthias Corvinus, King of Hungary. A laurel-tree and the word *Semper* were stamped upon his bindings.

His relations with artists were those of a patron who was never patronizing. Donatello's pupil, Bertoldo, was appointed keeper of his art collection in the gardens of San Marco, with a special commission to assist and instruct young students. The poorer students were supported by bursaries and premiums for proficiency. The *bottega* system of training was thus supplemented, for Lorenzo was not satisfied with the prevalent state of sculpture. Nearly all Florentine artists were trained in some *bottega*, a shop and school combined, which served as a painter's studio, a gold- and silversmith's shop, and a sculptor's and decorator's work-room. There was no division of labour. The pupil or apprentice might have to cast a bronze statuette, paint a merchant's signboard, enlarge his master's sketch for a fresco decoration, or carve a marriage chest. This variety of training helps to explain the remarkable versatility of Florentine artists. Besides frescoes and altar-pieces for churches, Baldovinetti painted household altars for private devotion, panels to decorate bedsteads and furniture, marriage chests and shields painted with arms and garlands and inscribed with mottoes, gesso frames, mosaics, cartoons for stained glass and inlaid wood. Verrocchio was a goldsmith, sculptor, painter, bronze founder, architect, mechanician and, like his greater pupil Leonardo da Vinci, he also studied mathematics and geometry and became an accomplished musician. Many of the greatest artists of the Renaissance, among them Donatello, Verrocchio, Luca della Robbia, Leonardo, and Michelangelo, never married. Their friendships were passionate and profound, but they seemed to find sufficient outlet for their energies in the numerous arts they practised.

In Lorenzo's time it is probable that Verrocchio's school took the lead in technical training. Verrocchio conducted all kinds of experiments, especially with the novel medium of oil painting; both he and Antonio Pollaiuolo, with their insistence on anatomy, perspective, and composition, set the standard for the next generation and established the Florentine school of art as the most scientific in Italy. Pollaiuolo concentrated on the muscular system and emphasized athletic energy; Verrocchio was more concerned with intellectual power. The former excelled in painting, the latter in sculpture: the mantle of Donatello descended on both of them. Their immense contribution to art, which Mr. Berenson has analysed in his indispensable essay on the Florentine Painters, was in the rendering of landscape, movement, and the naked human body. Verrocchio was chief sculptor to the Medici: his bronze *David* was originally made for the villa of Careggi, so was the buoyant bronze *Putto* with the Dolphin, now in the courtyard of the Palazzo Vecchio. It is significant that in the tombs he designed for Cosimo, Piero, and Giovanni de' Medici in St. Lorenzo, not an emblem of Christianity is to be found.

Among painters Botticelli stood closest to Lorenzo: he reveals the taste and sentiment of the period more vividly than those whose visions he interpreted. His *Birth of Venus*, his *Primavera*, his *Mars and Venus*, breathe the same atmosphere as the poems of Lorenzo and Poliziano. Here is the Tuscanized Hellas of the Florentine humanists in perpetual flower. For skilled portraits of the same humanists we must visit the frescoes of Ghirlandaio in St. Maria Novella and St. Trinità, commissioned by Giovanni Tornabuoni, Lorenzo's uncle, and by Francesco Sassetti, Lorenzo's agent at Lyons. They can be recognized among the guests at Herod's feast, among the crowds who throng the temple, in these thinly-disguised illustrations of public and private life in the Quattrocento.

Lorenzo asked Ghirlandaio to send his most promising pupils to work in the garden of San Marco, where he wished to form a finishing school for sculptors. Among these was Michelangelo, who had already caused his teacher to exclaim, "This boy knows more than I do." For the next four years Michelangelo lived in Lorenzo's palace and was treated like a son. Those who were first at table sat next to the host, no matter who came in afterwards, so that Michelangelo was often seated above Lorenzo's sons and other distinguished guests. There he came in frequent contact with Marsilio Ficino, Pico della Mirandola, Luigo Pulci, and Poliziano—regarded as the poet laureate of the Laurentian Age. The latter, "recognizing the lofty spirit of Michelangelo loved him exceedingly, and little as he needed it, spurred him on in his studies, always explaining things to him and giving him subjects. One day amongst others, he suggested 'The Rape of Deianira' and the 'Battle of the Centaurs', telling him in detail the whole of the story." The resulting high-relief, now in Casa Buonarroti, is the earliest work by Michelangelo to which an exact date, 1492, can be given; and it shows already that "power over rhythm of line in a crowded composition" which distinguishes his later groups— a prophetic masterpiece all the more extraordinary when we consider his extreme youth.

A short distance from the garden where Michelangelo was beginning to realize the full aesthetic significance of the naked human body and the ideal grandeur latent in physical expression, Savonarola was preparing for the wrath to come from the Convent of San Marco. In 1491 Savonarola was elected prior of this convent, which had been under the special patronage of the Medici since Cosimo rebuilt it. Without Lorenzo's favour he could not have been elected, and he did not release his pent up furies until Lorenzo's death. For a few tormented years the dangerous demagogue from Ferrara was to frighten the Florentines out of their senses, but he could not entirely destroy Lorenzo's achievement.

The large-hearted Lorenzo could not have foreseen this ultimate catastrophe. He had overcome two major calamities, the Pazzi Conspiracy of 1478, when his brother was murdered in the cathedral and he himself narrowly escaped with a wound, and the two years' war with Pope Sixtus IV and King Ferrante of Naples which followed it. The war proved disastrous to Florence, and an outbreak of plague accompanied famine and financial ruin. Lorenzo's courage and diplomacy saved the situation. He sailed quietly to Naples and walked into the lion's den. King Ferrante would not have hesitated to murder him for any possible advantage; fortunately he was amenable to reason and susceptible to Lorenzo's charm. After three tantalizing months, during which Lorenzo had to maintain the rôle of a lavish and unperturbed Magnifico, the terms of a separate peace-with-honour were concluded. In March 1480 Lorenzo returned to Florence, a popular hero. Botticelli's *Pallas subduing the Centaur* commemorates this event. Vesuvius and the bay of Naples are seen in the background; in the foreground the Centaur, emblem of war and anarchy, cowers before the victorious goddess of peace and wisdom, wreathed with olive and wearing the interlaced rings of the Medici on her white robe. The anti-Medicean Machiavelli wrote: "If Lorenzo was great when he left Florence, he returned much greater than ever; and he was received with such joy by the city as his noble qualities and his fresh merits deserved, seeing that he had exposed his own life to restore peace to his country."

Lorenzo cannot be blamed if all his efforts for peace were to end in failure. The other Italian states were too involved in their petty differences to heed his arguments. Florence enjoyed exceptional prosperity during the last years of his life. Profits were high and the cost of living was low; great fortunes were invested in town and country houses, those well-planned villas with their formal gardens, farms, and orchards, which still add stateliness to the Tuscan landscape. The peasants, farmers, or hired labourers, were in many ways better off than the urban artisans. They paid no rent, were liable to no taxes, and only —but here came the rub—had to share the produce of the land with the proprietor. In good years they could put by sufficient profit to buy land of their own. Many an astute merchant found his peasants more astute; and they have changed little since the fifteenth century, when in kilted tunics and leather gaiters they drove the same type of bullock-cart into the city to sell their corn, oil, vegetables, and wine. Successful merchants also spent extravagant sums on churches, religious fraternities, and charitable institutions.

On 8 April 1492 Lorenzo died at Careggi of the same disease as Piero and Cosimo, though he was only forty-three. Even before he was forty he had tried various cures which had brought him but slight relief. His wife had died before him at the age of thirty-eight; his eldest son, Piero, had married another Orsini, and his second son, the future Pope Leo X, had been raised to the cardinalate at the age of fourteen. The dynasty seemed secure, and Lorenzo had always identified Florence with his own house.

"The splendour not only of Tuscany, but of all Italy, has disappeared", wrote the Florentine, Bartolommeo Dei. "Every day we shall learn more what we have lost. As yet it cannot be calculated, but time will show." And in Naples his erstwhile enemy, King Ferrante, said, "This man has lived long enough for his own immortal fame, but not long enough for Italy."

PLATE 19

PALLAS SUBDUING THE CENTAUR
Painted by Botticelli to commemorate the peace made by Lorenzo the
Magnificent with the King of Naples

PLATE 20

NICCOLO MACHIAVELLI
Terracotta bust, Florence, 16th century

BURNING OF SAVONAROLA IN THE PIAZZA DELLA SIGNORIA, FLORENCE
Painting by an unknown Tuscan painter, 1498

Under the influence of Savonarola there was a brief and bloodthirsty return to the Middle Ages. It was a tragic end to the most glorious century in Florentine history. Individual liberty was destroyed for the sake of what Savonarola considered a greater liberty: the secrets of the confessional and the privacy of family life were violated, and servants were encouraged to turn informers against their masters. Hideous tortures were devised for such offences as gambling, and costume was made the subject of severe legislation. Fasting became the order of the day; the Burning of Vanities replaced the Medicean festivals. Street urchins were organized into moral police, who trotted from house to house to collect "luxuries" such as ornaments, mirrors, cosmetics, and bric-a-brac, profane writings such as those of Pulci and Boccaccio, and, above all, any representation of pagan deities and of the sinful nude for the virtuous bonfire. It was the reign of religious mania and militant puritanism, and again the city was divided as of old. Yet many a historian has been devoted to Savonarola and indulgent to his excesses. The revulsion of the public was ferocious when it came in 1498. "Prophet! now is the time for a miracle!" shouted the mob, when Savonarola was hanged from the gibbet and a fire was kindled beneath him. In contrast with the yoke he had laid upon poor nature, the so-called tyranny of Lorenzo seemed positively Utopian. For as Guicciardini wrote in the 1530's, "Florence could not have had a better or a more delightful tyrant."

Rome of the Popes

15TH–16TH CENTURY

CECIL SPRIGGE

THE Emperor Constantine, after his conversion to Christianity, ordered the erection of a basilica on the traditional site of the tomb of St. Peter. That great church, consecrated in the year 324, embellished and enlarged and repaired throughout the centuries, survived in some form until the ruthless spirits of the sixteenth tore it down in order to erect on its place:

> . . . the vast and wondrous dome
> To which Diana's marvel was a cell,
> Christ's mighty shrine above his martyr's tomb
> Power, glory, strength, and beauty, all are aisled
> In this eternal ark of worship undefiled.

That the sixteenth-century construction could strike such a response in Byron cannot console Christendom for the destruction of the venerable edifice of which a clearer-souled pilgrim of the "dark ages" said: *Lumina stringit et corda laetificat:* it takes hold of the eyes and delights the heart.

The Roman empire was soon shared out between an eastern and a western Caesar, and the last western Caesar threw up the struggle against the barbarians in the year 476. The commanding figures in Christendom were now the eastern emperor who from Byzantium claimed the succession of the whole empire, and with this, in course of time, the headship of the Church; the Christianized barbarian kings who established sway over parts of Italy; and the Bishop of Rome

who progressively claimed to wield the highest of all human
offices as not only the successor of Peter but the vicar of Christ.
The eastern emperors gradually lost all hold upon Italy and
in 1053, a few years before the Norman Conquest of England,
all relations between the eastern and western Churches were
formally broken. Two and a half centuries before this the
Frankish or Germanic Charlemagne had claimed by his conquests to have restored the western empire. He was crowned
in St. Peter's in Rome on the last Christmas day of the eighth
century. Historians still discuss whether Charlemagne asked to
be crowned, or was taken by surprise when the Pope placed the
golden circlet on his head. The doubt is symbolical of the whole
history of the popes up to the time on which, in this short essay,
we have to concentrate.

All through the Roman middle ages, masterful popes strove
to make use of emperors as their chief policemen for holding
the world in obedience to the vicar of Christ, and masterful
emperors strove to reverse the relation by employing the Pope
as principal chaplain to the successor of Caesar and of Charlemagne. A few names and episodes remain in the memory of the
general reader. Who has not heard of Pope Hildebrand
(Gregory VII), keeping Emperor Henry IV shivering in the
snow as a penitent outside the castle of Canossa in 1077? Or,
moving on a century, of the Pope Innocent (the Third) to whose
legate King John, in Shakespeare's version of the episode,
swore that "no Italian priest shall tithe or toll in our dominion",
only, before the play ends, to yield "the circle of his glory" into
the legate's hand who returns it to him "as holding of the pope
your sovereign greatness and authority"? And readers of Dante
may remember half a dozen texts on the towering pope who
bridges the thirteenth and fourteenth centuries, Boniface VIII.
In his Bull "*Unam sanctam*", Boniface speaks of the two swords,
the spiritual to be wielded by the Church, the temporal to be
wielded for it, and he declares, "It is necessary for every man's
salvation to subject himself to the pope." He had lately excommunicated the Hohenstaufen claimant to the imperial

dignity, and the Bull was a sharp warning to the rising power of the French monarchy.

Alongside of these formidable popes there are remembered the emperors who bent the papacy to their will or defied it, Barbarossa and his grandson, Frederick II, though the former found in the English pope, Nicholas Breakspere, a man he could not trifle with. Finally, in the medieval fortunes of Rome, there are ever-memorable figures who were neither popes nor emperors, but echoed the never quite extinct tradition of the ancient republic: Arnold of Brescia, Cola di Rienzo (Rienzi in English verse and fiction), Stefano Porcaro.

Those were the times in which classical temples, tombs, arches, and the old city gates served as the foundations of high towers from which the proud Colonnas, Orsinis, Caetanis, Frangipani and other clan chieftains warred on each other, and in the name of emperor or pope dominated different quarters of the seven-hilled territory within the city walls, far the greater part of which was then, and substantially remained until late in the nineteenth century, orchard or waste land. There were said to be at one time nine hundred towers, and Brancaleone, one of the reforming "Senators", ordered the destruction of a hundred and fifty of them in the thirteenth century.

With the passing of Boniface VIII, who is said, when receiving certain imperial emissaries, seated with the tiara on his head and a sword in his hands, to have shouted, "I am Caesar. I am Emperor", the city of Rome entered upon one of the worst of her centuries, the fourteenth after Christ, a kind of epitome of her darkest experiences in the departing Middle Ages. The Roman-German emperor was now eclipsed as the dominant secular power by the King of France, and the story of the papacy in this century is one of French dominated conclaves electing popes who went to reside in Avignon, on geographically, but not politically, French soil, the semi-voluntary exile being varied by brief attempts to bring the head of the Church, or some ostensible head, back to Rome, and ending in the "Great

PLATE 21

JULIUS II, 1503–1512
Painting by Raphael

LEO X, 1513–1521
Painting by Raphael

CLEMENT VII, 1523–1534
Painting by Sebastiano del Piombo

PAUL III, 1534–1549
Painting by Titian

PLATE 22

MICHELANGELO'S CUPOLA : ST. PETERS

Schism". For more than a generation, two, and sometimes three, rival popes contended for the obedience of Christendom. The process of sorting out which of the contendants were genuine popes has gone on right to our own time, for in 1947 two popes of the early fourteen hundreds whose effigies appear in the nineteenth-century series of mosaic portraits in the Roman Basilica of St. Paul were dropped from the list in the Pontifical Annual.

The canonical chapters and religious Orders of Rome, the merchants, and the populace clamoured for the return of the fount of honour and the magnet of pilgrims from what resentful Romans called the "Babylonish captivity" of Avignon. Feelings were indeed tense. The Avignonese pope, Gregory XI, having in 1378 shifted to Rome and died there, a conclave was held on the spot, with French cardinals in a majority, while the Roman population demonstrated for the election of a Roman pope. The cardinals elected a non-Roman Italian, but in sheer fear for their lives pretended to have chosen an aged Roman, who was accordingly dressed up in the pontifical vestments and made to pass for pope until the cardinals could repair to safety. Only then was the real election result revealed.

The plurality of rival popes, together with the clamour of Christendom for a general reform, led at long last to the great Council of Constance in 1414 at which, after a series of abdications, a Colonna of Rome, Martin V, appeared as the more or less universally acknowledged Head of the Church. Martin entered Rome in 1420. "As the pope entered the city", wrote the humanist Platina in the following generation, "what remained of the people and the princes came with great joy to meet him, saluting him as the star of salvation, the last hope. Martin found Rome in such extreme decay that it hardly seemed a town at all, with shaky and tumbling houses, temples destroyed, empty streets. . . . The faces of the inhabitants themselves bore the sad marks of want and misery." And he added, "No trace remained of the beauties of ancient Rome." In a Bull published in 1425 nominating certain citizens as *Magistri*

Viarum, the Colonna pope described some of the consequences
of the disasters—plague and earthquake, as well as civil warfare—which had overtaken the city since the fierce but culturally active reign of Boniface (for the late thirteenth century
left abiding memorials in church architecture, mosaic, cosma-
tesque work, and even painting). In the stricken city found by
Martin V the butchers were huddled in the classical forum of
Nerva, the fishmongers in the ruined portico of Octavia (where
they stayed for five centuries). Martin lived to see many fallen
churches restored to worship and may be regarded as the first
pope of the Renaissance. His epitaph termed him *temporum
suorum felicitas.*

What followed upon the definite return of the popes to Rome
was—as we shall try to illustrate in a few brief excursions—
first a sort of Antonine age of learned and artistic enthusiasm
not divorced from moral purpose and a sense of historical
responsibility; next the tumultuous splendours and horrors of
the Borgia period; the power politics of Julius II, and the "not
inelegant sloth" (as Macaulay termed it) of the Medici popes,
drawing down upon Rome appalling civil and ecclesiastical
disasters, which however were largely made good in the mid-
sixteenth century by the constructive moderation of Paul III
Farnese. The long life of Michelangelo, a Roman by election
and residence, links the worldly first half of the sixteenth
century with its earnest and rigid, but eagerly active conclusion
under the banner of the new Jesuit Order. Then this militant
moralization in turn yields to the sentimental devoutness,
aesthetic exuberance, and aristocratic politeness which with
little difference characterized the Rome seen and enjoyed by
John Milton before Cromwell, and by the delighted Stendhal
after Napoleon. Rome had by then become the religious and
artistic sanctuary, and the political rarity, which it remained in
the childhood of very old men still living today. How the last
age of the temporal power appeared to the hundred thousand
or so plebeians of Rome, the unpolished but shrewd and proud
children of a unique historical dispensation, has been powerfully

registered for posterity in the two thousand Rome dialect
sonnets of G. G. Belli, an early nineteenth-century work in
which some have found an affinity with the ribald pre-classical
chants of ancient Rome, but which in fact, along with the
ribaldry, bears witness to the well-known saying that no one
can live in Rome without conceiving a universal idea. Rome, in
fact, is itself a universal idea which throughout the centuries
has moulded men to incarnate it, and stones to illustrate it, in
richly various but intimately continuous succession.

Although the papacy, after Avignon, never seriously laid
claim to the temporal command of Christendom, there still
hung about the sovereignty of Rome the implication of a
universal dominion in which the imperial was scarcely distinguished from the apostolic inheritance. This is well shown in
the concluding pages of the excellent guide-book, remote
ancestor of Murray and Baedeker, penned by Flavio Biondo, a
scholar attached to the court of Martin Colonna's successor,
Pope Eugenius IV. "Rome today", reflects the fifteenth-
century author, "is not immensely powerful, as it was in
antiquity. But it is still held in much reverence not only in all
Europe but in many parts of Asia. Attached though I am to the
Roman name, and respectful of that more than of anything else
except religion, I will not let enthusiasm blind me to the great
decline in Rome's majesty and estate since ancient days. Yet
neither will I accept the view of those who regard the Rome of
today as of no account, as if the disappearance of the legions,
the consuls, the Senate, the beauties of the Capitol and Palatine, had put an end to all things. No! The glory and majesty
of Rome still stands, and if less ample than before, it is better
founded. Rome still exercises some jurisdiction over the various
nations and kingdoms, and to uphold this requires not armies,
horse, infantry, volunteers or conscripts of Rome or all Italy,
nor frontier guards, for the security of all this really lies not in
armed bloodshed but in our most holy religion . . . its emperor
is not the successor of Caesar but the successor and vicar of the
fisherman, Peter, adored and revered by the princes of the

world. . . . Do we not see almost all Europe sending its tributes and tithes to Rome, as great a sum, perhaps, or more than was sent, in antiquity? And all other cities come to receive benefices from the Pontiff and the Apostolic See. It is true that this could happen in Avignon or other places where the Roman court lately sojourned, but Rome has great and wonderful things which cannot be found or transported elsewhere, and he who has not seen Rome, what has he seen? To see these things there come almost every year visitors from Hungary, Mysia, Macedonia, Acarnania, France, Spain, and even the Island of England, utterly severed from our land. They all come to Rome as the revered head and mistress." And Biondo goes on to mention visitors from Asia arriving in their scores of thousands "thanks to thee, Holy Father Eugenius".

In Biondo's remarks we may notice how the Roman-German emperor is gently elbowed out of the scene; then, how Rome's modern position in the wide world is asserted to be independent of military power, a kind of anticipatory criticism of the power politics of coming Renaissance pontiffs; finally, the repeated mention of "Asia". This alludes to the recent triumph of Pope Eugenius in receiving the formal submission of the Church of the eastern empire from a delegation of seven hundred Greeks headed by the Emperor John Palaeologus. This official healing of the east-west Schism in truth signified nothing more than a desperate appeal for help by the eastern empire in the last days before its extinction by the Turk. But for a few years it gave to the restored papacy in Rome an accretion of prestige at the expense of all those in Europe who were striving to establish the authority of General Councils over the Bishop of Rome. At the same time it brought a notable body of Greek scholars to Italy, a number of whom stayed on, seeing the fate of their own country already sealed.

In Rome, interest in classical antiquity had been waxing for a century. The page quoted from Flavio Biondo sounds a note of appeal to the classical enthusiasts not to despise too greatly the living at the expense of the dead—an appeal which might well have been directed to antique-struck French travellers in the following century, like Montaigne and Du Bellay, and to English and German travellers up to the times of Walpole and Goethe. The Roman authorities were already fired with classical ardour. A fine of ten gold ducats with confiscation of cart and horse was prescribed in 1452 for those tipping refuse upon the *theatri et edifici antiqui* of Piazza Navona, where the outlines of the circus of Domitian had been slowly vanishing for centuries. (A year or two earlier a citizen had complained of the disappearance of antique stone seats familiar to him in his childhood.) But the growing critical knowledge of antiquity had on the whole stopped short of direct communion with things Greek. The arrival of the delegation of Greeks, some of them soaked in the tenets of a romantically nationalist revival of ancient philosophy in the face of the Turkish menace, enriched the sensibilities of the Italian soul with the tradition of mystical Platonism of which Florence became at once the centre.

The pope who best of all stands for the enlightened humanism which preceded the age of the Borgias and the Medicis was Pius II. An erudite historian not too classicized to study the Middle Ages, yet a famed and elegant Latinist, and the only autobiographer among all the popes, Pius ("Aeneas Sylvius" as an author) died in a tower on the distant sea-coast of Ancona, waiting for a fleet from the united nations of Christendom to convey him on a crusading cruise against the Turks. The dying ambition of this pope who had the imagination and courage if not the realism of a leader of a civilization in peril, bore no immediate fruit. Yet this example may well have helped to fire Pius V, a century later, to throw his resources into the fateful and fruitful campaign of Lepanto, which saved the Adriatic for Christendom.

Pius II, with one or two of his predecessors and successors, shows the artistic and learned enthusiasms of the early humanism still nobly allied with a sense of historical responsibility. In art, the enlightened pieties of this age are illustrated, at its outset, by Fra Angelico's Chapel of Nicholas V (the first great papal patron of art and letters) in the Vatican, and towards its end by the great frieze of the Sixtine Chapel by Botticelli, Perugino, Pinturicchio, Signorelli, and others—the works to which Michelangelo in the next generation had to match his ceiling, and, later, his colossal altar-piece of the Last Judgment. Rome's share in these artistic glories of fifteenth-century Italy was wholly due to the popes. Not a man among these artists, and few of the architects whose walls they adorned, belonged to Rome by birth or permanent election. The art of Renaissance Rome, like the literature of classical Rome, is essentially the work of guests and visitors drawn by that genius of the city which has furnished the successive supreme magistracies of our civilization with a seat and a home on the seven hills.

It was Nicholas V who attracted the new class of "Humanists" to Rome, men versed in the literatures and philosophies of antiquity. He filled the Vatican Palace—of which his architects devised the features now visible from the Piazza of St. Peter's—with clerks, copyists, calligraphers, translators, a host of servants of the classical learning which was soon to take wings from the newly-discovered art of printing. In Nicholas's reign (next after that of Eugenius IV) came the great shipment of Greek manuscripts from the disappearing eastern empire. His successor, the first and relatively respectable Borgia, appears as an interloper in the line of humanist popes, and cared so little for these things that he tossed a present of manuscripts to a cardinal, retaining only the gold and silver cases. His was a purely political papacy, not unworthily preoccupied with military leagues against the Turk. His successor, in turn, was the Pius whom we have picked out as the noblest of these humanist popes for the conjunction which he realized between a rich culture and a wide-ranging policy. The last, and the most crudely ambitious of the early humanist popes is the Sixtus IV who left his name to the Sixtine Chapel, and was the true founder of that Vatican library which has drawn scholars for ever after from the whole world.

Under these popes, Graecists and Latinists swarmed around

those treasures, vying with each other both in knowledge of antiquity and in the classical versification which, as in a later age of the Church of England, had become a recommendation for ecclesiastical advancement. Lorenzo Valla shone as the out-standing figure in the Roman revival of learning. He had made his name, before coming to Rome, with a utilitarian or "Epicurean" ethical theory, and he ranks for the great free-thinking historian of papal Rome, Gregorovius, as "immortally potent in science, a pioneering genius, the glory of Rome", but for the Catholic historian, Pastor, as a leader of that "false Renaissance", which according to a modern Catholic school of criticism sprang up and obscured the legitimate Christian-spirited revival of the arts and learning.

But the papal Rome of Nicholas V was augustly tolerant. Valla had asked for trouble by exposing the falsity of the "Constantinian Donation", an act by which papal lawyers claimed to trace to a gift from the emperor the possession of those lands around Rome and up to the Apennines and the Adriatic which the diplomacy and military energy of Church men had hammered into fairly stable shape as the States of the Church. Valla's anti-papal polemic, penned, as he said apologetically, in the interests of the King of Naples, and with backing from the reforming Council of Basle, did not prevent Pope Nicholas from bringing him to Rome to translate for him Herodotus and Thucydides into the vigorous and supple Latin of which he was a famed master. Aeneas Sylvius also impugned the Donations, and played with the Conciliar cause, without prejudicing his later ascent to the papal throne. It was only in the next century, with the consolidation of "iron curtains" between the worlds of orthodoxy and reformation, and corre-latively between mundane and spiritual culture, that variations of opinion and the controversies of ecclesiastical politics came to leave an indelible smear on the careers of men of great mind. Valla, without apparently delivering himself of any recantation, died and was buried in Rome as a canon of the Lateran Basilica.

The later strictness was, of course, supported by reference to the licentious paths along which unbridled classical enthusiasms had developed. There was a narrow snobbery, and ultimately a shameless corruption, among the unreflective devotees of antiquity. The Italian language, which had been moulded to the highest uses by Dante and Petrarch, was scorned by the lesser fry of this cosmopolitan assemblage which wrote, talked, and thought in Latin and struggled with Greek, aided by a team of Greek refugees. In Florence there was a development of a kind of Platonic church in which sermons were delivered to "Dear brethren in Plato". In Rome, the Greeks had a sagacious guide in the Greek ecclesiastic, Bessarion, who was raised to the cardinalate and was a serious and respectable candidate for the papacy.

In Raphael's famous fresco of the *School of Athens*, painted in 1509, when the artist was twenty-five years old, we may see a backward-looking glance at the noble inspirations of the first and more temperate zeal for antiquity. On the opposite wall to the *School* is the companion fresco of *The Disputation of the Sacrament*. It has been asserted that the *School* with its portrayal of the branches and gradations of human inquiry, leading up to the dominating figures of Plato and Aristotle, has a sincerity of inspiration lacking in the *Disputation* in which all eyes turn towards the mystery of the Eucharist and the Deity revealed in Heaven. It has been noted, moreover, that the guide-book used by Goethe devotes pages to the *School* and a bare line to the other. This valuation is strenuously rebutted by Pastor. But the balancing of the Christian and the Greek wisdom is what in truth makes of the twin paintings the grand memorial to a vision which had shone with haunting radiance in the fifteenth century, doomed to fade out ingloriously when a baleful contempt for the historical spirit of Christianity roused new and terrible human problems, forcing the greatest spirits of the next age to range themselves under antagonistic banners of tradition and reform, liberty and morality. It remained for great artists to portray the grandeur

PLATE 23

THE SCHOOL OF ATHENS
Fresco by Raphael in the Vatican

THE SISTINE CHAPEL IN THE VATICAN

PLATE 24

THE SENATORS' PALACE ON THE CAPITOL
Built after the design of Michelangelo

of their indignation and anguish, or the complex tenderness of an escape into ecstasy, but no longer to express the self-confident balance of a modest and serene virtue.

The harmonization of antique and Christian ideals, no longer attempted in heartfelt artistic creations, was echoed by inferior spirits in a grotesque verbal syncretism. The deities of Olympus, portrayed in the vases and medals of which the popes had become eager collectors, entered into literature as *noms-de-plume* of the objects of Christian devotion. The usage extended from the poems and letters of the humanists to sermons (which provoked the ridicule of Erasmus) and even works of theology. Paolo Cortesio, secretary to the second Borgia pope, published a dogmatic treatise in which Christ was called the God of Thunder and Lightning, Mary the Mother of the Gods, Saint Augustine the Pythian oracle of theology, and Aquinas the Apollo of Christendom. In these combinations which term was in truth adjectival and which substantial? For spirits who were not merely elegant but penetrating, and could not hide from themselves the deep-lying fissure between the uncriticized body of Church dogma and the uncritically resurrected pagan imagery, there came into circulation the escapist theory of a "double truth", though this, indeed, was no special invention of that age.

A mild foretaste of coming storms in which intellectual licence would be punished by harsh and undiscerning regimentation, was vouchsafed as early as 1468 when the papal police arrested twenty adepts of the "Roman Academy" or Humanist club which had gathered around Pomponius Laetus, a veritable ascetic and mystic of Roman antiquarianism, disciple and moral successor of Valla, but unlike his master a Latinist and Roman nationalist to the exclusion of all interest in things Greek. Among the charges levelled against him was, however, that of indulgence in the "Greek vice" to which, whatever may have been his conduct, he retorted by observing that Socrates, too, had admired manly beauty. In the following reign of Sixtus IV the academy resumed its learned garden parties and kept them up until the final downfall of the early and uninhibited humanism in the Roman disasters of 1526.

The counterpart to this failure, by the most gifted and privileged secular society in Europe, to repossess the wisdom of antiquity without loss of the finer Christian sensibilities, was a growing loss of reverence for the historical heritage of Christianity on the part of the highest leadership of the Church itself. The lusts of the Borgias would seem more forgivable than the destruction, by the truly magnificent Julius II, of the Constantinian Basilica of St. Peter, did we not feel that this sacrilege was incidental to a noble, though partially perverted, ambition to celebrate a new age of prodigious human achievement by the stupendous symbol of a new central temple of Christendom.

In the mid-fifteenth century our proto-Baedeker Flavio Biondo, a representative of the early humanism at its best, gave high praise to Eugenius IV for his repairs to old St. Peter's. "Buildings now already six hundred years old", he writes, (here thinking of St. Peter's as dating only from a ninth-century restoration) "were about to tumble to earth and crumble to nothing, but thy goodness, blessed Pope Eugenius, has allowed us to see them all repaired." Very shortly afterwards Pope Nicholas conceived, and actually began, the construction of new external walls. Then these plans were laid aside for a half century. "Of the old monument," says a recent devout critic, "Pius II and his three successors had made the richest museum of the early Renaissance. An open-air loggia for Benedictions had been built at the entrance to the sanctuary. New chapels, altars, tabernacles, tombs of choicest marble now mingled their fresh colours with the Byzantine splendours of John VII's Chapel of the Virgin, and the mosaics of the earliest centuries. . . . The ancient temple had been rejuvenated and its walls stood firm despite the pessimism expressed about them in quarters not wholly disinterested." It would indeed have been asking a great deal of the great architects at the court of Julius II that they should be disinterested in their master's and their own thirst for glory.

The second Borgia pope, Alexander VI, and his frightful son had at this time vanished from the scene with their brutally brilliant family politics, their wild amours, their bull fighting. Their part in history had been to introduce the papal state resolutely on to the scene of Italian politics as a temporal and dynastic power, one among many, its ambitions the largest and its methods the bloodiest and most soulless of all. Alexander was also the pope privileged first to take cognizance of America, and to assign the New World to Spain and Portugal with the pleasure of a half-Spaniard who had filled Rome with the sound of his mother tongue and the sight of Spanish costumes. Julius II, who called his Borgia predecessor "the boar", was in still greater measure a military statesman. Politically his career began with the enlistment of French and Venetian aid against the relics of the Borgias, and ended with a humiliation of the Venetians and a league of all Italy to drive out the French "barbarians". These wars, in the perspective of after events, appear as the preface to the direct and indirect Spanish domination of Italy in the next century and a half. But no doubt the Borgias and Julius both impressed upon Europe that the papal state, with its religious prestige superadded to the ordinary resources of a small kingdom, while it no longer had power to intervene authoritatively in the great affairs of the world, could yet sustain a place in the balance of Europe.

Of Julius II we are, however, more likely to remember that his will to astound the world by an incomparable new central temple of Christianity, enclosing also his own sepulchre wrought by the greatest genius of the age, is primarily responsible for the dominating feature of the Rome that has now been known for several centuries. In 1506 Bramante—first architect of the new St. Peter's—began the necessary work of destruction. In a few years he had smashed age-old columns, shifted the tombs of the pontiffs, hauled down walls laden with mosaics and even with quite recent masterpieces of painting, smashing to pieces, incidentally, the monument of Nicholas V who had been the first to think of replacing the old basilica. No inventory was kept, and our knowledge of old St. Peter's comes from chance records and sketches. The truly great architect who thus earned the appellation "the destroyer", and the reprobation of his successors Raphael and Michelangelo, lived only to see the four supporting piles of the projected dome rising amid ruins. The operation begun in such frantic haste took over a hundred years to complete, and Michelangelo, whose name chiefly lives in it, did not himself see more than the tympanum of his marvellous dome when he died aged all but ninety. No more than a fragment of the vast tomb of Julius II was ever completed, and this—the famous statue of Moses—stands over the bones of the *Papa terribile* ("tremendous" rather than "terrible" translates this epithet), not in the great St. Peter's but a mile away in the quaint old basilica of St. Peter in Chains. The spectacle of the unfinished temple of temples, towering behind the surviving medieval porch, accompanied Romans through extraordinary political and religious convulsions to well beyond the Holy Year of 1575. Something very unlike the life of the humanist age then surged around it. The city had lately mourned the death of a Borgia, third general of the new Jesuit Order, thereafter to be raised to the honours of the altars as a saint. He was the great-grandson of the pope in whom not only Luther, but the people of Rome, had discerned the lineaments of a devil or trafficker with devils, and an old man might in his life have seen both the diabolical and the saintly Borgia. But let us look back from this anticipatory mention of expiation, to the epoch of Renaissance Rome's unblushing luxuriance.

At the coronation procession in 1510 of Leo X (Medici) one of the triumphal inscriptions ran "Venus has had her day, and Mars his, now comes the turn of Minerva." The two former deities stood for Alexander VI (Borgia) and Julius II, whose reigns had been highly profitable to the careers of courtesans and swordsmen. That of Leo, the priest of Minerva, bade fair to be the golden age of literates, scholars, poets, and actors, who under Venus and Mars had enjoyed only a tolerable degree of favour.

One of the best Latinists in Italy, who fortunately cultivated
Latin letters only as a pastime—otherwise Italian literature
would lack one of its chief glories—a friend from youth, moreover, of the new Florentine pope, was bustled by his friends
from Ferrara to Rome to try and profit in good time from the
connection. A string of needy relations wanted their distinguished brother, though a layman, to net a bishopric. But for
all his court connections at Ferrara, Ludovico Ariosto was at
heart a rather simple bluff gentleman with views not unlike
those of Chaucer on what a priest should be. He was useless at
place-hunting. Instead, his visit to Rome inspired him to write
a series of Horatian epistles which are the best record of clerical
and business life in the high Renaissance. The first epistle is
supposed to be written in advance of his arrival in Rome, to
his brother who is already there.

"I mean to be in Rome", it says, "what time the cardinals
like snakes change their skins." (In Advent they exchanged
scarlet for mauve robes.) Ludovico gives instructions for a
modest lodging for man and beast, with simple cooking
arrangements, facilities for buying wine from an inn, and a
stock of water drawn off from the Tiber and left to settle at
least six days. And then, books. Books he simply must have "to
read during those hours in which the prelates bid the porter
admit no callers". "Please, sir," he expects to be saying to some
prelate's servant "do for God's sake let the most reverend
Monsignor hear a word from me." The servant will reply in
Spanish *mañana*, for since the Borgias Spanish customs have
penetrated everywhere. "That vile Spanish subservience of
calling everyone Sir obtains even in the brothels." Requested
again, the servant will say, "No, no, the master wouldn't stir
for Peter or Paul, not even for the man of Nazareth." And the
poet supposes that Monsignor is very probably employed in a
way which it is much better for nobody to see.

The poet then plans a business excursion up the Aventine
hill. Here he has got to sign and seal an important document
concerning family business. The Ariostos in fact have an

12

ecclesiastical investment. They enjoy the right to certain revenues from a sanctuary in Milan. Ludovico shows an evident sensitiveness about the morality of this income. He tells his brother that he means to induct an honest educated priest to serve as curate. But in no circumstances whatever, after what he has seen of prelatical life, will he seek in this benefice the beginning of a church career for himself.

"People say this is the path to great honours and often puts a humble man in the way of receiving the obeisance of princes." But what is the lot of the average prelate? "It is not everyone that can lay hands on offices, abbeys, or a rich enough church to meet the cost of stable and kitchen." As a bishop one has the pleasure of putting a green lining in one's hat. But there are many mouths to feed, and the revenues of the first two years are earmarked for induction fees. Then one has a sudden call to St. Peter's, but the cook and the steward are not at hand and it is out of the question to go out without an escort. Then, when you are a bishop, you begin wanting to be a cardinal, and when a cardinal you long to be pope. And supposing you succeed in becoming pope? The first care is to lift your own sons and nephews out of private life, and the next, not—as it should be —to summon all Europe to roll back the Turks but to settle local accounts with the Colonnas and the Orsinis. Willingly a new pope will barter Italian lands to France and Spain to ensure that something may remain for one's own bastard off-spring. Then the new pope will shower forth excommunications and plenary indulgences. Without these, where would the funds come to pay for Swiss and German guards?

The other epistles describe Ariosto's actual encounter with the priest of Minerva, who treated him not unkindly, kissing him and taking his hand, and remitting the papal rights to a tithe on the Milan sanctuary. Then—silence, and with an Æsopian fable Ariosto recounts how little chance he really had of drinking at the fount of honour with all the thirsty Medicis around him.

The last of the Roman epistles shows Ariosto's relatives still at him, to have him get from the second Medici pope, Clement VII, what he would not or could not get from Leo. "Get yourself named Ambassador in Rome by our Duke (the Duke of Ferrara). You have such a pull with the Medici. You may well get some fine fat preferment for yourself."

This time Ariosto tells them that if they want him to return to Rome they must give him some better motive. And he indicates the happier possibilities of Rome for a poet.

"Tell me there will be leisure to revisit the sacred Muses and to go poetizing with them once more beneath the holy foliage. Tell me that with Bembo, Sadoleto, the learned Giovio . . . I may each day sharpen my wits. Promise that each of these in turn, book in hand, will guide me through the seven hills and display Rome in all her parts saying, here is the Roman Forum, there was the Suburra, that is the sacred hill, here was Vesta's temple, and there that of Janus. Tell me that in reading and writing I shall always have counsel at hand whether I wish to quote from a Latin, a Tuscan, or a bearded Greek: and recommend me that great store of ancient books gathered by Pope Sixtus for the public good of all the world."

But even if these delights can be offered, Ariosto ends by saying that he would sooner be back home in Ferrara. The Rome which he saw, and despite its pleasures for the humanist, disliked, was that of the same years in which Luther conceived his burning horror and Loyola his passionate determination to redeem and rescue. Leo X probably cared little for any of these attitudes, and on his death the popular muse of Rome sang:

> Favours from you buffoons alone could hope,
> Be off and get your own reward, damned Pope.

This was hardly fair, for the reign of Minerva was in later and grimmer times often sighed for as "the golden age".

Leo X died suddenly and the whole world saw how precariously the policy of the papal state had been conducted by this Florentine magnate on a thin margin of independence from two contending and overwhelming great powers, the Emperor

Charles V and the French King Francis. At the conclave of
1522 there were many candidatures and no obvious worthy
choice: it was at this juncture that the Englishman, Wolsey,
hoped to profit by the backing of the emperor. But the emperor,
with the agitations of Luther behind his back, pressed the cause
of the unwilling Dutchman, Hadrian of Utrecht, his family
tutor, intending him to initiate in Rome what afterwards
became known as the Counter-Reformation. Hadrian, duly
elected, arrived in Rome and looked upon the feasting, versify-
ing, art-worshipping city with much the same eyes as Luther.
Consternation reigned among the humanists at the report of
court poets dismissed, Raphael's paintings suspended, and the
threatened destruction of the masterpieces of frank or voluptuous art. But the "barbarian" pope, the last non-Italian ever
elected, died within a few months. With hectic rejoicing Rome
learned that a new conclave had elected a second Medici,
Clement VII.

This meant that Rome and the Church were back on the
razor's edge between the pressures of France and of the empire,
for the rise of French power was now countered by an emperor
in whom family ties had united the sovereignty of Spain,
Naples, and the Netherlands with that of his German domains.
Clement sided with the emperor and then switched to France,
Charles swore to avenge himself, but events took a far worse
turn, such, indeed, that the trump of doom prophesied by
Savonarola and prayed for by the Lutherans seemed really to
have sounded for the old capital of Christendom. An imperial
army, compounded of Germans, Spaniards, and Italians, got
out of hand and marched in a state of growing mutiny, hunger,
and recklessness down to Rome and before rescue could arrive
from any quarter sacked it with a wild thoroughness such as no
barbarian horde had ever displayed. A diarist among the German troops put the story with the utmost succinctness. "On 6 May
1527 we took Rome by storm, killed 6000 people, plundered
the whole city, took everything that we found in the churches
or in the streets, and burned a good deal of the place down."

The ignoble circumstances of the sack seemed to bear witness to the rottenness of the papal government and of the civic leadership. The aggressors, ill-armed and undisciplined, were led by a brave but reluctant adventurer. Had he not been killed in the first assault on the walls he might have kept the destruction within limits. They were pursued by enemies and they faced supposedly impregnable defences. The pope, who had tried to meet the danger by complex diplomacy, believed the Vatican quarters to be in no danger, and when the walls were breached had only just time to scurry across the moats into the Castle of St. Angelo with a dozen cardinals and remnants of his troops. Even then the invaders held only a stretch of the west bank of the Tiber and the main city might have been saved by destruction of the bridges. The fact that this was neglected has been ascribed to the hatred of the west riverside for the wealthy citizens across the water. Several cardinals believed themselves safe from outrage because of their imperial sympathies or connections, and waited in their palaces. But the 40,000 invaders spared nothing and nobody. Imperial, German, and Spanish palaces were destroyed or held to ransom with all others. It is said that some of the Lutheran fanatics among the German troops held a "Conclave" in the Sixtine Chapel, and proclaimed Luther pope in the place of the fugitive Clement.

There was far more health and energy in the old city, far more resilience in its institutions, than the collapse of 1527 first let believe. Architectural and political decorum were regained with amazing speed. Clement made peace with Charles and performed the archaic ceremony of crowning him—the last emperor so to be hallowed by a pope—at Bologna. In 1536 Clement's successor, Paul III, received Charles with full honours in Rome. It was the beginning of a truly noble pontificate, inspired by a new kind of moral endeavour—even amid the horrors of the sack the traces of a sort of Red Cross activity by Roman nobles had become apparent—but unsoured by contempt for the free creations of art. The old pope's lively temperament and aesthetic enthusiasm, balanced by the ripe moral seriousness of one who had seen and weighed many vicissitudes, seems to echo in the late dusk of the Renaissance the similar qualities of Pius II in its morning hour. Like old Michelangelo, whose powers as an architect and painter he taxed as ruthlessly as the tremendous Julius had done before, Pope Paul Farnese was a survivor from the heyday of humanism. But the peacocks and butterflies of the Renaissance, the Roman Academy, the paganizing Latinists, had had their day. The new tempered humanism of the first Counter-Reformation reign was too finely balanced to endure. The Farnese era was a breathing space before an age of moral revolution.

The disorders of the Christian world which inspired Martin Luther to pit his wounded conscience against the easy-going and corrupt sloth of Medici Rome, inspired in his close contemporary Ignatius Loyola the ambition to renovate traditional Christianity from within, by the heroic exercise of a soldierly obedience to the vicar of Christ. Both came and saw the worldly heyday of Rome before the sack, the Rome of Ariosto's satires. Luther shook the dust of Babylon from his feet for ever; Ignatius, after a decade of gruelling studies and intrepid adventures of body and soul, returned to stamp upon the Church and the venerable city a new and revolutionary aspect. *Romae vobis propitius ero*, a mystical figure had told him in his prayers.

It fell to Pope Paul Farnese to receive and grant the petition of Loyola for recognition of an Order pledged to serve the pope's cause in the lands of the Turks, in America, or among the new Protestant infidels: *"sive miserit nos ad Turcos, sive ad Orbem Novum, sive ad Lutheranos"*. The Order, at first a group of young Spaniards, expanded and waxed at a prodigious pace. It was formally constituted in Rome in 1541 with a small church at the foot of the Capitol, the historic hill for which Michelangelo was then devising the exquisite architectural arrangement we admire today. Ten years later a notice went up near by: "School of Grammar, the Humanities, and Christian Doctrine —Free of Charge." A year or two after that the Order had

1500 members, organized in one hundred houses scattered through the world. In another thirty years it had over 10,000 members and nearly 300 schools, numbers which were about doubled in the following century.

The early obstacles to the Jesuit advance came not so much from frightened worldly interests (though the first school was invaded and ravaged by Roman schoolmasters and their pupils) as from other zealous reformers who sought to redress and moralize the Roman Church on more traditional lines. The Jesuit discipline departed from all precedent by not requiring from the members of the Order a regular choral recitation of the offices of the Church. Late in the sixteenth century the two austerest pontiffs seen since the high Middle Ages (Dutch Hadrian only excepted) forced the reluctant Jesuits to institute choral offices. The most difficult pontiff for the new Order which offered itself as a veritable life-guard or commando troop for the pope was Paul IV (Carafa), himself the founder of the new ascetic Order of the Theatines. Added to his suspicion of the innovations of the Jesuit Order, that pope cherished a hatred for all things Spanish, and even conducted a brief and hopeless war against the Spanish régime in his native Naples.

The friction of the Jesuits with the older Orders arose fundamentally, perhaps, from a suspicion which has always hovered around these great educators, organizers, and politicians, in the eyes of their emulators and fellow-believers. It has been felt—and Carafa must have felt it—that their style of devotion and culture, brilliantly adapted to changing climates of opinion and fashion, leaves the ancient beliefs of Christendom, which they so fervently assert, isolated from the aesthetic and sentimental accompaniment which had historically grown around them. The neglect of liturgical worship in favour of lively and appealing popular cults, and argumentative, emotional preaching, appeared to the zealous and unworldly Theatine to forebode a new sort of religious *désinvolture*. The fullest and most revealing display of such suspicions occurred late in the next century in the shape of bitter charges formulated by the Dominicans against the Jesuit tolerance of "Chinese rites", or more properly of non-Christian observances in many parts of the East, where the Society of Jesus found it more opportune to put a Christian complexion upon ancestor worship or other popular customs than to seek to implant upon alien ground the forms historically associated with Christianity. The inner nucleus of dogma and ritual, faithfully and indeed fiercely guarded by the Jesuits, has to their critics seemed to have the facile neatness of an abstraction or formula too easily transferable to new settings and irreverently divorced from the historical atmosphere in which the most intimate ideas and ideals live and grow. The Jesuit appeared as a heroic soldier, pledged to "do and die", but not encouraged, beyond a given point, to "reason why"; argumentative, practical, efficient, polished, devoted, but consciously withholding his inner thought both from the inspection of constituted authority outside the Order, and from that of a freely ranging human criticism.

The full glory of this brilliant and intrepid movement was celebrated in Rome in 1587 with the consecration of the Gesù, the resplendent central church of the Order. The aged Michelangelo, who appears to have been on warm terms with Ignatius Loyola, had delighted him by undertaking to design the new church "for pure devotion, without charge" as the saint wrote to a friend. But work was delayed, and the existing noble church follows another plan. Originally a severe structure, it was soon made brilliant with perspective frescoes of what came to be known as the "Jesuit" style, breath-taking in their technical perfection and luxuriance.

A few hundred yards away there soon rose the other great Jesuit edifice dedicated to St. Ignatius, and still more astonishingly adorned by the painter, Father Pozzi. Between the two the stately building of the Collegio Romano, the centre of the higher education of Rome until 1870, bears the inscription of Gregory XIII, another of the line of ascetic popes whose name is important for the annals of the Order, to which he committed the care of the great institution.

Other influences, besides that of the Jesuits, accompanied the transfiguration of the festive and voluptuous city into the severe home of the Inquisition and of ecclesiastical censorship. Rome remembers with particular affection, as "Apostle of the City", St. Philip Neri, founder of the Oratorians, who shares a remarkable memorial with the tormented emulator and successor of Ariosto, the poet Torquato Tasso. This is a withered oak-tree on the Janiculum hill flanked by the inscription: "In the shadow of this oak Torquato Tasso close to glory and death silently meditated his sorrows, and Philip Neri, amid joyous shouting, played as a child among children, wisely." Or *sapientemente* should perhaps be translated "deliberately", a fitting term for the mood of the best spirits of that autumnal epoch.

An aspect of Roman life in which the change from elegant magnificence to severe sobriety was particularly sensible was the activity of the theatre and of other spectacles dear to Romans high and low. Under Alexander Borgia, Pomponius Laetus had laid on performances of Plautus and Terence in the courtyards of great houses. More than these Latin plays, the rough vernacular comedies, in which the non-Roman characters purported to speak the dialects of Venice, Naples, France, and Spain, delighted Julius II and in particular Leo X. And in imitation of the Latin comedians, Ariosto and Machiavelli produced elegant Italian comedies of light intrigue with a bitter and sardonic undertaste. There is no record of performances immediately after the sack, but popular comedies were played before Paul III. The grim Paul IV himself did not disdain to witness vernacular farces.

Still later in the sixteenth century a ban was placed on the theatre by the ultra-scrupulous Pius V. Yet at the same time Latin dramas were permitted in the Jesuit college. Gregory XIII enacted a still stricter ordinance against performances of any sort, but with an exception for those supervised by the Jesuits. Sixtus V in 1585 withdrew the ban, and little interference was afterwards experienced in the theatrical life which became a notable attraction in the mundane and cosmopolitan Rome of the sixteen hundreds.

The Counter-Reformation popes, Paul IV, Pius V, and Gregory XVI, remain in the memory of Rome as exponents of much grimmer restrictions than these. Paul forced the ancient Jewish community of Rome, indigenous ever since the classical empire, to wear the yellow cap and to inhabit a locked Ghetto. The Jews of Rome had enjoyed various fortunes in the Middle Ages; in the main, perhaps, a tolerance tempered by boisterous horseplay and minor bullying. Several great popes of the Renaissance treated them with affability, or at worst amused condescension. In some reigns Jewish physicians were prized and well rewarded and probably did well under Paul III. But the next Paul forbade the practice of medicine by Jews and annulled all privileges and permits granted by his recent predecessors.

The fourth Paul goes on popular record as the inquisitor and tormentor of heretics. He is the arch-villain of the monumental compendium of anti-papal propaganda drawn from all the ages and published by the radical agitator Guerazzi after the frustration of the Mazzini-Garibaldi republic. "Foaming at the mouth Pope Carafa prescribed steel and fire to extirpate the evil before it could take root: suspicion was to suffice for punishment: no regard for birth or rank: prince and plebeian, protected and protector were to tremble equally." The Roman people of 1559 judged him no differently, for on Paul's death they stormed the premises of his Inquisition and applauded the prank of a Jew who crowned the dead pope's statue with a yellow cap. Catholic apologists seem to be shyer of recognizing this unpopular pope's services in the Counter-Reformation than Macaulay.

Little better does Pius V fare in popular memory if Stendhal, in his annotations on the popes, can find no more to enter about him than "Saint Pius V: Grand Inquisitor when elected Pope: his sanguinary zeal won him canonization." Such an epitaph wholly ignores the great historical merit of a pope who was the political animator of that campaign of European defence against the Turk which culminated in the great naval victory of Lepanto, denying to eastern invaders for ever an access by sea to western Europe. Haloes have surely been won less worthily. In that great battle a papal navy fought with great courage and success under the leadership of the Colonnas, Orsinis, Farneses, and Della Roveres, princely families which only the discipline of the Counter-Reformation could have induced to such a brotherhood in arms. And Gregory XVI goes down in Stendhal's notes, and other epigrammatic judgments, as the celebrator of the massacre of St. Bartholomew among the glorious episodes of Church history. He was also, however, the reformer of the calendar.

The great age of the Counter-Reformation closed with Sixtus V, the preoccupations of whose short pontificate were finance, town planning, water, and banditry. The straight streets through which we now walk across central Rome, the good water supplies until recently enjoyed by the Romans, and the keen lines of many an obelisk cutting the Roman sky at visual points of vantage bear witness to the zeal of this great constructor. The memory of his ferocious police measures, however, occasioned at his death a popular tumult to demolish his monument, and a decision that never again should a statue be erected to a pope while he was living.

It was by the builders of Sixtus that the dome of St. Peter's was at last finished, and the event must close this brief passage through the great and varied age of Rome from the end of the Avignon Schism—when she was a chaotic assemblage of antiquities and venerable sanctuaries pervaded only by the haunting suggestions of an immortal right to stand before all other cities of the world—to the time of her physical and moral renovation, coincident with the restriction of her authority, thenceforth, to the exercise of a specialized religious control over the newly-narrowed European boundaries and the vastly-widened missionary fields of Catholic Christendom.

By contrast with other cities which have attained a culmination, and then decayed, or which give a merely local connection to a disconnected series of historical phases, Rome has been the centre of one great human experiment after another, each of which has taken over site and stones from its predecessor, to reshape them to a new but not entirely new end. Christian Rome took over the basilicas of antiquity. The Middle Age which in Rome cannot possibly be termed an age of chivalry took over the massive relics of wall and temple to people them with its own fierce history. The Renaissance rediscovering the grace of antiquity absorbed it for its own uses and ate up also many venerable remains of early Christianity. Something of this phase and of its decadence, eclipse, and repudiation has been described in these few pages. After the Counter-Reformation the scene again changes. The ferocities of religious dissension are largely forgotten, and Rome becomes the drawing-room of polite Europe. This is the age when Lord Chesterfield enjoins upon his son "the study of that extraordinary government, founded originally upon the superstition and ignorance of mankind, extended by the weakness of some princes and the ambition of others: declining, of late, in proportion as knowledge has increased, and owing its present precarious security not to the religion, the affection, or the fear of the temporal powers, but to their jealousy of each other". His Lordship very confidently (in 1749) and with reasonable accuracy, foretold the extinction of the papal state within a century.

But as, in the Napoleonic Age, the system of the great powers hardened, and the blood shed in tremendous wars illustrated, in lurid colour, the absence from the competition of the nations of any conscious care for the general good of mankind, papal Rome developed a new appeal for sensitive spirits. Its very existence, so precariously poised on the play of rival national cupidities, pointed back to what once at least had been the living ideal of a coherent Christendom. Does not this recollection echo even today beyond the boundaries of particular ecclesiastical confessions?

The conception of a central theme running through history and incarnated in a particular tradition may become swollen, may harden itself into an intellectual tyranny. But some such line of reference remains none the less necessary if history is not to crumble into autonomous fragments which in conclusion will be so much dust. It was surely because no other historical tradition displayed any claim of comparable dignity, because, in fact, the empires and kingdoms of the nineteenth century represented by comparison the pursuit of secondary, superficial, and short-term purposes, that physically disarmed papal Rome called forth such lyrical devotion from a noble mind like that of Louis Veuillot. But in truth the papacy was in no position to put the Great Powers morally in the dock. Its own moments of greatest achievement and glory were quickly followed by one of corruption and cynicism. From this it fought its way back into a high political and moral standing at the cost of an invisible amputation more serious even than the visible sundering of western Christendom into Roman and Reformed. The consequence of that mutilation is shown in the estrangement, for generations, of the intellectual and creative genius of Italy and France from a Christian tradition which was represented in the form of an authoritative and unquestionable imposition. That the amputation was less absolute than has been believed in the liberal world, and more susceptible to repair than had been feared, is surely shown by the emergence in Italy of a Catholic liberalism which can look other contemporary movements squarely in the face. With such signs in the sky, it may be permissible to hope for a day when the traditions of Christian as well as those of classical Rome may be cherished by all the children of Christendom without chilling reserves.

The Venetian Republic

16TH CENTURY

VICTOR CUNARD

JUST as the geographical position of Venice and the nature of the city's construction are unique, so the political and artistic contributions she made to the development of European civilization differ profoundly from those of any other state.

From the emergence of an organized community amongst the islands of the lagoon at the turn of the seventh and eighth centuries, until she achieved her constitutional maturity at the end of the thirteenth century, Venice had been a purely maritime power preoccupied solely with increasing her wealth and prestige through the activities of her merchants. The fall of Constantinople and the partition of the empire after the Fourth Crusade had left Venice mistress of the eastern Mediterranean, and her attempts to maintain her position had led to long and costly wars with Genoa, and thus occupied she had played little or no part in European politics.

While her fleets were engaged in maintaining her commercial prosperity abroad, the growth of her constitution and the codification of her laws had proceeded at home, comparatively undisturbed by influences from the mainland of Italy. The direction taken in the development of this constitution was determined by the new commercial aristocracy, which had acquired wealth and power by the opening of the Levantine markets after the fall of Constantinople. It lay in the curtailment of the doge's absolute power, and the gradual exclusion of all but an hereditary minority from the Maggior Consiglio or

Great Council, election to which had, since its foundation in 1172, been open to all classes of citizens. An extremely elaborate system for electing the doge, in which the chances of the ballot played almost as important a part as the votes of the electors, made the establishment of a ducal dynasty impossible, and the great majority of the population was effectively disenfranchised by the so-called "*Serrata del gran Consiglio*", or closing of the Great Council, in 1297. By this law, only those who had sat in the Great Council for the last four years, and those who could prove that a paternal ancestor had sat in it after 1176, were eligible. The people had lost all voice in the government of their country, and the oligarchy, or close caste, which was to rule Venice for the next 500 years, had taken shape.

At a time, then, when nearly every Italian city was ruled by a despot, and subject to the political instability which such a system involved, Venice, which alone had escaped the long struggles between the pope and emperor, and which, moreover, had never come under the yoke of the feudal system, found herself in possession of a mature, a strong, and a stable constitution. It was perhaps to be expected that she should, in these circumstances, be tempted to lay hands upon the territories of the weaker neighbours as occasion offered. Nor was the ambition of territorial aggrandizement at cheap cost the only reason which brought about Venetian expansion on the mainland. So long as the Venetian republic was purely colonial, only complete naval supremacy in the Mediterranean could ensure the food supplies necessary to the lagoon-encircled city, and already by the end of the thirteenth century the Genoese wars had shown how precarious such supremacy could become, and how expensive it could be to maintain. But, however desirable and indeed necessary territorial expansion may have seemed to the Venetian government at the time, there is no doubt that the adoption of this policy was the great turning-point in the history of the republic, and determined perhaps more than any other single fact, its rapid decline and final disappearance as a great power by the end of the sixteenth century.

During the fourteenth and fifteenth centuries, Venice became further and further involved in those clashes and intrigues of European politics from which she had hitherto held so successfully aloof. As she pushed her frontiers northwards to the Alps, and westwards to the Adda within striking distance of Milan, so did envy and hatred of Venice grow until, in 1508, she found herself with her coffers empty and all Europe joined together against her in the League of Cambrai. Only an astute if disingenuous diplomacy, which took advantage of every disagreement amongst her enemies, and the natural protection afforded her by the lagoons, saved Venice from annihilation at this juncture, but she never recovered from the effort it cost her, although she sufficiently rallied her forces to take a decisive part in the battle of Lepanto in 1571.

To form a just estimate of the extraordinary genius of the Venetians it must be remembered that during the fourteenth and fifteenth centuries, while they were perfecting one of the most beautiful cities in the world, while one of the greatest schools of painting was emerging, while architectural monuments of unexampled magnificence were arising on every island of the lagoon and in every town and village of the mainland dependencies, the republic was not only engaged in the continual European wars already mentioned, but was waging a series of costly campaigns against Genoa at sea, and standing single-handed against the ever-increasing power of the Turkish empire in the Levant. The Golden Age of Venetian Culture thus started in a period of incessant turmoil and uncertainty, and reached its apogee just as the political importance of the republic was disappearing, and its commerce staggering under the blows struck at its very foundations by the discovery of the New World and the opening of the route round the Cape of Good Hope. The maintenance of a sufficient internal stability to permit of so extraordinary a development of the arts of peace, however harassed by wars the republic may have been both on her continental frontiers and in her colonial possessions, was made possible only by the peculiar nature of the Venetian

PLATE 25

VIEW OF THE QUAYSIDE IN VENICE
Detail from a painting by Vittore Carpaccio
belonging to the St. Ursula series

PLATE 26

PROCESSION IN THE PIAZZA SAN MARCO
Painting by Gentile Bellini, 1496

DOGE LEONARDO LOREDANO
Painting by Giovanni Bellini

constitution: a constitution which was the despair and envy of other less fortunate Italian states.

As we have seen, the part of the new commercial aristocracy, which had risen to wealth and power during the thirteenth century, succeeded, by the law of 1297, in eliminating all traces of democratic representation from the Great Council, which had until then maintained at least some semblance of an elected Chamber. From then on the membership of this Council, which formed the base of the constitutional pyramid, was confined to the members of a small patrician caste, a caste which by the beginning of the fifteenth century included not more than 1,000 out of a population of 200,000. Gradually the representative and judicial powers originally vested in the Great Council passed from it, and it retained only the function of electing the great officers of state.

Immediately above the Council stood the Senate, the chief legislative body which was responsible for the conduct of foreign affairs. Above the Senate stood the six *Savii* or, as they would be called today, the Secretaries of State, above them again the six ducal councillors, and at the apex of the pyramid the doge himself.

It was not to be expected that the adoption of so rigid a constitution, by which the vast majority of the population was disenfranchised, should be accepted without some protest, and the conspiracy of Bajamonte Tiepolo in 1309, though ruthlessly and successfully repressed, opened the eyes of the new order to the existence of a strong opposition. It was their realization of this danger that led to the creation of a body which must be unique in constitutional history: "The Council of Ten". So many romantic stories have accumulated around this council and its activities that it is difficult to disentangle the true from the false and to give a faithful picture of its functions in the government of Venice.

Appointed originally as a temporary "Council of Public Safety" in 1310, and declared permanent twenty-five years later, it had no proper place in the constitutional structure of

13

Venetian government, but existed parallel with and on the
same level as the Senate. The very nature of the Venetian constitution, which had been carefully designed to prevent absolute
power falling into the hands of one man, demanded a rapid and
efficient executive power; it was to fulfil this function that the
Council of Ten was created, and it was by the shrewd exploitation of this necessity that it rapidly became the effective ruling
body of the republic. At its inception the Council was hedged
about with careful provisions to prevent it becoming too powerful, office was held for one year only, the three presidents were
changed every quarter, the doge and his councillors were
present at every meeting, powers of arrest were strictly limited
and an early jail-delivery of the Council's prisoners was insisted
upon. Its terms of reference, which included all matters affect-
ing the safety of the state and the preservation of morals, could,
however, be so widely interpreted that neither these, nor subsequent measures of a like kind, were enough to curtail its
effective authority, and the Council of Ten had not been long
in existence before ambassadors were reporting secretly to it as
well as officially to the Senate, and were receiving from it
instructions sometimes at variance with those given by the
constitutional body.

By the beginning of the sixteenth century almost the entire
diplomatic activities of the republic were indeed directed by
the Council of Ten and the negotiations by which Venice
extricated herself from the designs of the League of Cambrai
were entirely in its hands. In internal affairs the Council of Ten
first gave proof of the power it had attained by insisting, quite
unconstitutionally, on the abdication of the doge, Francesco
Foscari, in 1457. Such a usurpation of its prerogatives naturally
aroused resentment in the Great Council, and the hatred and
opposition to the Council of Ten which was then born, died
only with the fall of the republic. We need not here consider
the part played by the ten and by the three inquisitors of
state, who were created in 1530 to ensure even greater secrecy
and dispatch in the carrying out of their decisions, during the

last two centuries of the republic's existence. The history of those years is one of continual fear of external enemies, stronger than Venice in all but diplomatic ability, of their spies within the state, of suspicion, conspiracy, and intrigue, and it makes a sad epilogue to the golden age we are to consider here.

There is no doubt, however, that reprehensible as the methods of the ten may seem to us today, the vigilance with which they watched over the interest of the state contributed greatly to the stability of the government, allowed Venice to develop to the full her cultural and artistic genius, and assured her those long years of respected independence after the economic reasons for her prosperity had disappeared, and her political power had waned. If the period of highest achievement in the arts and sciences, in lavish and luxurious living, was not determined by that of the republic's greatest political development, neither did it coincide with a time of increase or even stability in the public wealth.

In 1474 the great *condottiere*, Bartolomeo Colleoni, whose bronze statue still rides so proudly before the Church of St. John and St. Paul, left the republic his entire fortune, estimated at 500,000 ducats. So dangerously depleted was the Treasury at that time, that this unlooked-for windfall had immediately to be applied to meet pressing needs, and 100,000 ducats were appropriated at once for the expenses of the Turkish war. Nothing could illustrate more convincingly than this the sorry state of public finance at the very time when Venice was gathering together her intellectual forces to lead Europe for 100 years in richness of artistic invention and in magnificence of display.

The great wealth still in private hands, which made this splendid civilization possible, had its origins in the remote past. From the beginning of the eighth until the closing years of the fifteenth centuries, the history of Venice is the history of a vast commercial enterprise.

Venice was destined by her geographical position to be the link between the east and the west, and the merchants who were also her rulers never lost sight of the fact that her prosperity, indeed her existence, depended on the establishment and consolidation of her position as the importer and distributor of all goods exchanged between the two hemispheres. By 740 we find her traders firmly established as far afield as Syria and the Black Sea, while, as a chronicler wrote: "To the fair at Pavia come the Venetians bringing with them overseas all the riches of the Orient."

At the end of the eleventh century the doge, Pietro Orseolo II, obtained unprecedented privileges in trading with Constantinople from the Emperor Basil, and concluded at the same time a commercial treaty with the Saracen powers. This was the first time that the republic made it clear that commercial considerations could be kept separate from, and even override, religious ones, an attitude which often, in the centuries to come, enraged those other Christian powers whose economic interests were not similarly involved.

At about the same time Venice obtained concessions for the erection of factories and warehouses in Imperial territory, through which she could establish and maintain contact with the traders from Germany and the north. Steadily Venetian commerce grew, receiving an added strength in the Near East from the fall of Constantinople after the Fourth Crusade; and by the beginning of the fifteenth century it may be said to have covered the whole of the civilized world. "Venetian traders", wrote Petrarch, "cross the Caucasus and Ganges and reach the Eastern Ocean." At the same time Venetian ships were carrying sugar to England, wool from England to Flanders, and cloth from Flanders for sale on the Dalmatian coast and the Near East. In 1420, at what was perhaps the moment of Venice's greatest commercial expansion, the doge, Tommaso Mocenigo, in his testamentary exhortation in which he vainly urged the electors to choose as his successor a doge who would not lead them into war, put the annual turnover of Venetian commerce at 10,000,000 ducats and the net profit at 2,000,000 (the equivalent of about £4,000,000 today).

This great trading enterprise was bound by strict regulations, and sea transport was, to a large extent, what would now be called "nationalized". Six squadrons of government-owned ships were chartered annually by private enterprise. They were of standardized construction and identical burden and rig, so that the efficient supply of refittings by consular agents abroad could be simplified; they sailed in convoy with adequate armed protection, and the observation of a predetermined load-line was rigidly enforced. Privately owned ships, sailing with convoys, were forced to comply to government specifications. This highly organized system, far in advance of anything existing in other countries at that time, not only ensured constant protection to Venetian trade, but, as all ships were convertible into men-of-war, provided a well-found navy when necessity arose.

So deeply rooted was the tradition of Venetian commerce, so able was the republic in re-establishing trade relations after even the least fortunate of wars, that there appeared to be no reason why Venetian prosperity should ever suffer more than temporary regressions, until the discovery of America in 1492 and that of the route round the Cape of Good Hope in 1486. In the space of a few years the whole economic balance of the world was changed and Venice, from occupying a key position on the main trade route, found herself in a backwater. The wealth of the Indies, which had hitherto reached Europe only after crossing the Isthmus of Suez by caravan, for reshipment in Venetian bottoms at Aleppo or Alexandria, could now be conveyed to Lisbon as unbroken cargo. Only the cutting of a Suez Canal, and the subsequent control of it, could have given Venice a new lease of life, but although this project is said to have been broached, it was evidently not thought to be practicable.

With the disappearance of her commercial monopoly Venice was left with two wholly inadequate sources of revenue, a few small industries, of which glass-blowing and silk-weaving were the most noteworthy, and the production of salt. These could not provide opportunities for reinvestment of the accumulation of wealth still in private hands. Some of the great families bought large estates upon the mainland, the less well-to-do settled down to live upon their capital until, in the seventeenth century, the existence of an impoverished aristocracy known as the "Barnobotti" presented one of the most serious problems the government had to face. But, as the great movement of the Italian Renaissance reached its climax, the political impotence and financial straits into which Venice had fallen were hidden from all but a few. To the general observer, particularly if he came from the north of the Alps, she was still the rich, the powerful, the "Most Serene" republic, and for more than 100 years she continued to dazzle Europe with the splendour of her public ceremonies and the ostentation of her private life.

Love of magnificent display seems to have been deep rooted in the citizens of Venice, and the government had long indulged this taste, as an easy way of distracting the attention of the populace from its gradual loss of political freedom. Every curtailment of popular power, every extension of the authority of the governing caste, had been accompanied by the institution of some new and more splendid function. Now, besides satisfying the people, these functions possessed the added usefulness of helping to conceal from foreign eyes Venice's declining prosperity and power.

Nor was it only the Venetian "Way of Life" which blinded the visitor to the real state of affairs. Throughout the sixteenth century the transformation of Venice, which had begun towards the middle of the fifteenth century, continued under the inspiration of a number of architects, sculptors, and painters of genius, and apparently entirely unhampered by lack of funds. Between 1450 and 1600 the city of Byzantine and Gothic houses, with their brightly painted façades, dominated by the "Golden" Basilica of St. Mark and the vast pile of the Doge's Palace—the city of which Carpaccio and Gentili Bellini have left such vivid impressions—took on a new appearance.

One by one huge palaces of silvery Istrian stone, in the classic taste, rose along the sides of the Grand Canal; great churches in whose design the rules of Vitruvius were applied, if not strictly at least as approximately as contemporary requirements allowed, appeared in positions of advantage; the Library of St. Mark sprang up to face the Doge's Palace across the Piazzetta; and finally the Piazza of St. Mark itself underwent radical change. In 1600 it remained only for the Baroque artists to give Venice, with the touch of their fantasy, the appearance which we know today.

To deprive Venice of her mainland territories had been one of the principal aims of the League of Cambrai, but after seven years of wars, she found herself, by the Peace of Brussels in 1516, with her old frontiers practically unchanged. From then until the fall of the republic nearly 200 years later, the ultra-montane traveller entered the Venetian state as soon as he crossed the Alps or, if approaching from the west or south, when he had passed the Adda or the Adige. After experience of French or Imperial rule, the cities of Venezia—Verona, Vicenza, Padua, to mention only the most important—had welcomed the return of the banners of St. Mark, and the firm but paternal government of Venice.

The sixteenth-century Englishman setting out to see for himself the wonders of which he heard so much would first have been impressed by the spirit of contentment which animated the people, the cleanliness of the streets, and the good order with which life was conducted in the towns through which his road lay. At Vicenza, had he passed that way towards the middle or end of the century, he would have received the first impact of the great revival of classic architecture which was transforming the face of northern Italy, and which was destined 200 years later to leave its mark on the English countryside.

In and around this little city lying amid the gentle slopes of the Monti Berici, and with the grandiose panorama of the Alps for background, were arising under the master-hand of Andrea Palladio palaces and country houses of well-ordered simplicity and impeccable elegance. The Gothic irregularities of the Palazzo della Ragione, or Public Building, were rapidly disappearing behind the colonnades—the lower Doric, the upper Doric—of a Roman Basilica, and the Olympic Theatre was nearing completion. Nothing, perhaps, would have impressed the English visitor, accustomed to the rough wooden structures of the Bankside, with their thatched galleries and unroofed pits, more than this masterpiece of theatrical construction and scenic art. Seated on benches rising steeply in a semi-ellipse from the sunken orchestra pit, the spectators faced a false perspective of palaces and triumphal arches adorned with statues, and so cunningly contrived that the streets of Thebes seemed to have been built upon the stage in full scale. The back wall of the auditorium was enriched with sculpture, and, above a balustraded gallery, the ceiling was painted to simulate such a "Velarium", slung between masts, as had protected the audiences of ancient Rome from the heat of the sun.

Spurred on by such foretastes of splendour, the traveller's next stop would have been Padua. If Vicenza had given him some idea of how the Venetian republic encouraged the arts, so would this university town have shown him in what honour and esteem it held the humanities.

The Venetian government had long taken an active interest in the education of its citizens, and during the sixteenth century, in addition to parochial seminaries, public grammar schools were opened in each "Sestiere" of Venice. On these, and on the numerous private schools which flourished at the same time, the Senate and, on occasion, the Council of Ten kept a watchful eye. Although the inculcation of the Christian virtues was not neglected, the greater part of the curriculum consisted of French and Latin grammar and literature, of rhetoric and poetics, of all those subjects, in fact, which the revival of learning had brought to the fore.

After the wars of the League of Cambrai, the government had set about the reorganization of the ancient University of Padua, and from then onwards the pursuit of all higher studies was concentrated in and around the Palazzo della Sapienza, familiarly known to this day as *Il Bo*, or The Bull, a name derived from the sign of an inn which had previously occupied the site.

In order to ensure the prosperity of this seat of learning the government had published an edict to the effect that all Venetian subjects desirous of pursuing their studies must do so at Padua. The university, however, was far from depending entirely on Venetian patronage, and students from all over Europe, and particularly from north of the Alps attended the lectures of its professors. Nor was religious denomination allowed to stand in the way of those who sought learning in Padua. The republic had always stood out against the worst fanaticisms of the Church of Rome, and the Inquisition never attained the degree of power within those frontiers that it enjoyed in other parts of Italy. Thus Lutheran and other Protestant students were admitted as members of the University of Padua, and practised their religious rites unmolested.

Besides its Schools of Classics, Philosophy, and Law, all of which left their imprint on European culture, the University of Padua possessed an advanced and famous Faculty of Medicine. It was in the beautiful little Anatomical Theatre which is still in use today that André Vésale first practised the systematic dissection of the human body, and that, later, William Harvey made those studies which led to the discovery of the circulation of the blood.

The Renaissance conception of a complete education was not, however, confined entirely to research and the development of the mind. The English traveller, had he been so disposed, would have found within the walls of the university city ample opportunity to refresh his knowledge of music and the dance, and to acquire some of those airs and graces to which more importance was attached in Italy than in his native country. It is unlikely though, that with the goal of his journey so near, he would have dallied long under those porticoes and streets, and we may imagine him after attending, perhaps, a lecture or two and visiting the then unique Botanical Gardens, embarking on the comfortably appointed barge, which would take him in nine or ten hours down the Brenta Canal and across the waters of the lagoon to Venice.

The Vision of Venice, as she seems to float in the opalescent waters of the lagoon, has taxed the descriptive powers of many poets, and has eluded the ingenuity of all but a very few painters.

The eye of the sixteenth-century traveller was certainly less attuned to the search for the picturesque than was that of his successor who made "The Grand Tour" in the eighteenth century, but even the most stolid Englishman must have felt a peculiar thrill of anticipation as the glittering domes of St. Mark's, and the pink marble façade of the Doge's Palace, first came into view.

The encouragement of what we now call "The Tourist Trade" had been undertaken by the Venetian government as early as the fourteenth century, and the traveller disembarking on the Molo would have found a *laquey de place*, whose job it was to find him accommodation at an inn where the charges were commensurate with his purse, strike a fair bargain for him and see he was not cheated by shopkeeper or gondolier.

The cleanliness and decency of the better class inns was ensured by periodic visits from government inspectors, and some of them, notably the *Leon Bianco*, or White Lion, near the Rialto had a high reputation to maintain. Here then we will leave the traveller, while we examine in greater detail the instruction and entertainment which await him when he has recovered from the rigours of his journey.

Few modern travellers who enter Venice from the Railway Station, the Garage, or the Airport, or who have made the journey by sea, arrive without some fairly clear idea of what they are going to find. The coloured postcard and the photographs of the Travel Agency folder may be misleading, but familiarity with them mitigates the shock of wonder and surprise which the earlier visitor must have felt when he first found himself in the basin of St. Mark's.

This great piece of water had not, at the time we are

considering, yet achieved the full magnificence which the pictures of Canaletto and Guardi were to make so familiar in the eighteenth century, and which it still possesses today. Three of the finest buildings which surround it—the Church of San Giorgio Maggiore, the Dogana de' Ma or Customs House, and the great dome of Santa Maria della Salute—had not yet been built, or were still unfinished; but what beauty it may have lost from their absence must, at least in some degree, have been made up for by the richness and the variety of shipping which filled it, from the Molo and the Riva degli Schiavoni on the one side to the island of the Giudecca on the other.

Venice's commerce, as we have seen, had sensibly diminished by the sixteenth century, but the great galleons of her navy were still afloat in large numbers, and ships of every conceivable design and rig still loaded and unloaded a continuous stream of cargo on her quays.

At Ascensiontide, when the doge went out to wed the Adriatic by casting a gold ring into her waters, or at other times when the arrival of some foreign potentate or ambassador demanded a particular display of pomp and circumstance, the Bucentoro, or State Barge, lay moored off the Palace. This fabulous vessel, which symbolized perhaps more than any other single object Venice's age-long domination of the sea, was wantonly destroyed in 1799 by Napoleon together with so much else that, by recalling the departed glories of the Most Serene Republic, aroused the hatred and envy of the Corsican *parvenu*.

"Larger than a great galleon"—the historian, Sansovino, tells us—the Bucentoro was propelled by three banks of oars. Every available surface within and without was enriched with fantastically carved and heavily gilt ornament. On the high raised poop stood the doge's throne under a canopy of crimson and gold, while an awning of crimson satin stretched the whole length of the deck to shelter the representatives of the *Signoria* who accompanied the doge on his progress through the lagoons. When the Bucentoro left her moorings she was escorted by a convoy of lesser craft, they too carved, gilded, and painted, and with long velvet trains buoyed up by corks trailing in the water astern. Barge-loads of musicians played, the men-of-war fired their guns in salute, and the bells pealed from the towers, as the doge moved slowly towards the port of the Lido to greet a distinguished guest or pledge his troth to the sea.

In order to satisfy the public taste for display and also to deceive the world as to the real state of Venetian finances, no opportunity, whether civil or religious, to stage a pageant was missed, and the traveller would have been unlucky indeed whose visit did not coincide with some great ceremony.

The most famous of these occasions ever to be recorded in the annals of Venice was the reception and entertainment accorded to King Henri III of France, and probably no state visit in modern history has been marked by such lavish and imaginative display. The king was on his way back from Poland to ascend the throne left vacant by the death of his brother, Charles IX, and had informed the doge and the *Signoria* of his intention to pass through the Venetian domi-nions. Alvise Mocenigo was then reigning and he and his councillors immediately took steps to ensure that the Most Christian King should be received with all the honour due to his rank. The state archives bear witness to the assiduity with which every detail of his visit was planned and every con-tingency provided for.

After a week's triumphal progress from the Venetian frontier, the king reached the shores of the lagoon at Mestre on 17 July 1574. The state entry into the city had been planned for the next day and, as it was to be made through the lagoons which lie to the seaward of Venice and not from the mainland, the royal party were taken in a flotilla of gondolas to the Island of Murano, where they were to spend the night. Murano had not then become the industrial island, devoted only to the blowing of glass, that we know now. Although many furnaces from which came the looking-glasses and drinking vessels that subsequently made it famous were already installed there, the greater part of the island was devoted to the pleasure gardens of the great families, and one of these, famous throughout Italy for the ingenuity of its lay-out and the variety of its trees and flowers, together with its palace, had been placed at the disposal of the king.

Not even this earthly paradise, however, could allay the young monarch's impatience to see the city itself and to taste of its pleasures. As soon as he had greeted the ambassadors and other dignitaries sent to welcome him, and satisfied the curiosity of the people by appearing on the balcony of the Palazzo Capello, he slipped out through the garden and, accompanied by the Duke of Ferrara and a boon companion or two, embarked in a private gondola and was rowed across the lagoon to Venice, where he passed the greater part of the night incognito.

On the morrow the doge, in the flagship of the home fleet with a convoy of fourteen other vessels, came out to Murano and carried the king to the Church of San Niccolò on the Lido, where the ceremony of the state reception was to be held. Here a triumphal arch, inspired by that of Septimius Severus in Rome, and a loggia of ten Corinthian columns had been erected for the occasion. Both were adorned with sculpture and pictures and hung with garlands, and the royal arms of France surmounted the arch. Some idea of the importance of these purely ephemeral buildings—destined to remain *in situ* for at the most a week—can be formed when it is said that the architect employed was Andrea Palladio and the painters none other than Paolo Veronese and Jacopo Tintoretto.

Flanked by two squadrons of the fleet, the forty barges of the Art Guilds, together with innumerable gondolas, lay waiting in the lagoon. The ingenuity of every artist and craftsman in the city had been expended in the decoration of this fantastic fleet, and each guild vied with the others to show the wealth and taste of Venice to the French king.

The Art Guilds, although they never achieved in Venice the political importance which they enjoyed in other Italian states, played a great part in the structure of society, and this we shall consider in greater detail later. On this occasion it was their function to dazzle the eyes of the foreigners with the richness and variety of Venetian commerce and industry. To judge from the descriptions of their barges given by several writers who were present, they must certainly have succeeded.

So brilliant was the scene, as the procession moved towards the entrance of the Grand Canal, that the young king could not keep his seat by the doge on the Bucentoro but, jumping up and running from side to side, kept exclaiming: "We wish the Queen Mother were here." As the vessel reached the basin of St. Mark's the accompanying barges drew off and, ranging themselves by the Island of San Giorgio, allowed the Bucentoro to proceed alone up the Grand Canal to the palace of the Foscari family, where the king was to lodge.

Three rooms on the first floor had been prepared as his private apartment. Their decoration, of a lavishness almost incredible today, was typical of the taste of the time and hardly more luxurious than that which could have been seen in many other Venetian palaces. The first room was hung, from ceiling to floor, with cloth of gold and crimson and with cloth of silver into which was woven the king's cypher; the hangings of the second were of yellow and blue satin embroidered with fleurs-de-lis; the walls of the third, which the king chose for his bedroom, were covered with gold and silver brocade. The bed was gilt and stood under a canopy of silk, the tables were of alabaster and marble, the chairs were upholstered in cloth of gold, and silken carpets covered the floor.

Having taken stock of the accommodation and requested that a secret staircase, to enable him to come and go un-observed, might be immediately constructed, the king appeared on the balcony over whose balustrade a trapping woven with gold thread had been thrown. The sight that met his eyes was one which no other city in the world has been able to offer, before or since. The Palazzo Foscari stands just where the Grand Canal takes a sharp turn, and from its windows the whole of the noble waterway is visible, to the bridge of the

Rialto in one direction and almost to the basin of St. Mark's in the other. The older palaces of mellow brick, each with its characteristic central window of Gothic tracery, alternated with the newer classical buildings still in all their pristine beauty, some encrusted with plaques of many-coloured marbles, others decorated with frescoes from the brush of some great painter. Tapestries and other hangings of indescribable richness hung, as is still the custom on a day of rejoicing, from every window and balcony.

As the king watched, the barges of the Art Guilds, moving up from the basin of St. Mark's between the serried ranks of gondolas and other craft, once more came into view and passed before the palace to the sound of music. Foreigners from all over Italy had poured into Venice, gondolas were at a premium and every boat had been pressed into service that could carry the visitors or the citizens and their families. As far as the eye could reach the waters of the canal were hidden by the multitude of craft which they bore, and yet there was no confusion. On the water the Venetian feels himself in his element as other men do on the land, and the vast concourse moved up and down in an orderly and good-humoured manner.

As darkness fell coloured lights began to appear here and there amongst the boats, the little oil-lamps which outlined every cornice and window were lit in one palace after another, and soon the Grand Canal was a river of light. Venice had embarked on a series of festivities, unique even in her own long history, which was to end only on the departure of the king eight days later.

The descriptions in contemporary documents of the entertainments which followed—the state banquets, the balls, the ceremonial calls and inspections—produce a feeling of bewilderment, and almost a sense of surfeit. Even the Venetians, mad for pleasure as they were, found the pace a little fast and the expense alarming. Towards the end of the week the crowds were notably smaller and the illuminations less dazzling.

If the royal visitor's days passed in pomp and circumstance

and public entertainment, his nights seem to have been no less
assiduously devoted to enjoyment. The young king's truancy
on the night he spent in Murano before entering Venice, and
his hasty request that a secret staircase be constructed in the
Palazzo Foscari, had made it clear that he had no intention of
confining his activities to official occasions; and indeed hardly
a night passed that he did not set out, in company with the
Duke of Ferrara or one of his other companions, in search of
more intimate pleasures. He seems to have spent much of his
time visiting the courtesans, the profusion of whom had earned
for Venice the title of "The Gehenna of the waters."

Were it not for contemporary catalogues giving the names
and addresses, the prices and the accomplishments of these
ladies, it would be difficult to believe that the erotic demands
of citizen and visitor could have been so efficiently and satis-
factorily provided for. The courtesans of Venice's Golden Age
should not be confused with the inmate of a brothel or common
street-walker. Nor were they, it would seem, the equivalent of
the *grande cocotte* of the late nineteenth century, who usually
relied for her clothes and jewels on the generosity of one rich
man at a time. They lived comfortably and even luxuriously,
often with a retinue of servants, but were prepared to accord
their favours to any man who was ready to pay the established
tariff, which varied from half a scudo to thirty scudi. So
respectable was their appearance when they went out accompanied by their maids, that it was said to be impossible to
distinguish between them and their more honest sisters: a fact
which aroused the indignation of the latter and led to attempts
to prevent the courtesans wearing jewellery or silk dresses in
the streets.

Carpaccio has left us a picture, now in the Correr Museum
in Venice, of two courtesans sitting, richly dressed, upon a
terrace. One of them plays with her pet dogs while the other
watches a page feeding some tame birds. Though this was
painted somewhat earlier than the period we are considering,
it serves well to illustrate the prosperity and substance to be

PLATE 27

VENETIAN COURTESANS ON A TERRACE
Painting by Vittore Carpaccio

PLATE 28

THE CONDOTTIERE BARTOLOMEO COLLEONI
Bronze statue by Verrocchio

THE PALACE OF THE DOGES
in the Piazzetta di San Marco

found in the *demi monde* of the time. Montaigne, who came to Venice three or four years after the French king, found it "admirable to see as many as 150, with nothing else but their trade to live on, spending money on furniture and clothes fit for a princess". And this is how Thomas Coryat, in his *Crudities*, describes a visit to Margherita Emiliani, one of the most famous Venetian courtesans, whom, like a good Anglo-Saxon, he went to see not for any lascivious purpose but because, as he explained, *cognitio mali non est mala* (the knowledge of evil is not evil):

> "For when you come into one of their palaces . . . you seem to enter into the paradise of Venus. For the fairest rooms are most glorious to behold. . . . As for herself shee comes to thee decked like a Queen and Goddess of Love, in so much that thou wilt think she made a late transmission from Paphos. . . . In her cheeks thou shalt see the Lilley and the Rose strive for the supremacy, and the silver trammels of her hair desplayed in that curious manner besides her two frisled peakes standing up like pyramides, that they give her the true *Cos Amoris*.
>
> "Also the ornaments of her body are so rich that, except thou dost even geld thy affections (a thing hardly to be done) or carry with thee Ulysses hearbe called *Moly* . . . she will very near benumme and captivate thy senses, and make reason vale bonnet to affection. . . . For thou shalt see her decked with many chains of gold and orient pearle like a second Cleopatra. . . . A gowne of damaske . . . either decked with a deep gold fringe . . . or laced with five or six gold laces each two inches broade. . . ."

Towards the end of the sixteenth century Sanudo and Merlini, both reliable chroniclers, give the number of "public women" in Venice as 11,654. Of these, many were women of considerable culture and wit, well-read, agreeable talkers, accomplished musicians, and proficient in other arts as well as that of love. One of them, Veronica Franco, was a poetess of

14

considerable merit, who had been loved by Tintoretto, and it was she who captivated Henri III. On leaving, he took with him her portrait in enamels, together with some verses of her composition, in which she compares his sojourn under her "humble roof" to a visit from Jupiter in human disguise, and speaks of his "immortal and divine valiance". This remarkable woman, who at the beginning of her career charged but a modest two scudi for her favours and rose to the top of her profession, changed her way of life in old age and founded a house for the succour of fallen women. Her portrait, with those of other penitents kneeling before the Virgin, painted by Carletto Caliari, may be seen at the Accademia in Venice today.

It must not be supposed that after such merry-making as marked the visit of the French king Venetian life would sink back into a dull routine. The populace did not have to wait for such exceptional events as the enthronement of a new doge, the coronation of a dogaressa, or the celebration of a victory, to indulge its taste for pageantry and its love of pleasure. Such occasions were but the highlights in a continual round of public spectacle and popular entertainment. From St. Stephen's Day till Shrove Tuesday Carnival was in full swing, and the Piazza of St. Mark, the Campi—as the squares and open spaces are still called—and the streets were crowded with masked figures enjoying an almost unlimited licence to amuse themselves as they thought fit. Ascensiontide, when the great water pageant of the doge's marriage to the sea covered the waters of the lagoon, was a time of general rejoicing. On the Feast of Corpus Domini the doge went in solemn procession to St. Mark's, and on certain religious feasts visited other churches in state. The brilliance and variety of the costumes worn by the suite which accompanied him, the magnificence of the hangings which adorned the façades of the houses that lay on his route, the profusion of flowers and the quantity of the wax candles that decorated and illuminated the churches, taxed the descriptive powers of the most imaginative contemporary writers, and it is almost impossible, four hundred years later, to envisage such scenes of splendour.

Reference was made earlier to the Art Guilds which regulated the affairs of every industry and commerce. Their appearance at public ceremonies was, perhaps, their most picturesque but hardly their most important function. The very nature of the Venetian constitution prevented these corporations from exercising political power or even pressure, and the government, conscious of its own strength, encouraged their formation, and allowed them a large degree of autonomy. The affairs of the guilds provided to some extent an outlet for those political instincts which could not find expression in the jealously guarded direction of public business. The matriculation books, or statutes, contained provisions designed to maintain the professional efficiency of members, to guard, in the absence of an effective Patent Law, the secrets of each trade, and to ensure that the proper contributions and taxes were regularly paid. The guilds provided for the sick and aged, for the widows and orphans of their members, and for the burial of the dead. These self-supporting corporations, besides upholding the high reputation of Venetian manufactures, carried out many of the duties now assumed by the Welfare State, and by watching over the well-being of the working-classes helped to create the general feeling of contentment and satisfaction which was essential to the successful working of the constitution.

No class was too humble to be the object of the paternal care of the government, and no trouble to retain their affection and loyalty, or to provide for their amusement, was considered too great. Thus a healthy sense of rivalry between the inhabitants of one end of the city and those of the other was fostered by occasional gymnastic competitions—known as "Forze d'Ercole"—and unarmed combats between the Castellani, the centre of whose faction was the Arsenal, and the Nicoletti, who took their name from the fishermen's quarter around the Church of San Niccolò dei Mendicoli. The fishermen of this outlying parish had the age-long right to elect, in the presence

of one of the doge's secretaries, their own leader, who also, for
the year of his office, bore the mighty name of "Doge". Dressed
in red from head to foot, and preceded by his own standard-
bearers and guard of honour, this "Doge" for a year went on
foot to the real Doge's Palace and did homage to the head of
the state. On Ascension Day he and his subject-fishermen were
entertained to a banquet in the Palace. By such simple but
effective ceremonies the people were made to think that,
although wealth and power might be only for the great, they
too had their acknowledged place in the community and that
their part in the general economy was recognized and respected.

Although Venetian industry could not make good the losses
which the republic had suffered by the discovery of the route
round the Cape of Good Hope, it was sufficient to provide, at
least through the sixteenth century, full employment, and to
maintain amongst the people a standard of living that compared
favourably with that of other European countries. The rough
woodcuts of the period, and especially those which illustrate
books of devotion, give a good idea of the average working-class
dwelling. These houses, of two or sometimes three floors, often
possessed wooden *loggie* or balconies, festooned with creepers
and enlivened with potted plants. Most of them, like the larger
houses of the well-to-do and the palaces of the aristocracy, were
surmounted by open terraces, or *altane*, where the washing could
be bleached and dried, and the family could enjoy the evening
breeze. All but the poorest owned silver knives and forks, and
decent well-polished walnut furniture. The kitchen was then,
as it is now, the pride of every Venetian home, and the walls
of the humblest were bright with copper cooking utensils. The
women and girls contributed to the family budget by weaving
and dyeing, and many a house still bears the stone rings that
supported wooden poles on which the freshly-dyed materials
were hung out to dry.

The houses of the middle classes, on the other hand, would
have stood comparison with those of the nobility in any other
European capital, while the palaces of the great families were

comparable, in grandeur of conception and richness of decoration and furniture, only with the residences of crowned heads.

The Venetians were great collectors of works of art. Lorenzo Lotto painted the portrait of Andrea Ottoni surrounded by fragments of antique sculpture. This simple but prosperous merchant, whose name certainly did not appear in the Golden Book, lived in the parish of San Nicola da Tolentino, in a house whose façade was painted in fresco with scenes from Greek mythology. His collection contained, besides majolicas, bronzes, and gems, pictures by Titian, Bonifacio de' Pitati, and Palma il Vecchio. This collection, however, pales into insignificance beside those of such patrons of the arts as the Grimani of Santa Maria Formosa, the Vendramin of San Marcuola, or the Foscarini of the Carmini.

If the government encouraged the collection of works of art, as contributing to the wealth of the republic, it fought a losing battle against wanton luxury and extravagance. A series of "sumptuary laws" limiting the amount of money that could be spent on the decoration of any one room, and controlling the prices of clothes and jewels, continued to be passed throughout the fifteenth and sixteenth centuries. It is, indeed, to one of these that we owe the unrelieved black of the Venetian gondola. In a somewhat more successful attempt than usual to curb extravagance, the government laid down that only foreign ambassadors could paint or gild their gondolas and the Venetians, with instinctive good taste, accepted this edict without complaint. The curtailment of interior decoration was less willingly accepted—if it can be said to have been accepted at all—and the gilding of one room in Ca' Cornaro at San Maurizio was valued at 18,000 gold ducats.

Only the largest of the palaces were built round courtyards. In the majority a broad entrance hall traversed the ground floor from the *riva* or waterside to the door which gave on to a narrow street at the back. This entrance, which in earlier days was used, together with the store-rooms that opened off it, for the merchandise on which the prosperity of the family

depended, was in the sixteenth century kept clear and was often
hung with trophies of arms and the huge bronze lanterns which
had stood on the prows of the galleys. On the first half-landing
of the great staircase stood some fragment of classic sculpture,
or, let into the wall, a Latin inscription waited to be de-
ciphered. From here opened the mezzanine rooms, in which
some semblance of warmth might be maintained during the
short but intensely rigorous Venetian winter. On the first floor,
or *piano nobile*, were the great saloons, opening off a long gallery
which corresponded to the entrance hall below.

It was in these rooms with their vast proportions that the
splendour of Venetian taste could be judged. Carved cornices
lent support to ceilings whose beams were painted with delicate
arabesque designs. The walls were hung with damask and cut
velvet, or more often with painted and gilded leather. Massive
marble chimney-pieces, carved by the greatest sculptors of the
day, satisfied the eye if they did little to warm the atmosphere
of these lofty apartments; but resistance to extremes of temperature seems to have been highly developed amongst Venetian ladies, who, to judge from their portraits, wore the same
heavily brocaded gowns and elaborately jewelled head-dresses
through the rigours of winter and the stifling heat of summer.

The entertainments given on the occasion of a great marriage
or in honour of a distinguished visitor were worthy of these
sumptuous settings, and the feasting and dancing would go on
for three or four days at a time almost without interruption.
The *compagni della calza*, or "companions of the hose", came
into their own on these occasions. The appetites of so pleasure-
sated a society must have been somewhat jaded, and it was the
function of this company of well-born young men to see that
variety and novelty were not lacking from ball or banquet—a
task which they fulfilled with fantasy and imagination. Nowhere
do climate and surroundings lend themselves more readily to
open-air amusements than in Venice, and many are the
descriptions of supper-parties and alfresco concerts in gondola
and illuminated barge. The delights of nature, at least when

suitably tamed, had always appealed to the Venetians, and much time was spent in the gardens of Murano and the Giudecca.

By the sixteenth century, however, when the cares of the counting-house had become less pressing, and the rich were preparing to spend in enjoyment the fortunes which their fathers had amassed with such tenacity, these somewhat restricted properties no longer satisfied their owners. Along the banks of the Brenta canal, on either side of the Treviso road, and even farther afield, on the lowest slopes of the Alps or amongst the Euganean Hills, villas were built and gardens laid out where happy companies of friends could spend days or weeks in conversation, in playing games of chance, or in making music and love.

Of those already built or in process of construction at this period one stood out as the prototype of the Venetian country house, the perfect expression of the Palladian ideal. A few miles upstream from where the Brenta enters the lagoon at Fusina, the Foscari family built, towards the middle of the century, a house from the designs of Palladio, to be known to posterity as *La Malcontenta*, in memory, it is said, of an unhappy lady who spent many years alone there in expiation of some conjugal indiscretion. An outpost of Venice, an earnest of the splendours she had in store, the house stood in splendid isolation, flanked by groves of trees and reflected in the waters of the canal. Here, in the two noble flights of steps, in the faultless pillars of the portico, in the perfect purity of the proportions, lay embodied all that was best of the Venetian genius in its maturity.

Few others have survived with their original form unmodified and even fewer contain the contemporary decoration unimpaired. Of these, the Villa Maser, built by Andrea Palladio for two brothers of the Barbaro family, is the most outstanding, and here it is possible, as nowhere else, to form an impression of the amenities of country life during the High Renaissance.

The house stands on the lowest foothills of the Alps near Asolo, with the whole extent of the Venetian plain spread out before it. The central façade, with four engaged pilasters of the Ionic order, is flanked by long arcaded wings terminating in pavilions, the one bearing a painted sundial, the other an astronomical device. Here is none of that stateliness which marks so many palaces on the Grand Canal, and which the English noblemen did not leave behind when they brought the Palladian manner to the banks of the Thames two hundred years later. Dignified and noble, but without pretention or display, the Villa Maser fits into the agricultural landscape as simply and inevitably as the plainest farmhouse. The ingenuity and imagination which the Venetian artists brought to everything they touched is reserved for the interior. The central hall is painted with allegorical figures and trophies of arms; in the ante-chamber leading to the garden members of the Barbaro family lean over balustrades, or play with their pet dogs and birds. Gods and goddesses adorn the walls of some rooms in the long cool range of apartments, while in others landscapes with figures illustrate an Arcadian way of life. No lesser artist than Paolo Caliari, "Il Veronese", helped perhaps by his brother Benedetto, painted these frescoes, while Vittoria, one of the greatest sculptors of his day, fashioned the chimney-pieces and the stucco figures and ornaments of the fountain in the privy garden at the back. It was because the Venetian noblemen could call on such past-masters for the adornment of their houses that the art of domestic decoration reached a height that has never been surpassed.

To trace the development of Venetian painting throughout the Renaissance, or to estimate its significance and importance, is far beyond the scope of this study; but no sketch, however summary, of Venice's golden age would be complete without some attempt to describe how such artists as Giorgione, Titian, Veronese, and Tintoretto reflected the taste of the day and contributed to the magnificence of its life.

The painters of the sixteenth century were hampered by none

of the uncertainties and spiritual conflicts which had pre-occupied their predecessors. They expressed without misgiving or reserve the joys and beauties of the sensuous life. The men who look out from their canvases are no saints or ascetics, but men of the world—certain of themselves and uninhibited by ethical or religious doubt. In the treatment of sacred as much as of secular subjects, the pride of the flesh and the splendour of life are seldom absent. The *Marriage in Cana* and the *Supper in the House of Levi* as depicted by Veronese are sumptuous banquets in settings of unimaginable grandeur; and Tintoretto's *Miracle of Saint Mark* shows a background of loggia and trellised arcade such as beautified the pleasure gardens of the lagoons.

For the first time the works of great painters were appreciated for their decorative functions as well as for their aesthetic content. Giorgione was employed to cover the whole façade of the German counting-house at the Rialto with frescoes of mythological subjects. Tintoretto filled the great halls of the Scuola San Rocco—one of the larger charitable institutions—with canvases illustrating the life of Christ, and with Titian, Veronese, and a host of lesser artists, recorded the glories of Venice on the ceilings and walls of the Doge's Palace. These incomparable artists expressed with an easy mastery the beauty of sea and sky, the seduction of women arrayed in silk and velvet, the pride and nobility of the warrior. No sensual pleasure was alien to them, and the joy of life inspired and informed everything that they did.

If her painters furnish the finest reflection of Venice in her greatness, the works of her architects and sculptors are no unworthy adjuncts to the picture. We have already considered the villas of Palladio. The massive palaces of Sansovino and Sammichele are hardly less important as expressions of the classical ideal in the modern world. No nobler equestrian statue than that of Bartolomeo Colleoni, by Verrochio, exists on earth today. The figures which adorn the courtyard of the Doge's Palace, the tombs in San Giovanni e Paolo and the Frari and the exquisite decoration of Santa Maria dei Miracoli testify to the incomparable technique and the richness of invention of Lombardi, Rizzi, Vittoria, and other artists.

The tastes of the scholarly were no less completely satisfied than those of the less studious, and the books which poured from the press of Aldo Manuzio to fill the shelves of such humanists as Bembo and Bessarion set a standard of typography for the printers of Europe to follow.

Such then was Venice at the height of her glory: proud, resplendent, and serene; just and benign to those of her children who obeyed her laws and left politics alone; tolerant of human weakness, so long as it did not interfere with affairs of state; a lover of the arts and sciences; a respectful, but never subservient daughter of the Church.

She had learnt to divert the talents which had made her great to the task of making her beautiful, and the energies which had conquered her empire and amassed her wealth to the pursuits of peace and the enjoyment of riches. When she could no longer be a centre of business she became a centre of pleasure, and welcomed the hedonist as generously as she had received the merchant.

Greatness cannot last for ever any more in cities than in men, but, in the case of cities, adaptability can prolong its little day. Venice has never quite lost the art of turning her qualities and talents to the best account, and even the final extinction of the republic and the shame of a foreign occupation could not entirely break her spirit. She remains today, and will long remain, an indispensable stage in the grand tour of all intelligent men, and a destination for those who are not ashamed of devoting time and money to the pleasures of life.

The Golden Age of Venice has long passed; but a warming afterglow of the light that shone upon her then still shimmers over the waters of her lagoons and irradiates her palaces and towers.

Madrid under the House of Austria

16TH–17TH CENTURY

R. TREVOR DAVIES

EIGHTEEN emulous cities possessed the privilege of sending parliamentary representatives (*diputados*) to the Cortes of Castile. Many of them—such as Toledo and Burgos—had long disputed as to which was the greatest. Yet when Castile had gathered round her an empire covering a large part of the known world and Philip II had to choose a capital for it, his choice fell upon the least considerable of them all, the old town of Madrid that was not even the see of a bishop. Its chief value as a capital lay in its central position, about mid-way between the Atlantic and the Mediterranean and between the French frontier and the southern coast. Of merits it had few except its reputation for a healthy climate. The bare plateau upon which it stood some 2,500 feet above the sea-level was soon to be so denuded of trees that the bread of its inhabitants had to be baked with horse dung for lack of timber. Its river, the Manzanares, was too small even to supply enough water, and its bed was often half dry in the summer months. It had the "nine months' winter and the three months' hell" that was the tradition of the nothern *meseta* of Castile.

In some ways its creation as capital of the Spanish empire might be regarded as the eccentricity of a despot, like Peter the Great's creation of St. Petersburg. Yet Madrid was able to count the glories of its past. When the pride of France went down before the stubborn infantry of Castile at Pavia (1525) and the boastful young Francis I had written to his mother

"*De toutes choses ne m'est demeuré que l'honneur et la vie qui est saulvé*", it was to the Tower of Lujanes and the Alcázar of Madrid that he was brought a prisoner and there, worn down by the tedium of imprisonment, signed away some of the choicest provinces of his country. Charles V, who believed that the climate of Madrid was good for his gout, visited it frequently, held the cortes there twice (1528 and 1534) and allowed it to take a crown into its escutcheon since which time it has called itself proudly *Villa Imperial y Coronada*. Cabrera, the historian of Philip II, even says that Charles V intended to make it his capital. During his reign (1516–58) his fostering care had resulted in a growth of population from about 3,000 to nearly 30,000.

When, in 1561, Philip II made Madrid his capital (*unica corte*) he gave the impulse to an immense drift into the town of people of all classes. Building went on with alarming rapidity and little care for the levelling of the ground or planning. The nobles and the wealthy built their palaces and the poor built their hovels in the suburbs. Others built multitudes of houses of one floor only in order to avoid onerous dues to the court. The religious Orders set about the building of great numbers of monasteries with the assistance of the devout king, who also built various philanthropic institutions and hospitals, as well as the bridge of Segovia. In addition to all this Philip II gave his tireless mind to the project of making the Tagus navigable as far as Toledo—a gigantic enterprise, which, had it been carried out, would have led to an even vaster increase in the population of the new capital. As it was, its population had risen before the middle of the seventeenth century to an estimated figure of more than 400,000. If this estimate is anywhere near the truth Madrid must have been about the largest city in Europe. Paris, London, and Amsterdam would be its only rivals. Though Madrid soon came to possess buildings of the greatest magnificence it long continued to strike foreign visitors as ill-paved, dirty, and evil-smelling. Horses were said to sink to their knees in the mud and coaches to the butts of their wheels, as they attempted to make their way along the principal streets, while the privileged pigs of St. Anthony roved about everywhere grubbing for garbage in the gutters. But much of these descriptions must be discounted as the work of envious foreign humorists anxious to make the Spaniards look absurd in the eyes of the French or the English.

*

Though Madrid had its squalid places it was by no means devoid of Castilian pride. It was a common saying in the streets of the seventeenth-century town that the empire of Spain was twenty times as great as that of ancient Rome; that its size was so vast that the sun never set upon it; and that its slightest movement made the whole world tremble. This was not altogether the language of hyperbole. Philip II really did possess the largest empire upon earth. In Europe he held most of Italy and the Netherlands and many islands in the Mediterranean. In the New World the whole of America, North, South, and Central, was his, together with countless islands scattered over the oceans of the world. In addition to all this, Philip's conquest of Portugal (1580) placed in his hands another vast empire, which included the greater part of Africa—mostly as yet unexplored—and great territories in Asia and in the farther east, from which was derived the immensely lucrative spice monopoly.

But by far the greatest sources of wealth in the Spanish empire were the silver mines of Mexico and Peru. As for gold, moderate quantities crossed the Atlantic during the years after the discovery of America (1492); but before the middle of the sixteenth century about ninety per cent of the bullion imports from America had come to consist of silver in enormous quantities. Most of these discoveries of precious metal came by the merest chance. It happened that one day in the year 1545 a native of Peru was chasing one of his goats up a steep hill-side, and caught hold of a shrub to save himself. The shrub came out by the roots showing tiny beads of shining white metal, which proved on examination to be silver. Eager hands speedily dug into the hillside, which showed that beneath a thin surface of earth it consisted of little less than pure, solid silver. The countryside for miles around was found to have much the same consistency. Thus were discovered the famous mines of Potosi, from which poured into Spain those mighty torrents of silver that upset the entire economy of Europe and impoverished Venice and the other great cities of the Mediterranean. Before the end of the sixteenth century the King of Spain was receiving a revenue of some £4,000,000 a year from the American mines alone—a sum which amounted to about sixteen times the average annual revenue of Queen Elizabeth of England. The silver imports raised prices to dizzy heights in every country in Europe but most of all in Spain, which consequently became a good market to sell to but an extremely bad one to buy from.

These economic difficulties were intensified by the fact that the Spaniards—especially those of Castile—had a dislike of engaging in industry. They were proudly conscious of being the descendants of Catholic gentlemen who had driven the Moors out of Spain. They disdained any career except that of soldier, priest, missionary, or explorer. Hence while Castile possessed by far the finest soldiers in the world and many of the greatest saints, few of her sons were willing to work on the land or in industry. Moreover, poverty was not regarded as shameful as was money gained by ignoble pursuits like manual labour or trade. Many of the tall, thin, aristocratic-looking Castilian *hidalgos* (gentlemen) lived lives of semi-starvation rather than disgrace themselves with servile work. It was these lesser nobles who longed for employment in the king's service or for appointments in the army—only to find to their deep despair that the demand for such posts far exceeded the supply.

In a position of much greater dignity were the greater nobles of Castile, counts, marquises, and dukes, the most favoured of whom held the much-coveted rank of Grandee. It is characteristic of Castilian circumstances that the grandeeship carried with it no solid material gain but merely certain ceremonial dignities such as the right to wear one's hat in the royal presence or the privilege of being addressed as "majesty". Many of the greater nobles were, however, so wealthy as to constitute a political danger to the crown. Some, indeed, boasted that their lands were so extensive that they could ride from one end of the kingdom to the other without once leaving their own estates. Kings like Philip II parried this possible menace from the over-mighty subject by encouraging the greater nobles to reside at the court in Madrid. Here they would live out of touch with their faithful tenantry under the suspicious eyes of their monarch and waste their substance in extravagant living or in gambling for immensely high stakes. They would emerge from such a life too poor to play an adventurous part in politics or to attempt to assert their independence of the crown.

It is clear that the gap between noble and plebeian in Castile was not a narrow one. None the less it was bridged by one industry—the farming of migratory sheep, the staple industry of the kingdom. This lucrative sheep had been intro-duced by the Moors in the Middle Ages and bred solely for its wool. (Its mutton was almost uneatable.) The sheep owners, who consisted of men of all classes from great dukes, who owned tens of thousands, to poor shepherds, who owned fewer than half a dozen, had been formed centuries ago into a great nation-wide, democratic, self-governing guild, known as the Honour-able Company of the Mesta. The sheep spent most of their lives walking—an exercise which was said to be good for the quality of their wool. The summer they spent in the cool mountains of northern Castile and in autumn they set out for a cross-country march of many hundreds of miles in order to spend the winter in the warm south. The following spring they set out for the north again, the journey each way taking about three months. As may well be imagined the sheep, many millions in number, did no small damage to the crops through which they passed. But the Mesta, which had greatly increased its powers in the course of centuries, was strong enough to protect its flocks against the unhappy agriculturalists, whose complaints were loud and long and unceasing. The wool clip of the Mesta was collected at Burgos and sold by a system of national marketing —about the first ever practised in the modern world. Its destination was usually the southern Netherlands, where it was woven into cloth and sold back to Castile. Thence most of it was re-exported to the American colonies—a series of highly profitable transactions which help to account for the friendship that often existed between the southern Netherlands and Castile.

In discussing such matters as these it is frequently necessary to speak of Castile rather than Spain; because Spain consisted of five independent kingdoms each provided with its own parliament (the Cortes) and linked together by the mere fact that they had one and the same king. The King of Spain was, in fact, strictly speaking "King of the Spains". The kingdoms had not even a treaty of extradition or of free trade between them and they differed profoundly in laws, customs, and constitutions. Castile, the largest of them, occupied about sixty per cent of the whole Peninsula and possessed a population of some 7,000,000. To her belonged the whole of America, from which her fellow-kingdoms of the Peninsula were, as a rule, quite rigidly excluded. Navarre, the smallest kingdom, occupied about one per cent of the Peninsula and possessed a proportionately small population. The three kingdoms of the north-eastern part of the Peninsula, Aragon, Catalonia, and Valencia, known as the States of the Crown of Aragon, were far more independent than Castile in their attitude towards the monarchy. So much was this so that until the latter part of Philip II's reign (1591) Aragon was commonly spoken of in Europe as a republic with an elective king. At the coronation of an Aragonese king he knelt before the Justicia of Aragon, who placed the crown upon his head with the significant words: "We, who are as good as you are, make you, who are no better than we, our king; and we will bear true allegiance if you observe our laws and customs; but if not, not." As the nobles

PLATE 29

DON CARLOS, SON OF PHILIP II
Painting by Velasquez

PLATE 30

PANORAMA OF MADRID
17th century engraving

THE ESCORIAL
Erected near Madrid in 1563—84 the building is a combination of
monastery, church, palace and tomb

of Aragon enjoyed a unique measure of feudal independence, so its serfs endured the lowest serfdom, owing to the weakness of the crown, which was not remedied till Philip I put down the Revolt of Aragon.

*

Though much maligned in past centuries Philip II (1558–1598) possessed many virtues. Yet in spite of them all, this son of the Counter-Reformation showed an inborn secretiveness of temperament that transformed otherwise comparatively common-place events into dark, intriguing mysteries that have baffled the historians of more than a couple of centuries. Perhaps the most notable of these mysteries is the fate of Philip's unhappy son, Don Carlos. He was known to have been imprisoned by the orders of his father shortly after the Christmas of 1567 and to have died in the Alcázar in the summer of 1568. On the basis of these scanty facts that were allowed to be seen through the curtain of royal reticence was built a tangled web of rumours that spread from Madrid to every court in Europe, to be endlessly embellished by memoir writers, novelists, dramatists, and uncritical historians. The unhappy prince was a Protestant who fell a victim to the dread Inquisition; or he was the guilty paramour of his pretty young stepmother, Elizabeth de Valois, Philip II's third wife; or he had been discovered plotting with his father's discontented subjects in the hope of replacing him upon the throne. Imagination revelled in a subject which long remained an essential ingredient of the "black legend" of Spain. It has cost the scientific historians of the past eighty years no little research to produce a far less lurid story of the end of Don Carlos.

He was—to come to straightforward facts—like so many of the House of Habsburg, a victim of heredity. His father and mother, Philip II and Maria of Portugal, were first cousins and grandchildren of Juana the mad queen of Castile (1502–1555). After falling headlong down a flight of steps Don Carlos grew sicker in mind and in body.

15

He appeared to be dying in spite of all his father's frantic efforts to cure him. At last the surgeons tried the bold experiment of cutting a triangular piece out of his skull. Henceforth symptoms of mental disease became far more intense. On no fewer than six occasions he attempted in fits of maniacal fury to murder—by pushing through an upstairs window—some person who had thwarted his wishes. At other times he had lucid moments, in which he showed good traits of character—particularly reckless generosity. Consequently there were not a few who believed him to be sane and even his father sometimes ventured to hope for his ultimate recovery. In this hope he had induced the Cortes of Castile to swear allegiance to Carlos as heir to the throne, he had negotiated for his marriage to various princesses—including Mary Queen of Scots—and had admitted him to some share in the government of Spain. In spite of all this paternal care the young prince developed a furious hatred of his father and a "persecution complex".

Finally he made plans to leave Spain secretly, sending out secret agents to gather money for the purpose. When these plans were discovered the king saw that decisive action was unavoidable. The heir to the Spanish throne might easily, in that monarchical age, have become a deadly weapon in the hands of some unscrupulous enemy of his country, such as Elizabeth of England, Catherine de' Medici, or William the Silent. Immediately after the Christmas festivities the prince was arrested in his bedroom at the Alcázar by his father in person accompanied by various members of the royal household. The various booby traps that he had employed skilled engineers to construct in defence of his door were removed and he was closely imprisoned in the Alcázar. He was attended by great nobles : especial precautions being taken to prevent suicide.

Alternately fasting and over-eating, he also suffered from the intense heat of the Madrid summer; and, since medical men at this time had a strong belief in its curative properties, he was plentifully supplied with ice with which he strewed his bed and slept naked in the draught of an open window. The consequences of this reckless act were severe pains which ended with his death on 25 July 1568. That he received every possible care and consideration there is more than sufficient evidence. Yet later writers had a far different story with which to horrify their readers. Saint-Simon stated in his *Mémoires* that Carlos was beheaded. Llorente said that his father administered a slow poison; Pierre Mathieu, that the prince was strangled by some negro slaves, and Brântome that he was smothered. The death of his son cast a gloom over all the remainder of Philip's life and greatly increased his habitual gravity of manner.

All the same, Madrid had her moments of gaiety. She arrayed herself in holiday garb for the entry of the new queen, Dona Ana of Austria, Philip II's fourth wife, in 1570, and again in 1578 for the birth of the prince who was afterwards to succeed to the throne as Philip III. The following year Madrid was pleasantly reminded of her responsibilities as capital of the greatest of the empires of recorded history by the visit of three ambassadors from remote Japan, who presented Philip II with some curious pieces of armour that are still preserved in the Real Armeria.

*

When Charles II's London with its gaiety, colour, and freedom took the place of the drab, restrained, joyless city of Cromwell, it experienced something of the feelings of Madrid when the sceptre of the austere, laborious, parsimonious Philip II gave place to that of his son. For Philip III, though a valetudinarian and a saintly devotee, was much given to amusements; and his chief minister, the Duke of Lerma, set an example of lavish profusion in theatrical entertainments, bull fights, cane tourneys, masques, and balls. The theatre had suffered so much ecclesiastical opposition under Philip II that shortly before his death in 1598 he had made an order forbidding theatrical representations altogether. The town of Madrid begged Philip III that the theatres might be reopened, urging the excellent

influence of religious plays upon the spectators and the importance of the rents paid by the companies of actors to the hospitals
of Madrid. Moved by such arguments, Philip III, in 1600, when
the theatres had been shut hardly three years, summoned a
council of ecclesiastics and lay authorities to examine the whole
question. Following their advice—which still condemned in the
strongest manner the theatres as they had heretofore existed in
Spain—he allowed them to be opened anew; reducing, however, the number of actors, forbidding all immoral themes in
plays, and allowing representations only on Sundays and Church
festivals not exceeding three other days in the week.

Owing to the abundance of great dramatists which Spain
was at this time producing the Madrid theatres soon became
the most important in the world except only those in London,
which, however, met their death at the hands of the Round-
heads. At this time also, the organization of the theatre in
Madrid reached its perfection, about which fairly full information may be gathered from *El viaje entretenido* (1603) of Augustin
de Rojas Villandrando. Rojas enumerates all the kinds of
company from the simplest, the *bululu*, to the most complex,
the *compañia*. In 1603 there were only eight officially recognized
companies, but their number rapidly increased. In Madrid at
this time there were only two theatres, the Corral de la Cruz,
established in 1579, and the Corral del Principe, in 1582. These
theatres belonged to pious brotherhoods who collected hospital
funds from them. The performances, advertised by posters,
began at four in summer and at two in winter. The auditorium
consisted of the *patio* (parterre) for standing room; the *gradas*
(amphitheatre); *aposentos* (galleries); *desvanes* (upper gallery);
and at the rear, facing the stage, the *cazuela* (stew-pan), or large
box for women. The buffet was represented by the *alojero* where
aloja, a honey-and-spice drink, was sold. The mayor had a
special box on the stage, which alone was provided with a roof;
a canvas (*toldo*) was stretched over the *patio*, which was
crammed with a vociferous mob, the so-called *mosqueteros*,
infantes, or *alabarderos*.

The performance began with a *loa*, a prologue which some-times, but not always, had some relation to the play that followed. Between the first and second acts, and again between the second and third, two interludes (*entremeses*) were given, short farces usually of a popular character. After the last act came a *saynete* (tit-bit), with spoken dance.

Such was the mechanism of the Madrid theatres that stood pre-eminent in Europe for the greater part of the seventeenth century. This pre-eminence was mainly due to the luxuriant and protean genius of Lope Félix de Vega Carpio, a native of Madrid of Asturian origin (1562–1635). Lope, according to credible accounts, was an extraordinarily precocious child. He wrote more than one play by the time he was twelve, attended the University of Alcalá, formed a connection with Elena Osorio, the wife of an actor, and after she left him wrote such violent satires against her family that he was tried for criminal libel. He was sentenced in 1588 to eight years exile from Madrid and two from Castile. Yet at some time before 10 May 1588, he was able to elope with Isabel de Urbina, the daughter of a king-at-arms (*rey de armas*). For on that date he was married to her by proxy, after having been threatened with trial for abduction. Immediately after, he embarked on the galleon *San Juan* of the Invincible Armada, found time on board to write *La Hermosura de Angelica* and came back alive, though his brother was killed. After a stay in Valencia to complete the term of exile from Castile he entered service as secretary of several members of the higher nobility. In 1598 the death of his wife, Isabel, set him free to marry the well-dowered daughter of a rich butcher.

In 1609 he assumed the purely honorary title of "Familiar of the Holy Office of the Inquisition." In the same year he joined the Congregation of Slaves of the Holy Sacrament, in the Oratorio del Cabellero de Gracia, and in 1610, the Oratorio de la Calle del Olivar—*Cofradias* which were more like fashionable clubs than religious bodies. After being admitted to the Third Order of St. Francis in 1611, he was ordained priest in 1614.

His letters to his noble friend, and at times accomplice, the Duke of Sessa, show that in spite of his age and his clerical garb he had by no means renounced his gallant intrigues. His liaison with Marta de Nevares Santoya dates from 1616; she died in 1632 after a period of blindness. Lope continued up to his last days, which were embittered by severe family trials, to astonish the world with his literary productivity.

This brief sketch of Lope's life should serve to bring out its discordant mixture of romantic adventure, irregular passions, and domestic virtue.

"Who," writes Mérimée, "knowing only the first part of his incoherent existence, would have predicted that this man could be the tender father of Marcela and Lopito, the peaceable bourgeois who limited his horizon to his little garden in the Calle de Francos, the priest trembling with fervour as he raised the Host, or the penitent who scourged himself till the walls of his room were flecked with blood? And how, on the other hand, could one discover beneath the ascetic a brilliant cavalier, duellist, exile, soldier of the Armada, a Don Juan the list of whose conquests almost rivals that of his plays? In this multiple aspect, Lope is the type of his period. He experienced in turn, or even simultaneously, all the emotions known to men of his day; he lived many lives, and for that reason, doubtless, he was able to depict more completely than others the eternal human tragi-comedy."

Probably no writer recorded in history wrote so much as Lope. His non-dramatic works form twenty-one volumes; his extant dramas number more than four hundred, and yet most of those he wrote are lost. He boasted that he had averaged five *cuadernos* (twenty sheets) a day throughout the whole of his life, and that he had written more than a hundred plays in twenty-four hours each. Though pre-eminently a poet he produced many prose works, including novels that make pleasant reading as well as many accounts of festivals and *certámenes* (literary competitions). As a poet he touched every string in the lyre, composing in every branch, serious and light, odes, elegies, and sonnets by the hundred.

But Lope's fame depends most upon his plays, upon which at first he set so little value. He wrote about eighteen hundred. If to this number are added the four hundred *autos sacramentales* which Montalvan declared he wrote, we should have the incredible sum of 2,200 plays, and that without counting *entremeses*. Even if these figures go a little beyond the truth they exceed in size the output of any other European dramatist of the ancient or the modern world. They represent an entire literature. Their bulk exceeds the creations of all the Elizabethan and Jacobean dramatists put together. Lope had to satisfy an insatiable and critical audience and this he did successfully for over fifty years. Whatever blunders and anachronisms he committed, because of the speed with which he wrote, it is impossible to deny his versatility. One does not naturally associate his careless ease and sunny nature with tragedy, and in truth his tragedies are not oppressively numerous. Still he has produced sombre masterpieces such as *Las Paces de los Reyes* and *El Caballero de Olmedo*. Lope is always great when he attempts tragedy, and if he does not attempt it oftener, it is because the public insisted on something in his lighter vein. In this lighter vein, in pieces like *Las bizarrias de Belisa*, *La dama melindrosa*, *El anzuelo de Fenisa* there is an almost unparalleled measure of gaiety, wit, movement, realism, and portrayal of character.

All his work for the stage is inspired by a healthy realism. His dramatic conception is so powerful, his gifts of presentation are so alert and poignant that he makes visible the whole panorama of existence. No one's heroes are more seductive, no one's heroines are more delightful, no one's *graciosos* are more slyly humorous and roguish and quick in apt retort. His scope takes in all conditions of human beings. He portrays kings and serving-men with an impartial brush, he paints the average middle-class, to which he belonged, with all its picturesque outbursts of nonsensical extravagance, alternating with shrewd poetical instinct; he utilizes for dramatic purposes all the rich store of his nation's history, drawing on old chronicles, on old *romances*, on popular traditions. He has the secret of communicating a contagious emotion, of inventing appropriate dialogue gemmed over with a polite and debonaire wit.

In his own lifetime Lope's reputation was universal. As early as 1603, one of his plays, *La fuerza lastimosa*, was acted in the sultan's seraglio at Constantinople. Others were translated into the native languages, and performed in Mexico. In France Lope's dramas were imitated by all the dramatists of that country, both mediocre and above mediocrity, till the eighteenth century. In England signs of Lope's influence in the seventeenth century are less manifest but by no means lacking. Though he lacks something of Shakespeare's ample and embracing note, his power of appeal is intense. Nearly every Spanish dramatist and many who were not Spanish, derive from him. Almost everybody owes him much; he scarcely owes anything to anybody. No one in the world has contributed more lavishly to dramatic creation.

At the time when the theatres of Madrid were laden with the rising glories of Lope's genius the town received a sudden and staggering blow. In view of the financial embarrassments of the government and the country, Lerma proposed as a remedy the removal of the court from Madrid to Valladolid. He argued that the presence of the court in the latter city would do something to remedy the poverty of Old Castile. The plan was to the private advantage of Lerma who had recently been made perpetual *regidor* of Valladolid, in which city he possessed many interests. It is not difficult to imagine the overwhelming consternation in Madrid which the suggestion occasioned. None the less the order for the transfer was given on 10 January 1601. Madrid was ruined by the change. It resembled a vast poverty-stricken city of the dead. Its houses were emptied as population flowed out in search of subsistence elsewhere. It seems that the change brought no alleviation to the poverty of old Castile, for the presence of a great court served to make prices, which were already rising, soar.

The absence of the court from Madrid went on for more than five disconsolate years. At last, in the beginning of 1606, when the king and queen were amusing themselves in the Duke of Lerma's town of Ampudia, the *corregidor* and four *regidors* of Madrid presented themselves with a petition that the court should return to their town. As an inducement they offered 250,000 ducats payable in ten years, together with a sixth part of the rent of the houses during that period. At the same time they offered great gifts to Lerma and his family. The bribe did its work in an age when such payments were not so regarded. The court and government were gradually brought back to Madrid, which soon regained its life of gaiety and prosperity. It also regained its crowds of beggars. Fernández Navarrete wrote fifteen years later: "It makes one think to see all the streets of Madrid full of idlers and vagabonds, playing cards all day long, waiting till it is time to go and get food at the monasteries, and to set out to burgle houses."

With the return of the court the round of festivities returned—more gorgeous than ever in spite of the growing exhaustion of the country. They graced Lerma's diplomatic successes, such as the betrothal of the Dauphin of France to the Infanta Ann, the entry of the French Ambassador, with his promise of eternal friendship with Spain, into the town in 1612, and the arrival of Isobel de Bourbon in 1615 to marry the future Philip IV. A less festive entry, but one no less satisfying to the pride of Madrid, was that of Philibert of Savoy to make good, by a humble apology graciously received, the treachery of his wily and inconstant father, the Duke Charles Emmanuel of Savoy. Among the most splendid of the many ecclesiastical festivals was the celebration of the beatification of St. Isidro Labrador (19 May 1620), the devout medieval ploughman, who was shortly to become the patron saint of Madrid.

The *Justas Poeticas* which formed the substance of this celebration were presided over by the great Lope himself and participated in as competitors by the principal men of letters of the time. The Church of St. Andrew, in which St. Isidro's body rested, was ornamented with unexampled splendour. The merchants of Madrid encased its altars with pure silver. The goldsmiths enshrined the form of the saint, which in five centuries had not wasted away, in a sarcophagus also of silver elaborately wrought. Other classes brought their offerings, all typifying the wealth that had flowed in from the mines of Mexico and Peru. In front of the church a gorgeous stage was erected, from which the poems sent in for prizes were read to a vast and appreciative crowd. At the end of all there appeared a sort of masque, who under the assumed name of Master Burguillos "seasoned the feast in a most savory manner" with his amusing verses, caricaturing the whole like the *gracioso* in the popular theatre.

One more anniversary for Madrid—and that one never to be forgotten—was the death, in 1616, poor and neglected, of Miguel de Cervantes in a house—number two—in the street that now bears his name. If everything else that ever happened in Madrid had faded from the memory of man its fame would be immortal for two facts alone—that the First Part of *Don Quixote* was printed there in 1604, and the Second Part in 1615. The popularity of the book exceeded all expectation—most of all that of the author. It was hastily reprinted in Madrid and new editions appeared in many of the cities of the Peninsula the same year. It has been reckoned that the total number of copies of *Don Quixote* that issued from the press in its first year was in excess of the number reached by any book since the invention of printing. The Second Part is almost unique as an instance of a sequel that is superior to the original. Nothing is more fruitless than the various interpretations of a supposed mystery hidden in the novel (against Philip II, against the Church, against the Blessed Virgin Mary, against one or another politician, etc.). The book is simply a marvellously merry story of human foibles. Time has shown how this story has exercised an almost unique fascination upon all ages, all conditions, and all races; and to judge by the number and extraordinary variety of translations they have never wearied of it.

After finishing the Second Part of his great masterpiece Cervantes felt that his strength was declining and so hastened to finish his last novel, *Persiles and Sigismunda*, anxious that enough life should be left him to complete it. On his return from a short holiday he wrote the Preface, full of a delightful and simple humour, in which he tells how on his ride back to Madrid he was overtaken by a medical student, who gave him much good advice about the dropsy—the complaint from which he was suffering; to which the old novelist replied that his pulse had already warned him that he was not to live beyond the next Sunday. "And so", he writes at the conclusion of this strange Preface, "farewell to jesting, farewell my merry humours, farewell my gay friends, for I feel that I am dying, and have no desire but to see you happy in another life."

*

It has often been repeated that literature and art are the flowers that border the pathway of national decay. The saying has a peculiarly apt application to the Spain of Philip IV—the greatest patron of painters and dramatists in history and yet the ruler of a country that has become a byword for the steepness of its decline during his reign. He came to the throne (1 March 1621) a gay youth of sixteen, much healthier, abler, and more active than his father had been. It might, therefore, have been expected that Madrid would have started at once upon a period of unequalled gaiety. On the contrary the court began the new reign with a period of austerity and drabness reminiscent of the age of Philip II. For the new king had chosen at once as his chief minister Don Gaspar de Guzman, Count of Olivares, who was destined to rule Spain and its vast empire for the following twenty-one years.

Olivares was a type of ambitious man, who desires power not as a means to obtain wealth and self-indulgence as do most

politicians. He desired power for its own sake and out of an
honest wish to rescue his country from the morass of corruption
and economic decay into which he saw that it was fast sinking.
He signalized his entry into office by wreaking a ruthless vengeance upon Lerma, his son, the Duke of Uceda, and their
rapacious satellites. It was thus that Lerma's favourite, the
famous Rodrigo Calderon, Marquess of Siete Iglesias, met his
death on the scaffold in Madrid.

Rodrigo Calderon was only one of the victims of Olivares's
determination to arrest the economic decline of Spain. The
new minister set to work to cut down expenses in the most
drastic fashion. A law was promulgated for the reformation of
abuses. It forbade anyone, whatever his rank, to remain at
court for more than thirty days each year and ordered great
lords to reduce the number of their attendants. Extravagance
in living and clothing was sharply curtailed; and officials were
sent round the fashionable shops in Madrid in order to burn
ruffs, ruffles, lace, and other such-like forbidden luxuries. Ruffs
under Philip III had become enormous, and the costly lace
edging and elaborate devices for keeping frills stiff had made
them, perhaps, the most extravagant articles of dress for everyday wear ever donned in any country. It is significant that the
disappearance of the ruff from Madrid was soon followed by
its disappearance from all fashionable Europe.

The ruthless economies of the Count-Duke, as Olivares was
called, acted as dampers upon the splendid displays of Madrid
society, but only for a short time. Events constantly called for
celebration and for the lifting of the repressive laws. Such a one
was the visit of the Prince of Wales and the Duke of Buckingham
for the wooing of the Infanta Maria.

All rules about economy were cast to the winds in the Count-
Duke's anxiety to keep the friendship of England without giving
the Infanta to the "heretic" prince. Gorgeous bull-fights and
cane-tourneys and processions of gaily-clad nobles through the
decorated main streets were the order of the day, while the
Prince of Wales tried hard to get on more friendly terms with

the Infanta and to triumph over the stiff etiquette of the stiffest court in Europe. It was not till the end of August that this unexampled period of wild extravagance ended with the departure of the disappointed Charles and the indignant Buckingham.

Ten years later Olivares himself, in his desire to retain the king's favour, planned a piece of extravagant splendour that ill accorded with his former demands for economy. This was the Buen Retiro which soon became so famous a part of the theatrical and artistic life of Philip IV. The most popular promenade in Madrid was the Prado on the east side of the town. Along this spacious avenue, two thousand feet in length and one hundred and twenty broad, the señoras in their stiff attire drove up and down escorted by their cavaliers on spirited Andalusian horses. Under the three rows of poplars, festooned with flowering rose branches, music was played of an evening, while the air was refreshed and the dust laid by the sparkling waters of four fountains.

This superb promenade was overlooked by the Convent of St. Gerónimo with its Gothic church, spacious garden, and olive grove crowning the eminence over against the city. Near the church stood a royal residence, the *Retiro de St. Gerónimo,* whence kings and queens with their princely guests and envoys set out for their state entry into the city and whither the royal family withdrew for periods of court mourning or during Holy Week. It occurred to Olivares that here was some land highly suitable for being turned into a rustic retreat for royalty under the very walls of the capital. He acquired from various sources the rising ground that skirted the Prado in its entire length from the Alcalá highway to the Atocha Church.

Olivares's plans were kept a profound secret. It only gradually became apparent that he was constructing not only a park and gardens but also a palace and a theatre. On 1 December 1633 all was finished so that the king, with the whole court, could inaugurate the new villa with a tournament in the square facing the theatre. Mounted upon an Andalusian palfrey he ran a tilt with Olivares.

The glory of Buen Retiro was not the house, which was a flimsy structure, but the theatre, where the use of scenery on a prodigious scale seemed to make all the marvels of fancy into realities. The greatest masters of scenic decoration in Europe were brought from Florence. In 1628 Cosimi Lotti, a pupil of Bartolotti, the inventor of theatrical shifting scenery, had arrived in Madrid accompanied by Pier Francesco Gandolfi, as "master carpenter", and two gardeners from the Boboli Gardens. Lotti planned the theatre with apparatus for opening the back of the stage towards the park, where could be seen a vista of flower gardens and grottoes illuminated by artificial light, pageants, and masquerades. In a performance of Pedro Calderón's *Circe*, for example, the islet in the lake in the park was transformed into a fairy-like scene of groves with fountains and volcanoes, animals and shades of Avernus, where Circe on the dolphin chariot rushed through the water to break the spell. Nowhere else in Europe was anything on so splendid a scale attempted. The younger dramatists of this great age of the Madrid drama began to assume as a matter of course elaborate scenery for their new plays.

The age when this first appeared on the stage of the Madrid theatres is also the age when the Madrid school of painting gave to the world not a few of the very greatest paintings it has ever possessed. The greatest of this school, Diego Rodriguez de Silva y Velásquez, has been truly described as the first of modern painters and still the greatest of them. Two of his landscapes painted about 1630 might quite well be taken for Corots. For he seems from the very beginning of his life to see for himself and to paint only what he saw. And so he continued to the end, his art changing with his own development. For example *Las Meninas* (The Maids of Honour), painted in 1656–7, has a maturity and refinement that *Los Borrachos* (The Topers), painted some twenty-seven years earlier, lacks. That is the only difference. *Los Borrachos* remains one of the world's great masterpieces. His masters had little to teach him; he taught himself from the contemplation of nature. His first master taught him to use brushes with very long bristles. His second master, Pacheco, provided him with his daughter, Juana, as a wife. Even as a young man he was well known in his native Seville as a budding genius, tireless in his search for models and subjects, which he found in the streets, in the inns, and by the roadsides.

Pacheco was useful also in taking his pupil to Madrid and enabling him to meet Philip IV—a meeting which led to Velásquez's appointment as royal portrait painter and decided his future. The king, then about twenty, had a passion for painting. His grandfather, Philip II, despite his failure to recognize the supreme value of the work of El Greco, was a great patron of painters. His father, Philip III, though fond of painting, failed as a patron. He himself, Philip IV, was one of the greatest—perhaps the greatest—patrons of painting known to history. Velásquez seems to have attracted him not only as a craftsman but as a personality, and the king went so far as to promise him that no other artist should ever paint his portrait —a promise which he kept with but one lapse, when Rubens, as Flemish Ambassador, visited Madrid in 1628.

Velásquez's world-wide fame is of comparatively recent origin, dating from the first quarter of the nineteenth century. Till that time his pictures had lain immured in the palaces and museums of Madrid. During the past hundred years, time and criticism have established his reputation as one of the most consummate of painters. It was Ruskin who said of him "everything Velásquez does may be taken as absolutely right by the student". In modern times his marvellous technique and strong individuality have given him a supremacy in European art such as is exercised by no other of the Old Masters.

With the career of Velásquez Madrid reached the climax of her splendour and influence in Europe. The long-standing economic decline of Spain, the more recent military decline, with the decline of political influence in Europe, was followed by the cultural decline of Madrid. It had been heralded by the rise of Gongorism in literature and of Baroque taste in the arts. The Accession in 1665 of Charles II, grotesquely deformed in mind and body, as the last of the House of Austria in Spain, was the visible sign that the great days of Madrid were over.

PLATE 31

PHILIP IV
Painting by Velasquez

PLATE 32

COUNT OF OLIVARES
Detail from a painting by Velasquez

Paris, Versailles
and the "Grand Siècle"

17TH–18TH CENTURY

JACQUES CHASTENET

"Gentlemen, remember the greatness of France"
Maréchal de Luxembourg
at the Battle of Neerwinden, 1693

I T was during the seventeenth century, to be precise in the
second half of the seventeenth century, that French civilization reached its apogee.

True it is that both before and after that time France
experienced periods of great material prosperity, of great
political influence, or of intense intellectual and artistic activity.
But at no other time were prosperity, influence, and activity in
the arts raised together to such a pitch as was seen in the age
which historians know as the "Century of Louis XIV" or
simply "*Le Grand Siècle*—The Great Century". Nor has the
ascendancy of France ever been so generously acknowledged
by other nations, including even her enemies.

This ascendancy had a solid geographical and demographic
basis. In a world which as far as the western nations were concerned was limited for practical purposes to Europe and a
fraction of America, France seemed the most favourably-
situated country. Surrounded as she was by three oceans,
firmly supported by the Pyrenees and the Alps, it was only in
the east and north-east that she possessed no natural frontiers.

She had achieved national unity sooner than any other great European Power. Italy was dismembered, Germany a hotch-potch of petty principalities, Russia barbarous, while England and Scotland still had their separate Parliaments. On the other hand France, with her twenty or twenty-five million prolific inhabitants, was by far the most highly populated country in Europe—with a population equalling those of Britain, Germany, and Italy combined.

Finally she was the possessor of enormous territories in the New World, which, although their resources had been scarcely tapped, nevertheless constituted an immense reserve of wealth.

All this, however, does not suffice to explain the brilliance of the *Grand Siècle*. There was also the intense industry of the French people at that time, their military valour, the existence of an exceptional number of first-rate writers and artists, and finally the presence at their head of a monarch who possessed in a supreme degree two qualities which, when combined in the Head of the State, are more valuable than genius itself: namely the sense of greatness and common sense.

Louis XIV, the "*Roi-Soleil*—Sun King"; Versailles, seat of the court and centre of fashion; Paris, artistic and intellectual capital: here were the three poles towards which for more than half a century the eyes of every western nation were turned, always in admiration, sometimes in envy, but never with indifference.

When in 1643 the death of his father brought Louis XIV to the throne at the age of five, the kingdom was far from being firmly established.

The House of Bourbon—the royal House of France—had a redoubtable rival in the House of Habsburg, one branch of which ruled Austria-Hungary and extended its tutelage over Germany, while the other governed Spain, the Catholic Low Countries, two-thirds of Italy, and the greater part of America. Thus France was practically encircled by a hostile power and constantly threatened with invasion.

On the other hand, the French nobles were still very independent and quarrelsome, and knew no such sentiment as patriotism. To increase their power they were ever ready to rise against the authority of the king and to seek the support either of the English Protestants or the ultra-Catholics of Austria or Spain. The fact that such rebellions were fatal to national unity and the well-being of the masses, they completely ignored: their extreme individualism stifled every other feeling.

It is true that the policy followed in the preceding reign by the great minister, Cardinal Richelieu, had succeeded both in weakening the House of Habsburg and in holding in check the seditious nobles. But Richelieu had died shortly before the ascent of Louis XIV and the young king's minority was accompanied by a civil war complicated by a foreign war. The country was terribly ravaged and only its extraordinary vitality saved it from dissolving in chaos. Fortunately for France there arose another eminent statesman in the person of Cardinal Mazarin, who, using very different methods from those of Richelieu, pursued the same aims. Finally the Treaties of Westphalia, signed in 1648, marked the decline of the Habsburg power and brought to France, in Alsace and Lorraine, important territorial gains; at the same time the French nobility and the allies it had found among the bourgeois of Paris were at last brought to heel.

Mazarin died in 1661. Louis XIV was then twenty-three. He resolved to govern the country himself, without a prime minister. This decision he adhered to until the close of his reign which only ended in 1715. He was never to forget that his throne had been threatened by the Habsburg armies, nor that he had been forced as a child concealed in a shabby cloak to fly from a Paris that had risen in revolt. These two memories were the principal motive in all his policy.

At the time when he took the reins into his own hands, the king was a handsome young man, tall, robust, athletic, with ruddy cheeks framed by magnificent chestnut hair, dark and piercing eyes, a hooked nose dominating a proud upper lip, a

fine, virile voice, dignified but easy movements, and an air of
the utmost majesty.

He excelled in all sports, was a wonderful dancer, better still
as a shot, a skilful tennis player, fine horseman, and an agreeable
singer. He enjoyed an iron constitution, could hunt all the
morning, work all the afternoon, dance all night, still find some
time to make love, and yet be ready to begin again the next
day without showing the least sign of fatigue.

His appetite was gargantuan. "I have often seen the King",
relates Saint-Simon in his *Mémoires*, "eat four large plates of
different soups, an entire pheasant, a partridge, a large plate
of salad, two large slices of ham, some mutton with gravy and
garlic, a plate of pastry, and then some fruit and hard-boiled
eggs." Such a diet, which would soon have killed any ordinary
person, kept him in the best of health. Neither cold nor heat
nor rain seemed to affect him. He was always just as poised, as
calm, and as majestic, and this almost superhuman imperturb-
ability astonished all who approached him.

His manners were exquisite. "Never", writes Saint-Simon,
"would he pass the humblest female without lifting his hat,
even to the chambermaids whom he knew to be such." He made
this politeness serve as a means of government, modifying his
marks of courtesy according to the quality of those to whom
they were addressed or to what he hoped to obtain from them,
putting a price on his slightest remark, distributing his glances
and his smiles as so many rewards, and inflicting his silences as
terrible punishments. He never showed impatience, never lost
his temper, the nearest he came to it being the occasion when,
after the celebrated amorist de Lauzun had treated him with
insolence, he threw his cane out of the window and remarked:
"I don't want to strike a man of quality."

His punctuality was proverbial. "One knew", writes Saint-
Simon, "to within a quarter of an hour exactly what the King
was going to do." And yet he was the opposite of a stuffed
shirt. Until he grew old he was passionately addicted to violent
exercise and was an ardent if somewhat inconstant lover.

PLATE 33

LOUIS XIV
Painting by Hyacinthe Rigaud

PLATE 34

MADAME DE MAINTENON
Painting by Mignard

MAZARIN
Painting by Ph. de Champaigne

LOUIS XIV'S BEDROOM IN THE CHATEAU DE VERSAILLES

To seal the provisional peace with Spain, Mazarin had arranged the marriage of the king with the Infanta Maria Teresa. It was not long before this blonde, sallow, and insignificant young woman started to bore her youthful husband and he turned elsewhere for his pleasure. Several favourites succeeded, the gentle La Vallière, the witty and haughty Montespan, the beautiful and stupid Fontanges, and others, until at the age of forty-four, when he had become a widower and was overtaken by religious scruples, he secretly wedded the astute and pious Madame de Maintenon, who was then forty-nine and to whom he remained faithful till the end.

For Louis, sport and women were a necessary recreation. His one real passion was the state with which he identified himself. His supreme object was to achieve the status in history of a "great and glorious King", and in his memoirs he would describe with enthusiasm the job of "being a King" which he spoke of as "grand, noble, delicious". Although he possessed natural good taste and exceptional common sense, he was not particularly intelligent and his education had been neglected. But on reaching manhood he set to work to study, and he had the knack of employing first-rate ministers. Distrusting the great nobles whose rebelliousness he had not forgotten, he insisted on their presence at his court where he could keep them under his eye; while they were impoverished by the expenses they were obliged to incur, he flattered them with marks of distinction which were purely honorary. But except with the army he never gave them any important employment, and it was among the bourgeoisie, the people of "base birth", as Saint-Simon indignantly described them, that he chose his effective collaborators. As the latter owed him everything, he could be sure of their loyalty and could keep them well under control. "It was not my intention", he wrote later, "to make use of my more eminent subjects; I had above all to establish my own reputation and to make it clear to the public, through the rank from which I chose my ministers, that I did not propose to share my authority with them."

During the first part of his reign the most famous of these ministers were Hugues de Lionne, Michel de Louvois, and particularly Jean-Baptiste Colbert.

Lionne, a disciple of Mazarin, was the Secretary of State for Foreign Affairs. He was an amiable man, very subtle and with great experience, who directed French diplomacy with a skill and a tenacity that were equally admirable. Louvois, the Secretary of State for War, was a rough and impulsive character; but he was a first-rate administrator who transformed the French army, until then badly organized, into the foremost army of Europe. As for Colbert, he controlled finances, commerce, the navy, and the colonies. He was a tireless worker, as hard on himself as with others, reserved, brusque, and utterly devoted to the king. But in contrast with Louvois he wanted Louis to win glory, not by military conquests and extravagant undertakings, but by increasing the wealth of his kingdom.

To Colbert is due the ordering of the state finances and the civil administration, the codification of the law, the creation of hundreds of industries, the organization of the postal service, the magnificent network of roads and canals, the prodigious expansion of the navy and the merchant marine, and also the exploitation and expansion of French colonial establishments. Under the impulse given by him Canada, or New France, Acadia, and the Antilles—the Isles, as they were then called— experienced a real prosperity. It was acting on his orders that Cavalier de la Salle explored the course of the Mississippi and annexed to France an immense tract of country which in honour of Louis XIV was named Louisiana. Colbert's policy was strictly protectionist and to borrow a word which only came into use much later, *dirigiste*, i.e. based on a planned economy. It was the first appearance of State Capitalism.

After the death of Lionne, Louvois, and Colbert, the men who succeeded were not in the same class, but the difference was not noticed at first, since in the eyes of the world the sole chief and driving force of the French government machine was Louis XIV himself, the "Sun King".

Surrounded by sycophants, living continually in an atmosphere of adulation, convinced that he was made of a different stuff from that of other men, could it be said that Louis XIV was a despot?

In one sense the answer is certainly "yes", for he looked upon the kingdom as his private property which he was free to manage as he wished under the sole guidance of God, and he took good care not to convoke the *États-Généraux* (analogous to the English Parliament) which had not been summoned since 1614. And yet his authority, although absolute in theory, was in fact checked if not limited by the ancient customs and privileges of the French provinces, towns, and corporations. The orders of the king were received respectfully but they were not always carried out, and he found in practice that his government had first to negotiate if it wished to be obeyed. This was particularly so in the case of the Catholic clergy who, now that the nobility had been tamed, constituted the most powerful body in the state and was largely exempt from taxes, which it only paid in the form of voluntary gifts.

It was partly to please the clergy, partly from religious conviction and an innate love of unity, that in 1685 Louis revoked the edict of tolerance known as the Edict of Nantes, which authorized the free exercise of the Protestant cult. It was a disastrous act, and resulted in hundreds of thousands of Huguenots going into exile and taking with them, notably to Prussia, their talents and their industry.

Limited as it was to a certain extent at home, it was in foreign affairs that the absolutism of Louis XIV found freest rein; and it was naturally at the expense of the House of Habsburg—that is of Austria and Spain—that the king sought to glorify his reign.

At first all went well. He was served by great generals, of whom the most celebrated were the Prince de Condé and the Vicomte de Turenne (both of them formerly rebels); his troops, armed and trained by Louvois, were irresistible; his diplomacy, directed by Lionne, and alternately using threats and bribes, met with consistent success. Victory succeeded victory, one annexation followed another, even after peace—an "aggressive and predatory peace"—had been concluded.

But the tables were turned when his former enemies were joined by new opponents: the Protestants of the Low Countries and England, the latter now rid of the Stuarts who had taken his bribes. France then suffered serious reverses but the king met them fearlessly. In the end he was able to safeguard a large part of his conquests, namely French Flanders, Artois, Franche-Comté, Roussillon, and Strasbourg; and having placed one of his grandchildren on the throne of Spain he succeeded in maintaining him there. It is true the kingdom was impoverished and much of Colbert's work in ruins, but the influence of France remained considerable, French customs and French taste retained all their prestige, and French continued to be the polite language of all Europe.

"I was too fond of war and of building," Louis confessed on his death-bed to his great-grandson and successor.

His passion for war was certainly excessive; both in blood and treasure it cost his kingdom dear and many of the victories were precarious. By contrast the buildings, if they cost a lot of money, do at least still stand, and the nobility of their design and the magnificence of its execution explain better than any other reason why the age of Louis XIV received the title of "great".

The whole of France benefited from the king's taste for raising edifices which would bear witness in future ages to his glory. There are few French towns, however insignificant, which cannot boast of a church, a gateway, a hall, a castle or some military work constructed in his reign. They can be recognized by the beauty of their proportions, the classic purity of their line, and the simplicity of their decoration. In these buildings brick and stone are often happily married and the mingling of the white and the red has the effect of relieving any impression of austerity. The architecture of the time, like the literature, seems to reflect in its submission to the rules of reason the philosophy of Descartes which was then so fashionable.

It is naturally in Paris that the greater part of these embellishments is to be found. Until then anything but a beautiful city, and consisting of a labyrinth of narrow streets interspersed by the gardens of convents, it was far from being completely renewed by Louis. But he surrounded it with fine boulevards planted with trees and adorned by monumental gateways; constructed several wide roads and squares; made paving the general rule; provided lighting by means of five thousand lamps which gave some security to the town at night; laid out whole new quarters which included plenty of open space; regulated the course of the Seine; constructed quays and bridges and rearranged the Ile Saint-Louis. Above all it was in his reign that the many noble buildings in classical style arose that still give the capital its incomparable appearance; such buildings as the Hospital of Val-de-Grace, the Observatoire, Hôtel des Invalides, the colonnade and north wing of the Louvre, the Pavillon de Marsan, the College des Quatre-Nations, the houses in the Place Vendôme and the Place des Victoires, and many others.

Colbert, who liked to see the people thronging in the streets and crowding the shops and massing on the bridges, would have preferred to see even more done for the capital. But Louis XIV, who never forgot how at the age of eleven he had been forced by a rising to escape from it, had no great love for the city. He tended to avoid it, made his sojourns there ever shorter and less frequent, and in the end abandoned it altogether. He only liked châteaux surrounded by wide spaces where vast gardens could be laid out, merging into game parks. A city, however illustrious, did not seem to him the right framework for the greatest king in the world: he needed nature, but a nature "disciplined and embellished" by the hand of man.

At the beginning of his reign he divided his time between the Châteaux of Saint-Germain, Fontainebleau, and Versailles.

This last, built by his father, Louis XIII, to a fairly modest design, he was particularly fond of. He enlarged it and extended the park, which was the scene of magnificent fêtes. He came to use it more and more, and after 1678 it became his permanent residence.

From then on, Versailles, now the seat of the monarch and his court, although only a dozen miles from Paris, tended to form a world apart, very different from that of the *Ville*. As a consequence, the King of France, who had formerly been very accessible, lived separated from the nation. At the same time the nobility, attracted to the court by the hope of favours to be received there, took no part in local government and lost touch with the people. This twofold isolation of the sovereign and the nobles was to become, in the following century, one of the chief causes of the French Revolution.

Needless to say, once the court was installed at Versailles, the small château of bricks and stone erected by Louis XIII was much too small for it. In 1669 the architect, Le Vau, had begun its enlargement by building new wings on three sides. After 1678, under the direction of another architect, Hardouin-Mansart, the work was greatly extended. In 1685 thirty thousand labourers were still employed on it. The result was the vast conglomeration of buildings one sees today, whose proportions are so right that nothing seems out of place—a miracle of good taste and grandeur.

The walls of the Château of Versailles, as they were at the end of Louis's reign, have remained intact, but its interior decoration and furniture have for the most part disappeared. They were of an extreme splendour. Gleaming ceilings decorated with paintings depicting the victories of the king, tapestries representing further victories or mythological subjects, precious marbles, carved and ornamented woodwork, gilded furniture inlaid with mother-of-pearl, delicately chiselled bronzes, precious silver work, bibelots encrusted with rare stones, lamps and chandeliers of pure crystal, immense mirrors: nothing was too luxurious, too extravagant to frame the majesty of the monarch whose symbol—a sun—was displayed everywhere over the motto *Nec Pluribus impar* (it lights several worlds).

It is true there was very little real comfort. The vast rooms could not be properly heated, and in winter the wine froze in the decanters; the attics in which the courtiers crowded at night were deprived of light; and in the absence of any sanitary installation the corridors and stairways were filthy and evil-smelling. But it mattered little: one was not concerned with comfort: the aim of all was magnificence.

No less famous than the Château of Versailles is its park. Laid out by the great landscape gardener Le Nôtre, it was merely an extension of the château and constituted in itself an architectural work. The trees were not allowed to grow freely but arranged in rows, or staggered, or cut close so as to form a thick hedge. The lawns were laid out in geometrical forms, bordered with box and ornamented, in accordance with a complicated plan, with orange-trees or yews ingeniously shaped. There were statues everywhere, and long vistas were arranged giving a view either over the country, or of ponds and fountains. The flower-beds were in the form of stars, or arabesques, and resembled some cunning embroidery. At every turn there was some surprising effect, here a little wood, there a labyrinth, farther on a grotto whose walls were covered with a festoon of shells, or even a ballroom open to the sky half hidden by the foliage. And what gods and goddesses, nymphs and heroes! All the inhabitants of Olympus seemed to have been turned into stone and transported to this spot!

The Versailles of Louis XIV had also its annexes: the stables, Orangery, the Grand Trianon, the Château de Marly (no longer existing). Everywhere there was displayed the same grandeur, the same care for orderly arrangement, the same luxury at once refined and sober. Everywhere the King himself supervised the plans, himself gave the orders to the architects and gardeners, directed the work, concerning himself with the minutest details, and if necessary having it done again and again until he was finally satisfied. For the whole of his reign, a considerable part of his palace and its gardens was unfinished. But just as he enjoyed being with his armies, so he enjoyed being surrounded by his builders; in the latter as in the former he found matter for "glory".

It was against this background and ever circling round the monarch that the court moved. It consisted of an immense throng of lords and ladies, of chaplains, grooms, servants, workers, and various parasites—about six thousand people in all, in addition to an army of ten thousand bodyguards, musketeers, mounted escorts, and Swiss guards of the military household. At the beginning of the reign, the court reflected something of the youth of the sovereign. It was gay, brilliant, confident, dissolute enough and occasionally undisciplined. But later, especially after its definite establishment at Versailles, its activities took on the regularity of clockwork. Early in the morning the throng would gather for the *lever du roi*, then at the chapel, where daily he attended Mass; it would follow him as he went hunting; watch him as he sat alone at table devouring his dinner; wait for hours while he worked with his ministers for the sake of seeing him come out of his cabinet; accompany him on his walk; and watch him again at his supper, or playing cards or billiards or listening to a concert. And the day would end with the spectacle of the King going to bed.

There was, of course, every sort of distraction: fancy dress or masked balls, concerts, theatrical performances, lotteries, games of every kind, tournaments, fireworks, garden and water fêtes, military reviews and visits to other châteaux or to the armies. But these amusements, while they cost millions in costly dresses and ornaments, in the end became so many set pieces, in other words, tedious.

"Before I went to court", wrote a friend of Madame de Maintenon, the morganatic wife of the king, "I had never known boredom; but I have had plenty of it since." And she added: "At court, one yawns, one is bored, one is jealous and one tears his neighbour to pieces." For her part the Princess

PLATE 35

MEETING BETWEEN LOUIS XIV AND PHILIP IV OF SPAIN IN 1660
Tapestry after the design of Charles Lebrun

THE REVOCATION OF THE EDICT OF NANTES IN 1685
Contemporary engraving

PLATE 36

CLAUDE PERRAULT'S GREAT EAST FAÇADE OF THE LOUVRE UNDER
CONSTRUCTION, 1667–1670
Contemporary engraving

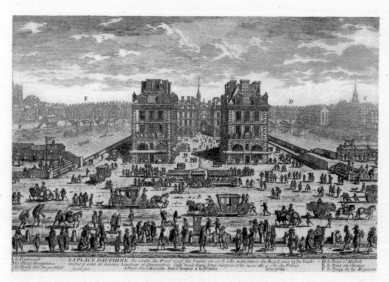

THE PONT NEUF IN THE 17TH CENTURY
Contemporary engraving

Palatine, sister-in-law of Louis XIV, complained that: "The women are so afraid of saying anything which may displease that they speak of nothing but gambling and clothes."

But in spite of all, such was the fascination exercised by Louis that nobody thought of abandoning a way of life which in the long run became boring. The Duke of Saint-Simon did not like the king and knew that the king did not like him, but it never occurred to him to leave Versailles. The Maréchal de Villeroy admitted that when his sovereign granted him an audience it was as though the heavens were opening. Madame de Sévigné, author of the famous letters, wrote: "What I like above all is to spend four entire hours with him." As for the Duke of Richelieu, nephew of the terrible cardinal, he declared: "I would rather die than to go two months without seeing the king." Finally La Bruyère, immortal author of the *Caractères*, was not ashamed to write: "Whoever considers that the visage of the prince makes the happiness of the courtier, whoever spends his whole life seeing him and being seen by him, that person will understand how the vision of God can make the glory and the happiness of the Saints."

This sort of spell made itself felt far beyond the French frontiers: there was not one German princeling or Hungarian magnate, or Polish nobleman, whose dream was not to visit Versailles, or if that was impossible, to construct for himself a miniature Versailles; in England, under the last two Stuarts, and even later, the fashions of the court of France had the authority of law; the Ambassador of the Elector of Brandenburg remarked that the French court served as a model to every other nation; the Grand Turk himself and the King of Siam sent ambassadors to the Sun King for the sole purpose of catching some reflection of his glory.

If Versailles was the shrine of the sacred cult of monarchism, and also the centre of fashion and refinement, Paris remained the economic and intellectual capital of France. With its 600,000 inhabitants, 25,000 houses, and 600 streets, by the second half of the seventeenth century it was the most populous and extensive city in Europe. It was also the most celebrated for its artistic and intellectual brilliance.

Mention has already been made of the embellishments which the capital received under the impulse of Colbert. "Beauty and luxury", a visitor wrote at the end of Louis's reign, "are here so lavishly diffused that anybody wanting to enrich three hundred empty towns would only need to plunder Paris." But what particularly struck foreigners as much as the splendour of the buildings was the vivacity of the streets and public places.

Your Parisian is by nature gay, inquisitive, and sociable. Living only too often in mean, comfortless, and unheated dwellings, he loved to sally forth and mingle with his fellows. Thus as soon as night fell the streets would be filled with citizens hurrying or strolling along without heed to the mud with which (in the absence of pavements) they were bespattered by passing vehicles. Above the buzz of talk and the clattering of horses' hooves on the cobbles would rise the traditional cries of the street vendors. "*Tous chauds, tous brûlants*", chanted the seller of hot chestnuts. "*A la barque, à l'écaille,*" clamoured the oyster merchant. "*Vieux habits, vieux galons,*" replied the old clothes man. "*Voilà le plaisir des dames! Voilà le plaisir*", from the girl selling biscuits. "*Harengs frais! Harengs nouveaux!*" from the fish merchant. In the midst of the hubbub would sound the trumpet of the public crier, announcing the loss of somebody's watch or purse; or the strident voice of a hawker selling lottery tickets; or a barrel-organ grinding out the latest tunes—the whole dissolving into the confused roar which constituted the voice of Paris.

The three points where the throng was always thickest were the Pont-Neuf, Place Royale, and Cours-la-Reine. The Pont-Neuf, constructed in the reign of Henri IV, grandfather of Louis XIV, bridged the Seine while bestriding the island known as the *Cité*, cradle and heart of Paris. Unlike the other bridges it carried no houses and gave an unrestricted view of the splendid river and its busy traffic of barges, lighters, and pleasure-boats. This was the favourite meeting-place of the Parisians. It was packed throughout the day with a chattering and jostling crowd through which carts, coaches, and equestrians had difficulty in forcing a passage. Among the crowd were to be found every type and class: gentlemen resplendent with plumes and ribbons, bourgeois in sober brown with white neck-cloths, fine ladies wearing masks and hampered by their long trains, men and women of the lower order in coarse woollen smocks and petticoats, doctors all in black and riding mules, monks, nuns, drug peddlers, tooth extractors, barrow boys, bookstall keepers, street musicians and singers, jugglers, chimney-sweeps, servants in livery, soldiers and beggars, without forgetting the ladies of easy virtue, and the pickpockets. It was an indescribable motley, a perpetual uproar, a joyous hurly-burly frequently enlivened by fights.

While the Pont-Neuf was the *rendez-vous* of all social classes, it was only the fashionable world that gathered at the Place Royale (afterwards renamed Place des Vosges). This was a vast quadrangle with a statue of Louis XIII in the middle and surrounded on all sides by rows of uniform houses overhanging a series of arcades which formed one continuous gallery. The houses belonged to members of the nobility and later, when most of the nobles took up their residence at Versailles, to wealthy bourgeois, especially those who were connected with the law. Under the arcades were installed the most elegant shops in the town. Here from morning till night there was a continuous procession of people "of quality" on their way to pay calls, to shop or simply to show themselves off. Fashionable young men, bewigged and raised by high red heels, and wearing, according to the mode of the moment, either the full-skirted "rhingrave" or the long and close-fitting coat adorned with buttons and crossed with a wide belt; fine ladies, generously *décolletées*, dressed in silk gowns embroidered in gold and silver, their hair fantastically arranged in one of the two prevailing modes, "à la hurluberlu" or "à la Fontanges", the whole scene producing an effect of luxury that was reflected in the gilded carriages and sedan-chairs with their brilliantly painted panels.

The government tried vainly to put a check to this extravagance by issuing edicts forbidding excessive luxury and imposing a fine of a thousand pounds on those who decorated their
coaches, and also forbidding the import of toilet accessories
from Flanders and Italy. These restrictions were laughed at,
and people continued to cover their coaches with gilt as well
as their belts, garters, hats, and even the bits of their horses.
The carriages and chairs continued to bring to the Place Royale
all the fashionable beauties of the day, while their admirers
either displayed themselves on horseback or strolled about like
peacocks, one hand gracefully resting on their swords, the other
ready to sweep the ground with a low bow as they met some
acquaintance. One moved from group to group, stopping to
exchange greetings or embraces, or to look at the shops where
the jewellers, swordsmiths, and the merchants of fine brocades
and laces displayed a profusion of goods. The Place Royale was
the glory of Paris.

Towards the end of the reign, however, the centre of fashion
moved to the newly-constructed Place Vendôme, and also to
the new quarter which was rising on the left bank of the Seine
in the neighbourhood of the Abbey of Saint-Germain-des-Près,
from which the name of the Faubourg-Saint-Germain was
derived.

From Easter on, and throughout the summer, the chief
rendez-vous for elegant society was the Cours-la-Reine.
Extending outside the fortifications this was a broad avenue
which started from what is now the Place de la Concorde and
followed the Seine for about a mile. It was about fifty yards
wide and planted with four rows of elms. Here, in the late
afternoon, could be seen a continuous procession of carriages
and horsemen moving slowly from one end to the other and then
turning and reversing the process. As acquaintances passed
each other they exchanged greetings and smiles, or waved their
hands. Many an intrigue owed its birth to this parade of
fashion, the Vanity Fair of Paris and "Empire of Ogles" as a
contemporary described it.

Sometimes the procession continued farther, across fields and market gardens, as far as the Bois de Boulogne, which was still fairly wild, and where the dauphin, eldest son of the king, often hunted the stag and even the wolf. In the middle of the forest there was a vast clearing which was used for military manœuvres and sometimes as a race-course. At the end of the seventeenth century, horse-racing, imported from England, was just becoming fashionable and beginning to eclipse the tournament. Professional jockeys did not yet exist, and it was the owners themselves who rode the horses.

In contrast to their social superiors, the ordinary people of Paris did not use the Cours-la-Reine and never went near the Bois de Boulogne. Their favourite promenades, apart from the Pont-Neuf, were those of the Tuileries Gardens, which had recently been laid out, and the Mail, which followed the right bank of the Seine as far as the Ile Saint-Louis. In winter, one of the most popular spots was the Saint-Germain Fair on the left bank. All trades were presented at the fair, which lasted for two months, and goods could be found there to suit every purse: silks and satins, stuffs and materials of every sort, ironmongery, toilet articles, furniture, jewellery, spices, drugs, cakes, and every kind of drink, including coffee, that new beverage which was so universally popular.

In summer, on days when bourgeois and artisans were not at work—and such days were pretty frequent, since in addition to Sundays there were numerous religious holidays—they liked to take the stage-coach to one of the villages situated on the river bank: Bercy or Charenton upstream, Chaillot, Passy, Surennes, or Saint-Cloud downstream. There they would instal themselves in some tavern or café, eating the meals they had brought with them, drinking the coarse local wine, and ending the day with dancing and singing to the tune of a violin. The gaiety of the French was proverbial, and even the poorest carried their poverty lightly. "In France", the saying was, "everything ends with a song."

This joviality, although noisy, hardly ever degenerated into

17

vulgarity. Jokes were ribald rather than obscene, and drunkenness was rare. Every foreign visitor was struck by the politeness of the common people of Paris and also by the refinement of their speech. The servants in Molière's plays bear witness to this.

One of the characteristics of the Paris of that period was that there was little distinction between the richer and the poorer quarters. Obviously the houses of the rich were more numerous in some parts of the town than in others, but even in the noblest mansions, although the principal floor would be occupied by the wealthy, it was usual for the upper floors to be divided up and let out to the families of artisans. Thus the different classes were brought closely in contact, meeting each other on the stairs, exchanging news about their families, and treating each other with an easy familiarity which was all the more natural because, the social hierarchy being solidly established, there was little envy on one side, or mistrust on the other. Liaison between the two groups was maintained by the servants who, while ministering to the needs of the richer class, belonged by origin to the humbler. They were, of course, extremely numerous. A bourgeois family would employ a butler, a porter, coachman, groom, cook, five or six maids and as many footmen.

The *étage noble*, or principal floor, usually consisted of a suite of vast rooms communicating with each other. The walls would be covered either with tapestries or some other rich material. The fashion for painted or gilded woodwork was spreading, and in the more expensive residences the use of marble was common. Ceilings were lavishly decorated. The style of furniture, which had been square and heavy at the beginning of Louis's reign, was developing in the form of graceful curves and fine carvings, sometimes encrusted with copper and mother-of-pearl. At the same time the taste for pictures, statues, mirrors, bibelots, fine books, and musical instruments was spreading rapidly: it was the first appearance of the connoisseur.

Ideas of comfort remained rudimentary. The rooms were so

large that it was difficult to heat them in spite of the immense fire-places which the servants kept continually stoked with wood. By night the only light provided was by tallow candles which had to be snuffed every twenty minutes, the more expensive wax candles being reserved for great occasions. Bathrooms, although not unknown, were still a rarity, and often there was not even a private closet. The *chaise percée* was an important and honourable article of furniture and refined gentlemen thought nothing of giving an audience while seated upon it. In fact, there was no privacy at all. Just as the king and queen dressed and undressed in public, so the nobility, the wealthy bourgeois and their spouses considered that people who came to see them getting up or going to bed were paying them a mark of respect. Maidservants would sleep on a truckle-bed in the conjugal chamber of their master and mistress, with a lackey bedded down outside the door.

There was no special dining-room. According to circumstances meals were served on trestles in one reception room or another. Although food was abundant, the culinary art which later on was so highly developed in France was hardly known; meat was served in great quantity and always highly seasoned. The wine most usually drunk was the thin, sour wine from the vineyards round Paris; occasionally there was burgundy or champagne (the sparkling variety dates from 1670), and after the dessert, sweet wine from Cyprus or Spain. For the dinner service, silver was replacing pewter more and more, and cut glass was quite common. On the other hand the fork was still considered a superfluous luxury. People used their hands to transfer food from the plate to the mouth. The smell of food and much worse was met everywhere, but the people of that day, even the most refined, do not seem to have possessed a very keen sense of smell, and cleanliness was not considered a cardinal virtue.

The dwellings of the humble folk were still less comfortable, and of course much more exiguous. It was common to find a family of several persons crowded in some single attic room which was also used as a workshop by the father. And yet there was no lack of housewives who took a pride in their home, polishing the few bits of furniture, or brightening the only window with a bowl of flowers or some gay curtains.

Below the workers who, however poor, nevertheless had a roof over their head, there existed a mass of unfortunates without any definite employment or secure livelihood who lived on alms (which the convents, at that time very numerous, freely distributed) and also on robbery. Among them were many blackguards who for long made the streets of Paris most unsafe at night. Under Louis XIV the police gradually cleaned up the capital. The male criminals were either imprisoned or enrolled in the army, or sent to the galleys; the women placed in convents where an attempt was made to teach them a trade, or deported to Canada. Many of them, however, succeeded in escaping the periodic round-ups, and continued to live their disorderly lives on the fringe of society. This sort of underworld was to be found in every great city of the time; it is the one depicted by Gay in the *Beggar's Opera*.

In spite of these darker corners the social and intellectual life of Paris was one of extraordinary brilliance. While it was success at court that put the seal on a man's reputation, it was the town that launched him on his career, and it was there that most of the men of genius lived whose work immortalized the *Grand Siècle*. Corneille, Molière, Racine, Boileau, La Bruyère, Madame de Sévigné—they all put in an appearance at Versailles, but their homes were in Paris. The great La Fontaine would never leave the capital, and if Saint-Simon resided at Versailles it was because he was a duke and had no wish to be taken for an author. However well they were treated at court, writers, unless they happened to be of noble birth, were still only regarded as entertainers. In Paris, on the other hand, they could mix with the aristocracy on a footing almost of equality. This was something new that had developed out of the *salons*.

The earliest of these *salons* had been initiated at the beginning of the seventeenth century by the celebrated Marquise de

Rambouillet, and it was in her famous "blue room" that the first gatherings were held where nobles, *grandes dames*, high officials, and men of letters met together. Others followed, notably those of Madame du Plessis-Guenegaud, Comtesse de La Suze, Mademoiselle de Scudery, Madame des Loges, the gay Ninon de Lenclos, and many more.

People went to these *salons* to exchange gossip, to discuss their friends, to exercise their wit, to listen to the latest madrigal, the latest sonnet, even the latest tragedy, to split hairs over linguistic and grammatical niceties, above all to argue interminably about love and friendship. These intellectual hot-houses, strongholds of the *précieuses*, had their ridiculous side which was satirized by Molière in one of his most amusing comedies. They contributed none the less to codify the rules of *savoir-vivre*, to purify the French language, making it an instrument of the most perfect precision, and finally to create that great art of conversation which was to reach its full flowering in the eighteenth century and remain for long the admired and envied attribute of Parisian society.

Louis XIV did not relish the idea that there was a centre of culture and influence apart from himself. In consequence he regarded the Paris *salons* with some suspicion. But realizing that the prestige of literature was as necessary to the glory of a monarch as military triumphs and splendid buildings, he was tireless in his encouragement of authors. And since he had naturally good taste, he seldom made a mistake in the men he encouraged.

He paid salaries to numerous writers, including even foreigners, upheld Molière against his detractors, appointed Racine and Boileau as his historians, and extended his patronage to the French Academy founded by Richelieu. The forty Academicians—the "immortals" as they were (and are still) called—held their meetings at the Louvre Palace and, subject to the royal pleasure, could co-opt new members. If some of them owed their seats more to birth than to talent, they were all regarded as equal: at their meetings a duke or a bishop was never addressed as "Monseigneur", but simply as "Monsieur", like the most plebeian of his colleagues. The Academy was to do much to establish the respect accorded in France to intelligence.

It was not only literature that Louis protected, but also the arts and sciences. The painters Le Brun, Mignard, Champagne, Largillière, and Rigaud; the sculptors Couston, Coysevox, Puget, and Girardon; the architects Le Vau, Perrault, and Mansart; the musician Lulli—for all these artists who were the glory of their age the king was the principal and often the only patron. Among the great painters only Poussin and Claude Le Lorrain remained independent of the royal favour. Many, too, were the *savants*, the engineers and the inventors who received subsidies from the treasury and were employed in the scientific institutions founded by the king. On the model of the *Académie Française*, Academies of painting and sculpture, architecture, and the sciences respectively were set up and installed at the Louvre. The prestige of these bodies rapidly expanded though-out Europe and with it that of Paris, which was their seat.

It was also in the capital that, on the instigation of Colbert, the royal manufactory of Les Gobelins was established, with the dual object firstly of making furniture for the royal palaces and secondly of setting a standard of technical proficiency and good taste in all the crafts concerned with interior decoration. The tapestries turned out by its workshops rapidly replaced those of Flanders in the esteem of connoisseurs. Moreover Les Gobelins did not merely produce works of art; it was also the school where the young craftsmen were trained who subsequently spread through the provinces of France and abroad to establish the style known as *Louis Quatorze*. There was scarcely a sovereign in Europe, nor even a rich individual, whose ambition was not to secure the services of one of these artists, and they were in-comparable instruments of French propaganda.

Needless to say, the theatre, to which the Parisians were so partial, was not neglected by their sovereign and the companies of players enjoyed special privileges although under conditions of strict supervision. By the middle of the century the two principal companies were that of the *Hôtel de Bourgogne*, which for the most part acted tragedies, and that of the rue des Fosses-Saint-Germain, which was directed by Molière and specialized in comedy. In 1680 the two troupes amalgamated and, under the patronage of the king, formed the famous *Comédie-Française*, which has continued to this day as a state institution and the leading theatre of Paris. A little later there appeared the *Comédie Italienne*, the home of light comedy, where the entertainment was often half-improvised.

The playhouses at this time were quite small. The *parterre*, where the audience stood, was reserved for men; behind these were the seats, while running the whole way round the amphitheatre were two rows of boxes. The lower row was the smarter, and it was here that ladies of quality competed in elegance with fashionable courtesans. A chandelier fitted with candles which had to be snuffed from time to time hung from the ceiling; on either side of the stage chairs were placed for the use of noblemen. They were expensive to hire and got in the way of the actors. Scenery, which was unknown at the beginning of the century, was making its first appearance, but it was still very simple.

Such as they were, the theatres were nearly always full. The audiences were quite unrestrained, showing approval or disapproval by loudly applauding or hissing, and indulging in passionate arguments about the merits of the play and the players, which occasionally ended in riots. A "first night" was an event, the news of which travelled abroad. All over Europe, and especially in England, there was a rush to put on plays which had scored a success in Paris.

About the year 1670 there appeared a new kind of entertainment which immediately had an enormous vogue, though it did not affect the popularity of the drama. This was the opera.

Opera already existed in Italy, but France up to then had only known the ballet. The Florentine musician, Lulli, the king's director of music, had staged a great number of ballets in which the most exalted members of the court and even the king himself did not disdain to take part. Feeling the need to introduce some novelty, this astute man obtained permission to found the Royal Academy of Music, and installed it in the theatre of the Palais-Cardinal (later the Palais-Royal), built by Richelieu. The place was elegant, richly decorated, brilliantly lit, and provided the perfect framework for the operas which Lulli presented, and which he described as "lyrical tragedies".

The whole town flocked to see this innovation. They were captivated by the beauty of the *décors*, by the surprising mechanical contrivances, by the charm of languorous or passionate verses sung to delicious music, interspersed with dancing by sylph-like ballerinas. In the intervals there were visits to neighbouring boxes, offerings of sweetmeats, and exchange of *billets-doux*. The aphrodisiacal atmosphere of the Academy of Music enchanted the Parisians, and soon the opera was all the rage—and one to which every visitor to the French capital rapidly succumbed. At once composer, producer, ballet master, and administrator, Lulli acquired both glory and a large fortune.

Fêted and petted as they were, actors and actresses, singers, and dancers constituted a world apart which was looked at somewhat askance. The Catholic Church regarded them as corruptors of morals and threatened them with excommunication. Because he was actor as well as playwright, the great Molière himself, when he died, was buried at night, almost furtively. The most illustrious actresses—la Champmeslé, la Duparc, la Béjart—were enveloped in an aura of scandal, which only enhanced their fascination for many of their admirers.

The Church might condemn the theatre, it did not diminish the passion shown for it by the court and the town. For religion, great as its influence still was on the minds of people, no longer exerted an absolute spiritual power. The vast majority of Frenchmen continued to be deeply religious, to go regularly to Mass, to fast, to confess, to follow processions, but they did not hesitate to criticize the ostentatious wealth of the hierarchy and the excessive numbers of monks. There were some even who, drawing from the philosophy of Descartes conclusions which its author never envisaged, maintained that religious dogmas should pass the test of reason, and went so far as to profess a secret atheism. It was in Paris chiefly that these bolder spirits congregated; they were called *libertines* or free-thinkers, and their audacity grew with their influence in the following century.

Louis XIV himself was a sincere believer, and it was this piety which influenced him at the age of forty-four to give up his mistresses and to marry Madame de Maintenon. At the same time he was passionately addicted to order and unity, and it was partly this obsession, as was suggested earlier, that led him in 1683 to revoke the Edict of Nantes and to forbid the practice of Protestantism in France. It was a hateful act which the resulting persecutions rendered still more odious. It has to be admitted, however, that most of his subjects thoroughly approved of the king's decision. Tolerance was regarded then not as a virtue, but as a weakness. In England at the time, Catholics and Nonconformists were also subject to persecution.

Moreover it was not only the Protestants that were out of favour; the Jansenists also experienced the rigours of the royal displeasure. Jansenism was a particularly austere form of Catholicism and since its puritanical adherents were also full of pride they were deeply suspect in the eyes of the Church. At the instigation of the Jesuits severe measures were taken against them. But in this case the king's edicts were opposed by a section of the rich bourgeoisie of Paris, which was at heart Jansenist. A prolonged quarrel ensued which took many years to heal.

Although a dutiful son of the Church, Louis XIV could not suffer that any foreign power, even a spiritual one, should pursue a policy in France independently of himself, and this brought him more than once into conflict with the Holy See. On one occasion he even forced the Pope to offer him a solemn apology. At heart his ambition (which was not very different from that cherished for a time by Henry VIII of England) was to constitute a Church of France in community with Rome, but enjoying a high degree of autonomy and of which he, the king, would be the temporal head. This conception was called *gallicanism*. Its eloquent apologist was the great preacher and bishop, Bossuet, and it was also officially adopted by the Sorbonne, which was then the centre of theological study. *Gallicanism*, which flattered the national vanity, met with considerable success in France, specially in Paris. However, it failed to take permanent root.

Religious questions were then exercising public opinion as a little later political questions were to do. They were eagerly debated in the street, in the stage-coach, at the inn, and an English traveller remarked that one could hardly exchange three words in France without being asked to what religious sect he belonged.

These theological disputes ended by producing a spirit of doubt and confusion very different from the conformist state of mind that Louis XIV would have liked to impose.

If to this be added the ruinous wars and financial difficulties which marked the end of his reign, it is easy to explain the awakening at the beginning of the eighteenth century of a latent opposition among the Parisians. When in 1715 Louis died at the age of seventy-seven, the city received the news of his death with relief, if not joy. Although Voltaire, that typical Parisian, wrote a fulsome tribute to the "Sun King" in his book, *Le Grand Siècle*, by the end of the century the French Revolution—an essentially Parisian revolution—could only see in Louis a hated tyrant and revenged itself by smashing his statues.

Such an attitude was less than fair to a monarch who, if he suffered from excess of adulation, was, nevertheless, one of the greatest whom France has known. When he died the country was tired but not exhausted, and in a short time it revived, more vigorous, more robust, and more prosperous than ever.

Louis XIV added several fine provinces to his kingdom, surrounded it with a solid ring of fortresses, endowed it with immense colonial possessions, and provided it with many valuable industries. On top of that, the French language, French manners and fashions, French organization and even the French way of thinking, conquered Europe, and France exerted the greatest intellectual and moral influence of any nation since classical times.

This supremacy was to last for a long time during which Paris—whose bourgeoisie ended by triumphing over the nobility of Versailles—would continue to be a pole of attraction for thinkers, writers, artists, and men of taste throughout the world. After two and a half centuries, and in spite of several world upheavals, there is still preserved to this day something of that attraction.

A century in which the national patrimony was enriched with so much beauty and so much glory, a century in which the capital of France became the centre of the civilized world, may well be considered great and it is understandable that not only the French but many other people choose to regard it as a "golden age".

Vienna under Metternich

19TH CENTURY

ALAN PRYCE-JONES

IT is odd, but undeniable, that those ages in which the sum of human happiness has been most evenly divided rarely have paid much attention to the privilege—itself rarer still—of widespread personal freedom. Gibbon has set the standard once for all. "If a man were called", he wrote, "to fix the period in the history of the world during which the condition of the human race was most happy and prosperous, he would, without hesitation, name that which elapsed from the death of Domitian to the accession of Commodus." And he goes on to link this sense of well-being to the intelligent despotism of the emperors.

In the last century despotism has fallen from fashion, if only because the reality of power is now a far more alarming, a far more penetrative reality than in the world before the industrial revolution. And, as we have seen during *le grand siècle* in France, the dynamics of power sooner or later produce exhaustion. In order to succeed in maintaining themselves, despots require power, and, if they refrain from using it, it is rather from force of external circumstance than from natural forbearance. The triumphs of Louis XIV at last wore thin, therefore; as well as its vigour he possessed also the parching quality of the sun. One does not associate his reign with so transparent a blessing as that of human happiness. But it is possible that Gibbon, had he possessed the gift of prophecy, might have reconsidered his verdict in favour of that period which succeeded the final disappearance, a century later, of the Roman empire; without

altering his reasons he might have substituted the names of
Francis (though it was not he but the empire which died) and
of Francis Joseph for Domitian and Commodus.

It seems paradoxical that this can be so. The Austrian empire
came into being as the child of disaster. The empire of Charlemagne had been shattered by Napoleon; in lands and revenues
the emperor found himself reduced with one massive blow; at
the same time much of the prerogative of the Holy Roman
Emperor passed into strange hands—the emperors of France
and Russia, the King of Prussia, even the King of England, each
performed an essay in subtraction upon the unique position of
the emperor in Vienna, until what remained was a kind of vast
family estate, extending from the archduchy of Austria to include Bohemia, Moravia, Hungary, Illyria, a part of Galicia;
and as well as material loss, the empire had to bear the abrupt
eclipse of a long afternoon glory still warmed by memories of
Prince Eugene and the Empress Maria Theresa. In a moment,
almost unnoticeably, nine hundred years of history dropped
from the map. Yet with a different title, on a diminished throne,
the same emperor sat; and in little more than a dozen years his
empire, illogical or retrograde though it might be, had returned
to sun itself in the last rays of the eighteenth century, as though
Napoleon had never been.

Of this pleasant tyranny the centre remained Vienna. And it
is easy to reconstruct both the appearance and the atmosphere
of the city once the noisy guests of the Congress had moved
away.

Let us imagine a traveller coming from the west. Driving
down from the low hilly woods, and cursing at the abominable
state of the roads, he would arrive, beyond the suburbs, at a
short avenue leading to the cream-coloured façade of Schönbrunn. Here, if the court were not in residence, he might turn
aside to visit the state-rooms, to stare into a world of gilding
and porcelain and crimson silk, and out again beyond the high
windows to the long pleached alleys which conduct a population
of statues towards the pillared hill at the end of the formal

gardens. But if the court were out of residence it was probably late autumn or early spring, and then there was little temptation to linger in the splendid melancholy rooms, warmed at best by a stove more delicate than cordial, and never forgetful of the white months in which the snow piled against the plinths of Mercury and Neptune and scurried against the hill-side in front of a searching wind.

For Schönbrunn was a summer palace. It needed to be seen when the citizens crowded along the lime walks and admired the Hungarian Guard, in red and silver and a tiger-skin at the shoulders, riding across the courtyard with Prince Esterhazy at their head. It needed the familiar presence of the emperor and the archdukes walking among the collection of Alpine plants or joining the imperial ladies at the Tyrolean châlet; it needed the double warmth which went with the summer light—and that, in Central Europe, at least, is as brilliant as ever—and with the paternal presence of the emperor himself, a simple, friendly figure who was perfectly ready to be stopped in his daily walks by anyone with a grievance, a request, a suggestion.

Our traveller, then, would not linger long. He would press forward into the suburbs, holding his passport ready, and prepared for exactly the questions which harass his descendants today. Had he any tobacco? Any foreign goods? And, above all, any undesirable literature? For, paternal though it might be, the emperor's government, under the cautious guidance of Prince Metternich, kept a watchful eye on the arrival in the country of new, and so possibly subversive, ideas; and therefore travellers were advised to jettison all books and papers so as to be on the safe side. The public libraries of Vienna, they were to know, would be plentifully supplied with wholesome or consoling reading matter.

But already, from the suburbs, a sight appeared which made the tiresome behaviour of the local officials seem inconsequent: the high polychrome roof of the cathedral, topped by an immense fretted spire, gathered the wandering roof-lines of the city to a single point; and when, after a mile or two, the outline of Vienna proper could be seen, pressed behind high brick walls in front of which lay a straggle of garden, palace, and dusty plantation, the traveller, keenly expectant of the comforts awaiting him at the *Erzherzog Karl*, or, better still, the *Kaiserin von Oesterreich*, anticipated as well the pleasures of a city second only, if second at all, to Paris itself.

He would drive in by the Josefstadt Gate. And then, in the centre of the city, he would find a Vienna which was to change surprisingly little in the next hundred and twenty years. Locked behind their walls, the inhabitants congregated into a maze of small streets and squares. The light and air came no lower than the attic windows; below, a thrusting, excitable, polyglot throng pattered over the cobbles, or drew back to the wall while some princely carriage rumbled by, preceded by a liveried runner with a silver-topped stick in his hand. In these years—the years of Metternich's greatness—Vienna played something of the part of modern New York: it set a pace, it stamped with its own pattern the different nationalities which came to it because it lay at the centre of a civilization; and yet it remained a small city in spite of its wealth and its influence; not much more than 300,000 souls lived in centre and suburb together, and of these seven-eighths in the suburbs.

Because all the activities of the court, the government, and the world of industry, as well as the palaces of the nobles, were crowded behind walls, the city, at first sight, seemed rather cramped and disappointing. The shops were small, the houses towered high, all the families of a vast cousinage were crammed into edifices which one visitor describes as resembling inns of court rather than private dwellings. The imperial palace itself was the reverse of cheerful; the state apartments had not been redecorated since the time of Maria Theresa, and the private rooms were dank and threadbare. Nevertheless, an extraordinary animation was in the air. The coachmen in the streets were famous for their skill and dexterity, and in the crowded hours—from midday to one and from six to seven—the press was so thick that slow-going foreigners were liable to be bowled over into the gutter.

Where, then, did the attraction of Vienna lie? It was not at all like the Vienna of Johann Strauss. It frowned upon unnecessary levity. It was cautious, subtle, rather dull. Music-making, conversation, and cards, filled a great part of the time; every evening the streets were deserted by eleven. Over the whole city an extraordinary attention to rules could be observed. Not only to minor rules, such as that against smoking in the streets, but to iron conventions of social behaviour, some of them handed down from medieval times. It was, to say the least, unexpected that it should be the emperor's duty to attend every fire, yet it was a duty punctually observed by Francis II in his capacity of chief citizen. And, in matters of daily conduct, the strictest laws of precedence were maintained, so that from the imperial family down to the slavey each place was known and kept, and every lifetime regulated in a series of concentric circles between which close communication was almost impossible.

And yet the fact remained: Vienna, on closer inspection, spread a snare so alluring that each traveller was caught in turn. It was not the *"tourbillon irrésistible de plaisirs continus"* —in La Garde-Chambonas's phrase—to which foreigners succumbed; such gaieties had been a temporary by-product of the Congress and died with it. But they had left something in the air: something, moreover, which had combined with a high sense of purpose. In a word, it soon became apparent to the sympathetic observer that the Austrians believed themselves to be set upon a business both important and enjoyable.

For consider: to the archduchy of Austria came North Italian noblemen and Triestine merchants; Jewish bagmen from Galicia and legendary magnates from the Hungarian plain; Moravian Brothers from Reichenberg and subtle Greeks from the Adriatic provinces; Unitarians from Transylvania and monarchist refugees from all over Europe. The local capitals played their part: Buda and Prague and Venice and Milan

PLATE 37

METTERNICH
Drawing by Anton Graff

THE CONGRESS OF VIENNA
Drawing by Jean-Baptiste Isabey

PLATE 38

VIEW OF SCHÖNBRUNN

THE TAPESTRY ROOM IN THE HOFBURG

kept their own state and often their own counsel as well; but at the higher level at which all those conflicting interests had to be reconciled and smoothed into a single policy Vienna stood as the single imperial centre.

Furthermore, while the different provinces of the empire looked to Vienna for guidance, the whole German-speaking world observed it with very different, but not less attentive, eyes. That world, spreading from Poland to the Rhine, across a multitude of kingdoms, principalities, grand-duchies, free cities, might turn up its nose at the absurd peoples upon whom the emperor wasted so much of his time: the incomprehensible Magyars, slavish Bohemians, facile Lombards, the clowns and Shylocks and rogues who ought to be put in their places and kept there. It might turn up its nose at such, but not at the Austrians themselves. For whatever the kings of Prussia and Saxony might say, it was the Emperor of Austria, not they, who held the inheritance of Charlemagne; and, on a lower plane, it was not Sans-Souci, nor Karlsberg, nor Ludwigslust which set the tone of German society—that indefinable tone which sounded in music and poetry and subtle talk—it was not they but the Hofburg and Schönbrunn. The Prussians might grumble at Austrian delicacy; the Bavarians might vaunt a greater purity of race. But the emperor could still afford to smile at such presumptions. He alone stood at the still centre of the axle round which all Germany revolved.

This accounted in part for the special relation in which he stood towards his peoples. It gave his power that paternal kindness which touched every aspect of government. Government could be arbitrary, certainly; it could be narrow-minded, over-cautious, old-fashioned; but those are all paternal qualities, and qualities evoked by a family growing up untidily, its members strongly individual in character and divided by wide differences of age. And always, above government itself, stood the figure of the emperor. It could not be said that Francis II was a very lively monarch. He was not clever, nor brilliant, nor dashing. His favourite reply to any concrete suggestion, "Let's sleep upon

18

it", reflects the embarrassed and pernickety caution which was so intelligently exploited by Metternich. But at least he accepted his position at the head of the German-speaking world. And so, during his reign, a constant attractive power was exerted upon it by his capital.

For this, no doubt, the Congress of 1815 was partly responsible. If the Congress splendours were only temporary they at least revived a forgotten standard among classes of society each of which had been exhausted by a whole generation of high political and economic tension. It had long been the fashion, for example, among the nobles to visit Vienna as little as possible. Now, however, the influx of distinguished visitors brought with it a fresh taste for the city. Neglected palaces were refurbished, and not only the nobles but plain citizens as well obtained such a reputation for civilized living that a marked industrial revival took place—a revival which attracted the ambitious and the forceful from abroad, especially from South Germany, and gave Vienna that air of fabulous promise which clothes the greater American cities today.

It is necessary to remember that Metternich himself had obeyed this attraction. Born in Coblentz fifteen years before the French Revolution, he had become a servant of the emperor as a result of the revolutionary upheaval which deprived his family of its Rhineland property. It is natural enough, therefore, that he should have looked to his master chiefly as an upholder of order. During the years between his first appointment as imperial representative at The Hague and his final accession to power after the disaster of Wagram, the old Europe had been swept away—or so we can now perceive. Yet at the time it cannot have seemed quite so certain. Revolutionary zeal had been stemmed; through the marriage of Napoleon to Marie-Louise two contradictory orders had been united in the fragile person of the King of Rome; the future—to one of Metternich's temperament—held a tantalizing balance between hope and fear: hope of an internal concord from which all threats to the imperial house could be progressively scotched, and fear of the strain and ferment which were still to be felt throughout Europe. "The true character of our age", he told Guizot many years later, "is that of an age of transition . . . I made myself a conservative socialist. . . ." And if Metternich's idea of socialism is remote indeed from the concept which gradually formed after 1848, the statement shows at least that his mind was neither inelastic nor conventional. Not surprisingly, therefore, he felt a particular sympathy for English institutions; not surprisingly, at the end of his life, Disraeli turned to him in affectionate admiration. And there can be no doubt that in the years of his power this intense (and sometimes blind) desire for order, tempered by a lively interest in the thought, the art, the applied sciences of his time, was the chief factor in the renaissance of Austria.

For under his rule a remarkable change occurred. Goethe's friend, Varnhagen von Ense, summed the matter up in the early 1830's: "The whole aspect of the city and its surroundings", he wrote of Vienna, "has something rich, pleasurable, and gay of heart about it. People here seem healthier and happier than elsewhere; the dark spirits which dog mankind, which harass us unremittingly, find it hard to breathe in this air, and seldom have tried to lodge here. Such an appearance has something uncommonly agreeable; it exerts a power for peace on every temperament, every humour, and promotes the feeling that thus should it be for every man among us; for everybody such an atmosphere is the right and natural one. And even if it is only an appearance, the appearance is not in vain."

It was, indeed, only an appearance—linked to the wave of prosperity which broke upon the city during the 1820's. A few years later, when the July Revolution in France had touched off minor insurrections throughout Europe and thus alarmed the Austrian government into redoubling a policy of rigid isolation from all liberal currents of thought, the dream was broken. But in the 1820's a youthful spirit of enterprise was abroad; and although the life of the city was quiet enough, a runnel of open good humour spread through a populace tired of war and poverty. The court, the nobles, the government officials, might oppose levity; but among the middle classes that spirit was now forming which later made the gaiety of Vienna a commonplace. Dancing suddenly became the fashion. In the Apollosaal, in the "Schwarze Bock", above all, in Dommayer's Casino not far from Schönbrunn, the sound of the waltz broke delightfully over the crowded tables; at Dommayer's, Josef Lanner himself, and the elder Strauss, began their years of fame; and it was not long before the mild pleasures of a Viennese evening became celebrated throughout Europe.

To what did they amount? Certainly not to excess. The emperor, like the middle classes, dined at the old-fashioned hour of two; receptions at the court were rare; and even though the nobler families might dine at four or five, they had little to look forward to except a reception which began at ten and ended soon after midnight. The opera and the theatres started at seven; a little whist or an hour of music closed the day well in time for early rising except during Carnival and in a short season of ball-giving after Easter. There was, in fact, not much in the Vienna of 1830 to support a legend of high living. But there was something better: an extraordinary diffusion of kindly temper, of ease, of mutual confidence.

That, perhaps, was the great contribution of Vienna to European civilization. It provided, in the Biedermeier period, a momentary suspension of history—a breathing-space before the great industrial struggle of the mid-century, in which men and women of different classes, religions, nations, showed themselves perfectly at home in a strictly hierarchical society, perfectly disposed to innocent amusements, and singularly free from the warping rancours which disfigured the more liberal countries of western Europe.

Perhaps it was a little stuffy, a little acquiescent, yet it is hard not to be touched by the crowds sitting under the trees at Nussdorf and Döbling, listening to the *Harfenisten*—musicians who, in earlier times, had sung comic songs to the music of a harp, but now played violin or clarinet, zither or guitar, under the nut-trees among the wooden benches; or again, hard to watch without affection the popular festivals, such as that in the Prater on 1 May, or at the Brigittenau on the first Sunday in July.

The Prater, it must be added, played its part every Sunday in the year. The *Ausflug*—the Sunday excursion—was already a settled habit among the Viennese, who flocked out, on any auspicious day, into the welcoming landscape which surrounded their city. But the Prater, because the nearest, was also the most animated of meeting-places. There, on a sunny day under the trees, a microcosm of Vienna assembled. The long shady avenues kept the heat away; in countless low buildings, each set in its garden, the tables were spread for a midday breakfast. The *Papagei*, the *Eisvogel*, the *Tracteur* competed for custom (for fashion, among these friendly little restaurants, was both absolute and changeable); and in the afternoon, after admiring the view from the Lusthaus, and watching the boats on the sweeping Danube, the traveller would plunge among the coffee-house tables, among the coloured shacks, crammed with young people singing and dancing, spilling out under the avenues, clapping the little trios which accompanied a singer, admiring the musician who blew a trumpet fixed to his violin and worked the drums with his feet, or gathering round a story-teller in the shade, while a Turkish band did its best to distract the kite-flyers, the exponents of optical illusions, the pigeon-shooters, the sausage-sellers at every corner.

Tired of these lowly pleasures, he might walk into the Haupt-Allee—a triple avenue devoted to elegant display. There, in the Sunday afternoons, the fashionable rode or walked; and in the middle avenue three to four thousand coaches followed slowly behind the bowing figures of the imperial family in an open carriage. If he were lucky enough to be present on 1 May, he would certainly (after watching the well-dressed display their spring gowns in the Augarten) stay to see the traditional race between the runners of the princely houses. These runners, in rich and brilliant uniforms, casqued in feathers, were maintained in the first instance to run ahead of the family coaches, two and two, torch in hand, both to light the road and to clear a way. Later they were cherished as objects of family pride, not unlike race-horses; and each 1 May an immense crowd gathered to watch a dozen or so of the best show off their paces. High wagers were laid, and tribunes were built to accommodate the families whose runners took part in the race. Excitement was immense. "Bravo, Kinsky!" the crowd cried; "Faster, Karoly! Keep to it, Auersperg!" And finally the winner was rewarded with a purse of gold.

The July festival on the Brigittenau was still more animated. There, on a quiet site occupied only by a chapel and a hunting lodge, a whole city of tents was built for the day, between which a kind of Feast of Unreason took place. All social distinctions were banished (although the leaders of society, it must be admitted, did not arrive till the evening), and until night fell the peculiar unity of the city was fully manifest, whereby the prince and the goose-girl, the magnate and the kitchen-maid, shared their pleasures without embarrassment.

Among these pleasures the theatre stood high; and in order to catch the flavour of the times nothing is more evocative than the pieces of Raimund and Nestroy. How can they be described? To what can they be compared? To the Keystone comedies? The Aldwych farces? Scarcely: for, though they may not seem very amusing today, they represent a kind of popular art which was solely Viennese. Its merits can be glimpsed through Nestroy's *Lumpazivagabundus*: merits of a strongly local, heady order, and meant for display by an author who was also a beloved comic actor. Dialect, verbal humour, imaginative fantasy—such are the ingredients. And there can be little doubt that it was largely by means of the *Vorstadttheater*—the light comedy stage, as it were—that the ebullience and the ironical bravura of the Viennese character were formed.

In part, no doubt, these traits can be attributed to the Italian strain in the Austrian nation, in part to the Slav. It is only necessary to look as far as Munich or Dresden to perceive how marked a difference lies between the popular world of Vienna and of any German city outside the empire. But the Viennese spirit did not show itself only in trivialities. At this distance it is very easy to feel too sentimental an affection for the frank merriment of the *Brigittenkirchtag*, for the open, humorous temper of the city populace. We see a Teniers without grossness— foreign observers were much struck by the fact that the Viennese so seldom became drunk—a Boucher without pretension. But the same mixture of blood which gave the Viennese so marked a taste for simple pleasures also gave them a quick appreciation of sensuous or evocative themes at however high a pitch. Thus the performance of Sophie Schröder in Grillparzer's *Sapho* became legendary; and the very presence in the city of such men as Beethoven, Schubert, or the painter, Daffinger, was felt to be a measurable honour even by those to whom their works made no special appeal.

And, indeed, to an art-loving people, the time was wonderfully propitious. Yet it contained a paradox implicit in the very name, Biedermeier. Biedermeier was originally a comic personage, the symbol of a truth as penetrating as that hidden in Colonel Blimp or in Marius. Biedermeier was the comfortable bourgeois, the timid, convention-ridden, respectful little citizen. And as the years of Metternich's rule succeeded one another the rôle of Biedermeier became more emphatic. He was the supreme counter-revolutionary, the exactest of adherents to Church and State. And yet the civilization of which he was representative nourished such unexpected ardours as the quartets of Beethoven and the great simplicities of Grillparzer.

Perhaps the dwelling-houses of the Viennese exemplify best the Biedermeier character. The palaces of the Herrengasse and the Wallnerstrasse are not representative. Kinskys, Czernins, Lobkowitzes, Wilczeks and the innumerable consanguinity of the *Almanach de Gotha* stood apart. Their vast houses usually dated from the eighteenth century (though the Clam Gallas Palais in the Währingerstrasse remained, until taken over by the American authorities in 1946, an unspoiled example of an early nineteenth-century palace, set in a little wooded park just beyond the walls); all round them, however, were the modest villas of plainer folk, many of which have still survived almost as they were built.

Their elevations were classical: in Hietzing, in Nussdorf, at Lainz, the sober milk-coloured façades still stand, their double windows bolstered against winter cold, or hidden from the July sun. The rooms inside were plain. No carpets hid the complex pattern of the parquet floors, and the sofas were the reverse of comfortable. Under elaborate pelmets the winter curtains retained the warmth of a porcelain stove, shaped like a vast inkstand and set in one corner; in summer the muslin draperies floated on a calculated draught from the garden brilliant with phlox and geranium. Commodity, not splendour, was required. But the furniture (unless it were modelled on French originals) was light and cheerful. Pearwood and cherry, Hungarian ash and mahogany, were set sparely round the walls; treasures from an earlier generation, imported or copied from abroad, had been replaced by a half-rustic simplicity; instead of the Georgian display which reigned in London, or the cosy elaboration of French contemporary taste, an Austrian household wore rather a conventual air. Plain living and plain thinking (so far as he could impose them) were Metternich's ideals for the subjects of the emperor.

In such settings the question of human happiness, as raised by Gibbon, became all-important. For if the Viennese were not happy they were nothing. The paternalism of the state took away much of their responsibility for their own welfare, the barriers established by a strict censorship between Austria and the rest of the world (not least the rest of Germany) gave them an unusual intellectual self-sufficiency. The empire could feed, amuse, and (between economic slumps) employ them. They lived, therefore, in almost a private world, moved by internal stresses but secured, for a whole generation, from the disturbing touch of the unexpected.

No doubt it was rather dull; no doubt the peaceful well-being of the Biedermeier years chafed the more restless spirits of the time to provoke the irascible temper of 1848; but the dullness had its charms while it lasted. It can be compared to the dullness of Adalbert Stifter, among the greatest and most unjustly neglected of Austrian writers—dull because static, careful, prosy, but at the same time drenched in warm sunlight and nourished on clear, bright air. Both aspects were reflected in the appearance of the people themselves. "I certainly", wrote Mrs. Trollope of 1836, "never saw the elements of what in most other cities would have constituted a mob, so decently clothed, so generally clean and *well-to-do* in appearance, and, in the midst of great gaiety and good-humour, so perfectly quiet and orderly." "A most happy and enjoying people", another traveller of the same period, Peter Turnbull, calls them. "With all their apathy and slowness . . . a very gay, junketing nation," Lady Londonderry wrote in 1840. And before dismissing Metternich's government as a reactionary tyranny it is worth examining in some detail exactly how it worked upon the daily life of the Austrians.

First, as to religion: although Catholicism prevailed, clerical power was sternly curbed, and equality of right was given to other denominations. The Archduke Joseph, Palatine of Hungary and brother of Francis II, was married in succession to a member of the Greek Church, a Calvinist, and a Lutheran; and when the Lutheran wife of his brother, Charles, died, her funeral rites were celebrated in St. Stephen's, at the emperor's orders, as a Protestant ceremony. Not surprisingly, the archbishop complained, with the support of the nuncio, that it was unfitting to use a Catholic cathedral for a Protestant rite. "Tell the nuncio," the emperor merely replied, "that this is no affair of his." And on every occasion (following the precedents established in the 1770's by Joseph II), he took care to assert the supremacy of the civil power, as vested in the throne, over the ecclesiastical—to the extent that no Austrian subject could be excommunicated without imperial consent, or, more striking still, that army marriages contracted without the permission of a superior officer were declared in every case invalid.

The emperor thus became, in his own domains, effectively head of the Church; even the monastic communities were removed from the authority of Rome; and an equal jurisdiction was exercised over other religions, which were classified under four heads, as Greeks, Lutherans, Calvinists, and Jews. Each community maintained its own independence; disabilities upon the Jews had been cancelled progressively, until they could fill any office in state or army; unauthorized sects could only meet in public by licence; in fact, the religious life of the country was used as a channel of communication between the emperor and his subjects to an extent perhaps unparalleled in history. For although he did not much care to which religion they adhered, the emperor insisted on each of them being registered as belonging to one or the other, in order (it can be surmised) to attach to the civil government the most intimate of all principles of order.

Not unexpectedly, the educational processes of Austria developed the same theory. To quote Turnbull once more:

"Aiming at the gradual and peaceful amelioration of her internal condition, the equalization of rights before the law, and the general development of the national resources, Austria views education in its larger sense, as a mighty engine to mould the public mind; to cement it together in a bond of cordial union with her existing institutions; to excite and to regulate its energies, so that it shall be neither a drag on the state machine by its ignorance and grossness, nor a spur to unsafe speed by its crude theoretical fancies. She strives at the creation of a happy, not a brilliant people. . . ."

Thus, again, the ideal of happiness is put forward. And again happiness is bound up with a sense of security. This may sound heavily pedestrian, yet its ideals must be measured against the uncertain and often violently changing background of the preceding generation throughout Europe. The French Revolution inevitably produced extremes of licence or restriction, and the foreign examples open to the Austrian government after the fall of Napoleon were not reassuring. In Germany the Romantics had impressed a surface of passionate, often of anarchic, feeling upon a habit of mind either military (as in Prussia) or casuistical; in France an uneasy compromise had been struck between the libertarianism of the Revolution and the cautious respectability of a restored monarchy; in Southern Europe a rigid clerisy controlled every branch of education. The Austrian authorities tried, therefore, to avoid the obvious pitfalls. Education was in the hands of the state, but it was closely bound to the five official religious denominations. Without testimonials from the religious body with which each pupil was registered, no educational advance could be made, but, under the supervision of rabbi, priest, or pastor (who were severally forbidden to proselytize), schools were free, varied in character, and universal. If education was not compulsory, the absence of a certificate made later employment, except as a labourer, illegal; and under Francis II a coherent attempt was made to weld the whole empire together by means of a uniform system.

It will be seen that the government was playing safe. Contentment was its chosen virtue, and anything which might disturb contentment, or foster ambitious inquiry, was banished from the schools. From this distance that sounds a comforting principle, if unexhilarating. The difficulty which arose, however, was that it weakened the Austrians in that faculty in which they were already weakest—the faculty of independent judgment. By making their formative years so snug, it gave them no defence against the outside world, it confined their intelligence to practical skills, and it required of their rulers a constant vigilance against the importation of vigorous ideas.

This vigilance, more than anything else, has darkened the reputation of Metternich as a wise ruler. It was not alarming —indeed, all contemporary travellers agree that police activities were less in evidence in Austria than anywhere else in Europe— but it had the disadvantage of cramping opinion within narrow bounds. True, the rules were languidly applied. The censors fussed, and then forgot. But, in a negative way, the police supervision worked a good deal of harm: by eliminating almost all home news from the newspapers, and by forbidding travel abroad except to the very important or to the professional classes who had a specific reason for leaving the country. Bad habits might be picked up abroad, and so it was wiser to be on the safe side.

But within the country itself there was no terrorism of any kind. Nor was the law in itself severe. Even the convicted criminal—and there were surprisingly few of them—only felt the paternal hand of a state which was more than a century ahead of the rest of Europe in matters of criminal jurisprudence. To begin with, the death sentence was extremely rare, and had in all cases to be ratified personally by the emperor. Otherwise the extent of the fault was measured by the extent of the public disturbance caused, except in cases of treason, first-degree murder, or forgery of currency notes. In every case, however, all possible excuses were allowed to diminish the crime; full responsibility was only admitted at the age of fourteen, and liability to the death sentence only at eighteen; and at a time when English children were being executed for insignificant thefts, the young Viennese were treated as unfortunates in need of care rather than punishment—indeed, the punishment, if exacted at all, often fell (and severely) upon their parents.

From the vantage-ground of modern England it is fascinating, and perhaps sobering, to see how nearly the Austria of the 1830's resembles the ideal of the Welfare State. A uniform education gave equal opportunity to all, and a vast civil service found place for all who did sufficiently well in their examinations. Then, a fatherly interest was taken in the citizen by his government. Better mechanism to deal with ill-health, old age, and unemployment existed in Austria than elsewhere in Europe, and the exchequer was permanently out of funds owing to the responsibilities shouldered by the state towards its citizens. The result should have been a paradise; in fact, however, it sustained the faults of the Austrian character at the expense of its virtues. By giving a paramount importance to peace of mind, it cramped initiative, and, as might have been foreseen, gave an exaggerated influence to those who refused to conform. For so long as all went well within the state, and above all, so long as contact with the outside world was kept to a minimum, the Viennese enjoyed, in no spirit of fervour or inquiry, their privileges as the citizens of a capital city.

They developed the scheme of life which played a considerable part in wrecking any possibility of unity within the empire. Under this, it was assumed that the hard work would be done by the Slav and Magyar populations, while administration was perfected by the Germans; or, worse, that it would be safe to tolerate the disparities of a feudal system as practised outside Austria proper, so as to make sure of the loyalty of the nobles.

Not that the Viennese administrators were wholly blind. They saw (or some saw) quite clearly the social changes which would have to be made in order to fuse together the different parts of a state not only sharply divided by variations of tradition and language but ranged between high urban fashion and the most primitive simplicity. They saw that the nineteenth century was married, within their frontiers, to the Middle Ages, and that the marriage was not going too well. Yet somehow the moment for introducing a change never seemed quite to come. "Let's sleep upon it", the Emperor Francis had said; and they slept, until the pressure of the outside world became too great, and with the coming of the railway round about 1840 it was found impossible to keep dangerous ideas at bay any longer.

The climax, after years of mounting unrest, brought about the fall of Metternich and the revolution of 1848. But the sleep, while it lasted, had been wonderfully pleasant—a light sleep, moreover, enlivened by exhilarating dreams. Was it really impossible to combine the best of the old world and the new? Round that question turned the brightest of Metternich's visions. Was it so hard to make people see that violent changes were of their nature impermanent? That out of order alone progress could grow? It is not odd that an instinctive friendship and respect should have grown between Metternich and Disraeli.

Both perceived very clearly the problem of the nineteenth century: how to guide a state through the coming industrial revolution without its breaking under the centrifugal pressure of rival
economies, policies, societies; how to use the revolution as a
creative, not a convulsive, force. But Metternich, who had
known the eighteenth century, was the warier man. Too wary,
no doubt. By knowing what had been good for the past he
conceived that he could prescribe for the future. Ease of spirit,
security from want, a quiet life: to these his own period, like
that in which we live, attached a perhaps exaggerated importance. In such a scheme there was not much scope for the nobler
virtues, but plenty of room for holidays, light music, cheerful
conversation. There was room, too, for judicious experiment.

Technical schools, for example, were warmly supported by
the government. In Vienna itself a Polytechnic Institute had
been founded in 1816; and beneath the foundation-stone laid
by the emperor was a roll which dedicated the building
above all to "*die gemeinnützige Ausbildung meines lieben und
getreuen Bürgerstandes*"—to the intellectual enlargement for
the common good of the faithful middle classes. The phrase
sums up an official attitude of mind in the Biedermeier period.
Things had to be *gemeinnützig*—for the common good—and the
middle classes were to be given as much attention as possible,
whether they liked it or not.

Certain things, however, though in themselves desirable, are
not particularly designed for the common good. The arts, for
example. And since a generation is chiefly recorded by the
books, the pictures, and the music it leaves behind, it must be
regretted that Metternich's personal pleasure in the arts offered
so meagre an encouragement to the Austrians. It is usual to
praise their extreme musicality; and so far as sheer volume of
music-making goes it is right to do so. But already the vitiating
flaw in Viennese musical life was apparent. The bad drowned
the good; and the good too often included whatever it cost an
intellectual effort to comprehend. Fascinated by brilliance, and
easily captured by charm, the Viennese knew no standard to

maintain except that of immediate pleasure. Furthermore, they were fickle. And if Beethoven was in high reputation at the time of the Congress, it needed his death, eleven years later, to make him once again the object of public interest. In the intervening years Rossini had become fashionable. The Italian opera outbid the German upon its own stage. In brief, it is easy to overpraise the musicianship of early nineteenth-century Vienna, in spite of its exceptional executants—Czerny, Thalberg, Moscheles, the young Liszt, among pianists alone—and of a small number of devoted amateurs who supported the quartets of Schuppanzigh and Mayseder.

In the other arts an absence of vitality was much more apparent. Among painters there was the romantic Moritz von Schwind, whose art has been compared, without much reason, to that of Schubert; but the general run of competent painting can be deduced from the fact that Daffinger—one of the most agreeable of portrait painters but no more—owed much of his fame to the albums of celebrities which he compiled for Princess Metternich's drawing-room table in the 1830's.

As for the writers, they were most skilfully discouraged by an oppressive censorship. Some, like the Count Auersperg who wrote under the name of Anastasius Grun, took refuge in satire at a safe distance; others, like Grillparzer, wore themselves out in alternations of bad temper and attempts to please the authorities. In general, however, Turnbull's verdict on the period stands: "in point of daring original genius, it is rare to see a work of literature, art, or science, proceed from an Austrian".

And yet . . . should one forget the wide diffusion of simple and pleasurable art throughout Vienna in his time? Should one overlook Fanny Elssler, the dancer, or be deaf to the haunting street-music under the trees on summer evenings, or turn away from the processional side of daily life inside the city walls? Suppose one were to catch sight of Prince Colloredo on his way to pay respects at the imperial palace. First, we are told, came four mounted guards in dark-green uniforms heavily embroidered in gold lace; next, two running footmen, carrying silver batons, in short jackets and tight pantaloons of scarlet and silver; next, half a score of liveries, striding through the mud in white stockings; then a fool; followed by the prince himself in a state chariot drawn by six black horses; and finally a troop of mounted guards to bring up the rear. Such sights were to be seen every day. Every day the German Guard, in black and gold and scarlet, or the white aigrettes of the Hungarian Hussars, might turn the corner into view; and it is arguable that the senses of this tranquil people were satisfied by the colour and vivacity of daily life, enhanced by a climate of extremes in which the world lay for weeks under a glittering cover of snow, or breathed, even on the verges of the city, the warm flowers and fresh-cut wood of the hills beyond the Danube.

Metternich would have argued thus. He would have preferred to see his people amused than stimulated. So much better for them, he would have said, so much less agitating. Let them leave the books alone and dance instead under the lindens. And there can be no doubt that the chancellor's caution, over a long generation, was the chief element which formed the character of his people. For it is to Metternich that all inquiries into the state of Vienna during the Biedermeier period eventually lead: to Metternich who shared with the emperor himself for over thirty years the status of universal father-figure to the subjects of the empire.

His reputation has not taken the turn he expected. He looked for fame to posterity, and posterity has rewarded him instead with an almost unqualified dismissal. Perhaps that comes partly from exasperation. Metternich was prolix, confident, and scornful. He declined to have doubts, but at the same time refused to hope. He foresaw, with rare clarity, the chaos of modern Europe, but in his search for a palliative he erected a rigid system of political conduct which was quite incompatible with the world before him. And so it is not entirely surprising that posterity should have taken an easy revenge by setting the failure of Austria in the nineteenth century too directly to his account.

PLATE 39

HAYDN 1732—1809

BEETHOVEN 1770—1827

SCHUBERT 1797—1828

JOHANN STRAUSS 1804—1849

PLATE 40

BEETHOVEN'S HOUSE
in Mödling near Vienna

SCHUBERT'S BIRTHPLACE
in Vienna

He possessed, moreover, that quality which brings discredit to any statesman unlucky enough to possess it: he pleased. He pleased by his manner, by his looks, his conversation; he pleased by his variety of interests—by having read so widely, cultivated the sciences so elegantly, trained so well a musical ear, and an eye habituated to whatever was best among pictures, furniture, flowers. He entertained so splendidly, got into debt so negligently, built up his estates in Bohemia and on the Rhine with so princely an intermittence; he loved so widely, he flattered so discreetly, that it was natural to accept a stern view of his character as soon as the presence of his charm was removed. "He believes", said Lord Liverpool, "that politics consists in finesse and tricks." It would be truer to say that he believed in Metternich. But such conviction, sustained to the point of fatuity and adorned with all the graces of a civilized mind, could hardly fail to irritate. Finesse and tricks—that was what it came to in the end. And perhaps Sir Charles Webster's verdict goes as far as anyone is likely to go in making amends to his shade a century later: "In diagnosis Metternich was without an equal in Europe. But no one would trust him to prescribe a remedy."

His diagnosis was more or less thus: After the French Revolution two main forces were abroad in Europe—the continuing spirit of the revolution and an anxious desire for social order. Metternich rejected the revolution out of hand; he saw, however, that social order was not to be defined once for all, and so he came to conceive a state of equilibrium between conflicting forces, an equilibrium which would allow necessary changes to be introduced into the national order by a series of minimal steps calmly undertaken.

But he had a logical mind. He saw also that there was an essential connection between the individuals within a state, and the state itself viewed as one member of a family of nations. In a multi-national state like the Austrian empire this connection needed no underlining, and it impelled Metternich to press his theory of a desirable equilibrium into international affairs.

19

"Political bodies", he wrote, "have an independent existence as little as the individuals who make up society." In his own mind, therefore, the nations of Europe bore at least some degree of responsibility for each other's well-being, as a condition of the well-being of their own peoples. How could this responsibility be maintained? Only by a strong personal rule. Monarch must speak to monarch as brother to brother. Throughout all Europe subversive ideas must be extirpated so that in tranquillity the brotherhood of kings might guide the ease and enlarge the privileges of their obedient subjects.

The concept was noble. But it was not compatible with two ideas held by Metternich with equal tenacity. One of them was the pre-eminence of Vienna among European capitals, the other a fastidious dislike of the middle classes. Metternich, let it be remembered, had come to Vienna as a servant of the emperor. His loyalties were closely bound, therefore, to the reigning house, and he was firm in his aim of making Vienna the centre of a European concert. The city lay, after all, at the physical heart of the Continent; why should it not become its spiritual heart as well? The fact that the power of the empire had declined once for all, the fact that its internal administration, however good in separate parts, was hopelessly cumbrous as a whole, the fact that to pacify the Hungarians and the Italians alone was almost beyond the resources of the centralized government—none of this weighed with him. And as for the middle classes, were they not the most obvious centre of disaffection everywhere? The poor knew their place; the nobles governed; it was from the intermediate class that revolution sprang. And his prevision that the dominance of that intermediate class was to be the prime event of the century filled Metternich with a kind of obstinate horror. At least they should not have their way in Austria. It is symbolic that although the upper classes mixed freely with the people at the fêtes in the Prater and the Augarten, they should have maintained a chilly distance whenever it came to mixing with their immediate inferiors. For example, during the carnival

of 1835, as the price of attending a public ball, Princess Metternich (the chancellor's third wife) insisted on a roped enclosure
being erected in the middle of the ballroom so that the noble
visitors present might not come into contact with the bourgeois.
And on another occasion, dining with a banker who had largely
financed her husband, she prompted one of her attendants to
bring her own gold plate and lay it on the table before her.

As the years went by—and especially after the upheavals
which shook all Europe in 1830—the position of Metternich
became harder. While Francis II lived, he could at least count
on the sympathy of his master. It was a sympathy offered on
terms, no doubt: so long as Metternich agreed with the emperor
on matters of principle, the emperor would give him the negative support of a benevolent inertia. He would at any rate keep
rivals away. But Francis II was succeeded in 1835 by the feeble-
minded Emperor Ferdinand, and almost at once Metternich's
absolute power within the state was limited by the creation of
a *Staatskonferenz*—a committee of three, in which Metternich
was given charge of foreign affairs while the internal conduct
of the state fell to an enemy of long standing, Count Kolowrat.

Perhaps it was already too late. Metternich was sixty-two
years old. His plans for Austria and for Europe might gain
conviction with the passing of time; they could not develop.
Now, however, after holding the reins of state in his hands for
a generation, he found himself abruptly diminished. And not
only that: he found himself vulnerable to the hostility of his
colleagues. His health was declining, his optimism sinking. And
during the twelve years which ended with the upheavals of
1848, the current of public opinion set finally against him. A
new life was stirring throughout Europe. Ideas which could not
be repressed by a censorship, however harsh, were crossing from
frontier to frontier. And when the end came, during a hurried
flight from Vienna, his wife wrote of him in her diary, "This
man whose daily habits and pleasures were the object of constant
preoccupation, in aid of whose comfort I was trying up to
yesterday to avoid draughts and chills, now, at 75, found

himself shelterless and with no knowledge of where he might be the next day. . . . He had seen in the space of 24 hours the collapse of all he had built up in a lifetime of work."

That, no doubt, is what it looked like at the time. And during the liberal century which followed 1848 it was natural to associate the defeat of Metternich's ideas with a notion of their impropriety. At this distance, however, we can see that Metternich was both wiser and more valuable as an example than he is commonly admitted to be. He saw clearly that the older Europe had been swept away, and that a period of deadlock must ensue before a new Europe came into being. His fault lay in the assumption that a weakened Austria could be the instrument of that new order, and that it would suffice to ensure internal and external calm for a replenished and harmonious concert of nations to be formed under the inspiration of Vienna.

The nineteenth century rejected him, certainly (indeed, the rejection was mutual). But he would have been perfectly at home in the world of President Wilson, and still more in that of Roosevelt. A concept like the United Nations would have been exactly what he liked most—an orderly, schematic ideal with plenty of scope for manœuvre. And a world which has seen the mounting tyrannies of the last twenty years might, paradoxically, have reversed the judgment of his contemporaries and regretted, not his conservatism, but his lack of an effective national power during the crucial years which ended in 1835.

As it is, we cannot deny that the price paid by Austria for her generation of tranquillity was in the long run ruinous. Yet at the same time, it is easy to allow some feeling of envy to rise. Periods in which history seems to be suspended are the most dangerous of all. Beneath the quiet surface, cracks are forming through which the angry forces of nature will one day burst. But at least we can say of the Viennese—as we might say of the Parisians in the 1880's or of the Edwardian Londoners—that they were happy while it lasted. And no architect of an age can ask more than that.

Jubilee London

19TH–20TH CENTURY

ROGER FULFORD

A S THE nineteenth century drew to its close, London was easily the largest city in the world. With a population of four and a half million, it exceeded the population of New York by one million, of Paris by two million, and of Vienna by three million. Anyone who had known eighteenth-century London —that thriving, self-reliant, and compact city admirably described for us in the pages of Boswell's *Life of Johnson*—would have been astounded by this colossal expansion, which had been experienced by the capital in the short space of a century. The two principal causes of this were the growth of foreign trade and the application of numerous inventions to our home manufactures which brought about the Industrial Revolution. But the natural energy and ingenuity of Londoners, which is one of their abiding characteristics, also has its place in any estimate of the reasons for the phenomenal growth of London. The long series of wars in the eighteenth century, which had ended with those emphatic triumphs for British arms— Trafalgar and Waterloo, had left England in possession of the cream of the European trade with North America, the West Indies, India, and the Orient. Her principal rival—France— had been decisively subdued in all these areas. Simultaneously with this huge increase in foreign trade came the transformation of England from an agricultural to an industrial economy. This change, which marked the difference between eighteenth-century and nineteenth-century London, could be summed up by saying that "the nation of shopkeepers" (as Napoleon had once described England) had been transformed into "the workshop of the world"—a phrase coined by the great Victorian Prime Minister, Disraeli.

The following facts illustrate the truth of this point. Until 1870 Great Britain raised more than half the whole coal supply of the world. In that year the combined trade of the United Kingdom and the British empire was greater than that of France, Germany, Italy, and the United States put together. The abandonment of the old Protectionist system of trade in the 1840's gave a great impetus to British shipping and magnified the significance of London as a port. In 1800 the tonnage of ships coming into the docks of London was nearly 800,000; by 1880 the figure had reached nearly 8,000,000. The fact that London was first and foremost a market and not the centre of a manufacturing district is shown by the value of the imports into London being more than double that of the exports. But the history of London during these years is but a reflection of what was going on throughout Europe at this time. The old courtly, traditional civilization, based on agriculture and petty manufactures, was being pushed on one side by the emergence of commercial nations, devoting their skill and endurance to the capture of markets. Of this London was the pioneer and on this her rise to pre-eminence was founded.

The first impression of any visitor to London during these years would have been of the vast dimensions of the town. This is illustrated by some comments made in his diary by a member of the United States Legation in England. Looking over the capital from some high ground to the south on a lovely evening in May in the 1860's, he was astounded by what he called "the magnitude of London"; in attempting to describe his impression he used the simple but effective phrase "London is illimitable". The great town stretched in an almost unbroken mass of bricks and mortar and stone to the hills of Hampstead and Highgate in the north, past the densely-crowded poor quarter of the East End to the flats of Essex, and through a great diversity of prosperous villas to the chalk and conifers of Surrey in the south, and to those historic fields in the west (where lay Runnymede) through which flowed the Thames.

The size of London showed at once that it was both the capital and a great commercial town, for this dual aspect is the true explanation of its size and power. Yet of these twin foundations the surest and the most important was London's long-standing pre-eminence both in commerce and finance. For that reason the curious observer was invariably anxious to see the City—because there, and in the docks which adjoined it, were congregated all the bustle and activity of money and of commerce. In the heart of the City, exuding confidence, respectability, and tradition was the Bank of England which had stood supreme among the banking houses of the world for two centuries. Possibly the best indication of what the Bank stood for in the life of London was to be seen on "Dividend Day". In the twentieth century the majority of people who own British government securities have them sent to their homes through the post; at the end of the nineteenth century, when the number of these investors was infinitely smaller than today, it was usual for many of them to go to the Bank and collect the dividends themselves. "Dividend Day" at the Bank in the closing days of the nineteenth century afforded a fascinating study in human nature—the rich, of course, predominating but yet varied by shabby-looking individuals of miserly habit, who owned perhaps thousands of pounds in Gilt-edged Stock, or nervous-looking widows clutching possibly their sole resources for the year. And out of sight lay all the glittering expressions of the wealth and might of London and England—the great ingots of gold and the sovereigns and half-sovereigns with the beautifully-designed head of the widowed Queen Victoria and, on the reverse side, the proudly capering figure of St. George. Nothing seemed to emphasize the financial dominance of London so effectively as this solidity of the Bank of England. Lying close to the Bank were the headquarters of the financial institutions of the empire—joint-stock and foreign banks, shipping and insurance companies, stockbroking firms and trust companies. All these great financial and commercial houses, no less than the streets which surrounded them, were an exclusively male preserve. Like the Houses of Parliament and like all Government Offices at that time, the City of London was kept inviolate from the advances of women. At the end of the century one or two progressive firms admitted women to work the recently-invented typewriting machines but broadly speaking all was masculine—top-hats were everywhere and even the humblest city clerks aped the subfusc clothes and formal attire of the financier.

Within the boundaries of the City was to be found the proof that the greatness of London and the survival of England depended on the flow of foreign trade, for in the establishment of London's supremacy trade played a part for which, in the history of Europe, Venice alone proves a counterpart. At the eastern end of the City were the great marts where goods were exchanged—corn in Mark Lane, rubber and tea in Mincing Lane, coal in Lower Thames Street, wool in Coleman Street, and diamonds and precious stones in Hatton Garden. Outside the City, on the other side of the Thames, were the exchanges for hops, butter, and bacon. Behind these exchanges were the docks—the arteries through which flowed the life and prosperity of London. Many years ago it was well said that England was balanced on the end of a collier's pick-axe, meaning that coal was the commodity by which the nation paid for its food and raw materials, and it was not less true to say that the life of London depended on the muscle and brawn of the dockers at the waterfront. The way in which the fortunes of the capital were bound up with the dockers was forcibly illustrated by the great dock strike in 1889. In the summer of that year almost all the dockers in London came out on strike with the demand that they should be paid at the flat rate of 6d. an hour. The Dock Companies obstinately held out against this scale of pay, but public opinion, perhaps conscious of how much turned on the dockers, was largely against the employers. When two of the strike leaders came to negotiate with representatives of the Companies in the City, they had the heartening but extraordinary experience of being loudly cheered by a group of business men in this stronghold of respectability. This is an example of that underlying humanity of London which was a powerful influence in moulding its history at this time.

Yet in spite of the fact that London was essentially a commercial city, life at the summit was conducted with a splendour which has not been exceeded in history. King Leopold I of the Belgians, who was familiar from boyhood with the courts and capitals of Europe, decided after staying at Buckingham Palace that there was no country "where such magnificence exists" as in England. The public functions of the English court at Buckingham Palace or St. James's Palace—such as a Drawing Room, a Levée, or a Presentation—were conducted in a style which was exacting but not finicky, awe-inspiring but not absurd. The richness and variety of the ladies' clothes on these occasions—the costly, silken trains of brilliant colours—amber, sky-blue, or deep green—were a reminder of the solid foundations of wealth of which the English court was to some extent the expression. An American who attended one of these functions confessed that his eyes ached with the quantity and richness of the spectacle.

But it was not only at Buckingham Palace that these impressive displays were to be seen. The leading members of the aristocracy had houses in Piccadilly, along the edge of Hyde Park, and in St. James's which were only slightly less magnificent than the Palace itself. In illustration of this, a remark of Queen Victoria's is significant; on arriving at one of these houses she remarked to her hostess, "I come from my house to your palace." Perhaps the most elegant and striking private entertainment of these times was the fancy-dress ball given by the Duke of Devonshire in Devonshire House, Piccadilly, during the celebrations for Queen Victoria's Diamond Jubilee in 1897. All the members of the Royal Family—except the Queen, who was not present—attended in Elizabethan dress and the general brilliance of the spectacle was shown by the delight and enthusiasm of the phenomenal crowd of sightseers in the street. The English aristocracy—and this famous ball illustrates the point—was never composed of an exclusive caste; one of the guests at Devonshire House, who appeared not inappropriately as a Puritan, was the son of a Yorkshire woollen manufacturer. (He was later to be Prime Minister.)

In this respect the English aristocracy was quite distinct from its counterpart on the continent of Europe; there *l'haute aristocratie* was an exclusive section of the community—possibly poor, but proud and slightly forbidding; but in England it was constantly recruited and refreshed by intermarriage with the manufacturing and City classes. One consequence of this merging of the classes was that the jealousy of the aristocracy, which often marked other European countries, was not conspicuous in London at this time. Indeed the feelings of most people at this time ran rather to imitation of their social superiors than to envy. Therefore the organization of the top strata of London life in these days had something in common with the kind of commercial oligarchy which flourished in Venice at its prime.

The solid dignity of the wealthy classes, which was marked both in the aristocracy and in those on the fringe of society, in London at the end of the nineteenth century was obvious to all, and it made itself felt in many of the activities of the capital. At Westminster—in the House of Commons and the House of Lords—the government of the country was conducted against an unchanging background of formality and tradition. Members of both Houses invariably appeared in the standard uniform of frock-coat and silk hat, and when in 1892 the first Labour Member of Parliament was elected, Victorian London was scandalized not so much by his election as by his appearing at Westminster in a tweed coat and a cloth cap. For their relaxation Members of Parliament belonged to clubs, chosen according to their political bias, where the surroundings and the countless liveried men-servants matched the splendours of the homes of the nobility slightly farther to the west. The chief professions in London then were the Church and the Bar, and these were both marked by a high style of personal comfort and even by profusion. A garden-party at Lambeth or at Fulham Palace (the homes respectively of the Archbishop of Canterbury and the Bishop of London) was one of the outstanding features of the London social season. But even the most successful professional man never lost sight of the value of money; once when the Lord Chancellor (and in those days his princely salary of £10,000 a year amounted to a very substantial private fortune) was driving in Piccadilly his horses bolted and he was heard shouting out of the window to his coachman, "For God's sake drive into something cheap."

The same solid and dignified standards governed those who carried on their business within the golden square mile of the City of London; they likewise had their maxims based on success and integrity and they were the first to despise fortunes made from unorthodoxy or from lucky speculations. They remained at the end of Queen Victoria's reign very much as they have been drawn for us by Charles Dickens in the middle years of the century. They were perhaps a trifle vulgar, indifferent to the arts and culture and too partial to the fleshly joys of eating and drinking, but with it all sound, dependable, and guided by certain rules of what could and could not be done. All these classes—the aristocratic, the parliamentary, the professional, and the commercial, with a huge retinue of shop-assistants, servants, and clerks ministering to them and copying them, provided the main-spring which regulated the mechanism which governed the great community of London.

In earlier times London had been governed by the City itself—by the Lord Mayor and Aldermen and Common Council. Gradually their powers had been confined to the small area of the City proper and to the control of certain large estates outside. In addition each London Borough, of which there were then about twenty-five, had its own local government. In 1889 a government for the whole of London was formed by the creation of the London County Council. This experiment in self-government was one of the great achievements of London in the nineteenth century. To many people Local Government is one of the more tedious parts of the machinery of democracy; but the advent of the L.C.C. drew forth an astonishing amount of enthusiasm from Londoners. The first elections were a proof of this and illustrate the variety of talent which was attracted to the task of governing the capital. Among several members of the House of Lords, Rosebery (the future Prime Minister) was elected: among philanthropists chosen was Quintin Hogg, virtually the founder of technical education in London: there were also some outstanding economists, notably the first Lord Farrer, socialists like Frederick Harrison and, what was especially striking, a powerful force of working men under the able leadership of John Burns, later a Cabinet Minister. Burns as well as being a forceful working-class leader was a great lover and student of London, and is generally credited with the fine phrase which describes the Thames as "liquid history". "Practicable Socialism" was the watchword of many of these men elected to the L.C.C., and the fervour with which the work went ahead gives some indication of the idealism of the average Londoner. It is likewise interesting because these men, by their work in the L.C.C., prepared the soil for much of the social legislation which was to flower in the twentieth century.

Certainly in any account of London at this time it is essential to emphasize that if there was great prosperity and if there were great prizes to be won these went hand in hand with deplorable poverty and desperate disillusion. The squalor and degradation of life in some quarters of the East End were scarcely to be credited. To working-class audiences, radical speakers were fond of pointing the contrast between the glories of empire and the horrors of life at its heart. A favourite question was this: "What is the good of belonging to an empire on which the sun never sets if you live in a court on which it never rises?" Nothing perhaps more vividly brought home to people how precarious was life for thousands of honest Londoners than the scene at a busy pawnbroker's on a Saturday night. Furniture, trinkets, and even the tools of a man's trade were marched off to one of these brightly-lit emporiums, with their swinging emblems of the three brass balls—supposed to be the sign of the old Medici family—in an effort to exist over Sunday with the hope that the new week might bring better times and regular work. The nicely-balanced economic mechanism of London was kept in place by what was unquestionably the curse of the day—casual labour. Any visitor to London was quickly struck by the sudden appearance of an abject, dishevelled figure—seeming to spring up from nowhere—eager to earn a copper by holding a horse, by sweeping a path across the street clear of dung and mud, or by fetching a cab. Similarly anyone who was astir in the morning would have been immediately aware of the sprinkling of casuals, waiting in the hope that the sickness of a regular worker—even an omnibus driver or conductor—might lead to a day's employment. Another illustration of the dire poverty which existed just below the surface is afforded by the aftermath of the famous Tooley Street fire. A huge storehouse, filled with butter, close to the docks, caught fire and burned for several days. Streams of melting butter were carried away by the Thames, and where it was deposited by the tides, urchins scooped it up and found a ready market for their mixture of burned butter and river mud.

Yet London at this time had a strong social conscience and was in this respect outstanding and remarkable among the capitals of Europe. Gone were the days when poverty was a crime; the point of view satirized by Bernard Shaw in *Major Barbara* that "our first duty is not to be poor" would have found small currency among intelligent citizens of London at the end of the nineteenth century. This is an important point because it was something new: in past centuries great prosperity had gone hand in hand with complete indifference to the fate of those who, in the economic struggle, were trampled to the wall. In London the man who crystallized attention on this subject was Charles Booth, whose scientific investigations into

conditions in London were published in the 1890's. His re-
searches were collected under the omnibus title of *Life and
Labour of the People of London*; they were based largely on the
reports of school visitors and on information amassed by various
charitable bodies.

Simultaneously with this attempt to analyse the problem of
poverty went a real effort to ameliorate it. To give two examples.
Unorthodox religion provided the Salvation Army which was
founded in Whitechapel in 1865; the stalwarts of the Army
combined a trumpet call to repentance with the tangible
earthly blessing of shelter and food. While it was easy to laugh
at the Salvation Army (as the author of *The Belle of New
York* found) such laughter, on closer acquaintance, was apt
to become respectful and affectionate. More conventional
religion provided Oxford House, Toynbee Hall, and Mansfield
Hall, where university and public school youths could live in
the East End and bring to its denizens some savour of a larger
and nobler existence. This social conscience also manifested
itself in substantial acts of private benevolence. The money
which individual members of the Rothschild family distributed
in charity for the benefit of Londoners was astounding. At
Christmas each year Lord Rothschild gave a brace of pheasants
to all the omnibus drivers and many of the cabbies plying in
Central London. The more grateful ones used to tie their
benefactor's racing colours to their whips.

Perhaps nothing brought home to people the pitiable conditions of the poor quarters so dramatically as the plight of the
immigrants from abroad. From the harsh countries of eastern
Europe, driven out by terrors, purges, and privations, they
drifted to London in the certainty that they would be free from
persecution and in the hope that they might be able to scratch
together a livelihood. The majority of these immigrants were
Russians, Poles, and Rumanians; for the most part they found
work as "sweaters" in the tailoring or boot trades. But here
again London showed that even for such people (whose claim
on its solicitude was only slender) the capital would not tolerate

gross abuses, and their conditions were the subject of special inquiry by a committee of the House of Lords at the end of the century. Many of them were, of course, Jews—by the end of Queen Victoria's reign the Jewish colony in London numbered at least 100,000—and they were to a large extent cared for by various philanthropic organizations run by members of their own race.

In addition to these hapless immigrants there was a steady stream to London of more fortunate foreigners—young Germans coming to work as waiters in restaurants, as bakers or in hairdressers shops, or merely to take an instrument in the then-popular German brass bands; Russians to take up work as tailors, cabinet-makers, or boot and slipper makers; Italians to work as waiters, ice-cream sellers, organ-grinders, chestnut-roasters, and those specialized trades such as polishing, mosaic work, and point-lace in which they excelled the members of other nations. All these elements made London a strikingly cosmopolitan city, its riches drawing people from afar.

For it should not for a moment be supposed that the wealth of London was only apparent to those who moved in the charmed circle of the court, the aristocracy, or the well-to-do business community. As the traveller from the provinces or visitor from abroad stepped out from one of the termini he was at once conscious of the thriving and bustling prosperity in which he was moving. In a passage in one of his letters Charles Lamb gives expression to his idea of the richness of London life. He writes: "O her lamps of a night! Her rich goldsmiths, print-shops, toy-shops, mercers, hardwaremen, pastry cooks. . . . These are thy Gods O London!" But what would Lamb's language have been if he could have seen seventy years ahead and looked into the shop-windows in Piccadilly, Regent Street, Bond Street, and Oxford Street in all their glory in the 1890's? Any visitor to London had but to stroll along those streets, gazing at the wonderfully-dressed shop-windows to his right and left, to realize the full force of worldly temptation and to see how easy it would be to fall down and worship the great god gold. In the twentieth century London shoppers are accustomed to windows, which may be arresting but which prove too often on examination to be grimly bare. At the end of the nineteenth century profusion was essential in order to catch the eye of the passer-by. "Everything into the shop window" was the ideal. The drapers' shops for instance were dazzling and tempting—huge rolls of silks, satins and velvets, carpets, dress-materials and woollens, linen, art-needlework and hosiery, lace gloves and mantles were all grouped and blended in a blaze of colour.

This appreciation of the importance of a well-dressed shop-window helps to explain the remarkable rise to popular favour of William Whiteley, who opened the first of London's departmental stores and was able to claim for himself the proud title of "Universal Provider". The scene outside Whiteley's (which was further west than the conventional shopping ground of the rich) would have struck any visitor as gay and splendid—especially about four o'clock in the afternoon. The pavement was thronged with smartly-dressed women gazing at the windows with a mixture of approval and longing. Every few seconds hansom-cabs rattled up delivering late shoppers. Carriages and pairs—the horses' heads held high with bearing reins—flanked the edge of the pavement. Each had a stalwart young footman, resplendent in livery and top-hat, ready to carry the purchases which his employer had made. In those days shopping was not something to be rushed through with a rapidly fraying temper, but it was a rite to be enjoyed with contemplation and leisure—something faintly mysterious and quite beyond the comprehension of men. To take full advantage of this desire by human beings to indulge themselves, no one was more richly endowed than the shopkeepers of London.

The prominence of business, of commerce, and of shopping would have been the most constant impression which any foreign visitor to London would have taken away with him. He would have felt that he had been a part of a community which was essentially money-making. Naturally this concentration on

PLATE 41

GLADSTONE
Painting by Millais, 1879

DISRAELI
Painting by L. Bogle after Millais

QUEEN VICTORIA AND THE PRINCE CONSORT IN 1861
Photograph

PLATE 42

FLEET STREET, LUDGATE HILL AND ST. PAUL'S ABOUT 1905

LAMBETH PIER ABOUT 1900

commerce was not without its influence on art and letters. Victorian London was certainly not completely dead to the importance of art, but to some degree art was smothered by the prevailing commercial characteristics of the time. Huge prices were paid to successful painters, and with the proceeds they bought or built unwieldy palaces in which they gave conventional parties for people who, like themselves, had achieved distinction in society. Lord Leighton, Millais, and Sir Lawrence Alma-Tadema, who were all prominent Royal Academicians (the first two being Presidents) all lived in substantial style in the inner suburbs—each a witness to the prosperity of Victorian art. The Private View Day at the Royal Academy—which, ironically enough, was generally held to mark the beginning of the social season in London—was an annual rendezvous for all the leaders of English society, politics, and the professions. The traffic in Piccadilly was disjointed for hours and the paintings hung somewhat neglected on the walls while the building rang with laughter, chat, and social courtesy.

In London there was no art quarter, and students, unlike their counterparts in Paris or Munich, had few chances of easily meeting together outside the art class-room. In spite of this somewhat unpropitious climate Victorian London yet succeeded in producing some fine pictures and buildings—the St. Pancras railway station is a case in point—which were not wholly unworthy of a great city at its prime. But in London, as indeed throughout the whole country at this time, there was a preoccupation with worldly success and an indifference to culture which even the warmest admirer of the Victorian age has to admit and regret. Ruskin once expressed this feeling in an outburst of characteristic vigour. He wrote: "This yelping, carnivorous crowd mad for money and lust, tearing each other to pieces and starving each other to death, and leaving heaps of their dung and pools of their spittle on every palace floor and altar stone." Though to some extent this language might seem exaggerated, it drew attention to that streak of the Philistine in Victorian England which left a decided mark on the life of

London. People found that it was only too easy to worship comfort and call it civilization. Matthew Arnold, who lived in London during these days and knew it intimately, expressed this point of view when he wrote that Londoners were inclined to think that they lived at the highest pitch of civilization because they could travel every quarter of an hour between Islington and Camberwell. He added that they did not seem to realize that the trains only carried them "from an illiberal, dismal life at Islington to an illiberal, dismal life at Camberwell".

Yet these strictures would have to be qualified by the admission that, at any rate on the religious side, Victorian London devoted its energies to something which was not commercial and which was not Philistine. In the fashionable and residential parts of London, the Sunday morning parade was virtually compulsory and the crowds thronged the churches in the 1890's in much the same way that their grand-children fill the cinemas today. On a Sunday evening it was only possible to be sure of a seat in Westminster Abbey by getting there at least half an hour before the service began. One consequence of this attention to religion was that the clergy were very influential in London. A large part of the feelings aroused over the conditions of the poor sprang from knowledge obtained by the clergy and church workers in the course of their parochial visiting. The politicians—even the Socialists—really worked on facts provided for them by the Churches. It was not chance that the Bishop of London and the Cardinal-Archbishop of Westminster were the two men largely instrumental in arranging the settlement of the Dock Strike in 1889.

And just as the people of London paid great attention to the authority of the Churches so they respected that other important (though more worldly profession) the Law. Walking along that part of London where the Strand merges into Fleet Street any visitor would have been immediately struck by the ponderous, important, and not wholly unsuccessful building on his left. These were the Royal Courts of Justice, which Queen Victoria opened in 1882. Sydney Smith once observed of the Pavilion at Brighton that it looked as if St. Paul's Cathedral had gone down to the sea and pupped. With that saying in mind a foreigner in London might have said that the Law Courts were the result of a union between the Bastille and a provincial town hall. But in their solid and mysterious way they seemed to sum up the feelings of the people of that time for the Law as something formidable, unfathomable but yet a buttress of property.

A visitor coming to London at the end of the nineteenth century would have searched in vain for those obvious and spectacular glories of architecture which had distinguished the cities of Italy, or for the preoccupation with learning and philosophy which had been a characteristic of many of the large towns of Germany. To some extent these things did exist but they were not obvious—not the essence of London. And perhaps after the impression of wealth, the predominant picture left on the mind of a foreigner would have been of the immense variety of London. Coupled with this and clearly perceptible through all the noise and bustle was the gaiety and vitality of the town. There perhaps lay the secret of London's individual character: there certainly lay its difference from many of the other capitals of Europe. For the overriding impression of London was of human beings, not of bricks and mortar. Again it is Charles Lamb who, in a telling phrase, puts into words this aspect of the life of London. He wrote: "All the streets and pavements are pure gold, I warrant you. At least I know an alchemy that turns her mud into that metal—a mind that loves to be at home in crowds."

Nor would it be any exaggeration to suggest that it was the streets which focused the attention of the stranger on the gay variety of London life. They were far noisier than is often supposed by people whose only acquaintance with horse-drawn traffic is through hearing it mimicked by an agreeable "clop-clop" produced behind the scenes at a theatre or cinema. At night an uneasy sleeper could hear the noise of a single,

quick-moving cart or carriage from a quarter of a mile away as
it rattled over the uneven granite setts with which the majority
of streets were paved. Many people wrongly suppose that the
roar of traffic is something which began with tram, motor-bus,
and motor-car, but that is not so. It was Tennyson who wrote
as far back as 1852 of "streaming London's central roar".
Although to the elderly and neurotic noise is doubtless highly
offensive, it is not scientifically untrue to say that it leads to an
increase of energy in human beings, and it was (and is) un-
doubtedly an element in the generally stimulating effect of
being in London.

The spectacle of the traffic in those days was memorably gay.
Although the pillar-box red of the modern motor-bus is fine
and striking, it is uniform. Sixty years ago the streets were
bright with buses and trams of varying colours. They might be
blue, green, white, yellow, brown, chocolate, black, or red, and
they were set off by the sober hues of the private carriages and
the distinctly shabby look of cabs or "growlers". The craftsman-
ship which went to the building and painting of London vehicles
was something of which the metropolis was rightly proud for
they helped to give a general effect which was striking and
elegant. This was enhanced by the hansom-cab, with its
glistening body and burnished metal, and with its pair of large
wheels generally picked out in yellow or scarlet paint. Cabs
were latterly fitted with rubber wheels and to give warning of
their approach they had a jingle of bells attached to the horses'
necks. Characteristic of that attention to trifles, which marked
the Cockney at that time, was the careful arrangement of a gay
little bunch of flowers inside the cab. The driver, perched high
at the top of his vehicle, had a wonderful command of the
streets and his comments on the passing pageant, relayed to his
passengers through a trap-door in the roof, was an education in
that quickness of wit which was developed by life in the capital.
It was Disraeli who summed up the excitement and romance of
a journey by hansom-cab when he called it "the gondola of
London". The full-throated songs of the gondoliers may have

been absent, but the mind of the traveller was soothed and diverted from the pressure of business problems by the raucous jibes and jests of his driver as he careered through the streets.

The vigour and liveliness of the streets spread to the pavements. Among the pavement *habitués* the most conspicuous were possibly the large army of shoe-shiners. The streets were less efficiently cleaned than in a modern city—partly owing to the horse-dung—and there was in consequence a big demand for shoes to be cleaned. The most successful of the fraternity offered their clients a comfortable chair, with a plentiful supply of periodicals, and really regarded themselves as being equal in importance with the hairdresser. They introduced an agreeable splash of colour with their jackets: red was the most common but it varied according to the district—blue in the East End, white at Marylebone, and brown at King's Cross. Like the hansom-cab driver they beguiled their patron's leisure with plenty of pungent chat. One consequence of the rapid tempo of London life on those born and nurtured there was illustrated by the speed and eel-like quality of the boys who acted as street orderlies. Armed with a hand-brush and scoop, and wearing a jacket of conspicuous red, they darted among the traffic whisking up the dung from among the *melée* of the horses' hooves. This process was not without danger, and if the boys were injured they were entitled to a pension of 10s. a week for life.

But if the streets were gay with life and movement, they could also remind the observer of the struggle to live which was never far below the surface in London. The crossing sweeper, shabby and dishevelled, his broom often having the bristles worn down to the wood, hoped to earn a copper by cleaning the path in front of some wealthy pedestrian. A dry wind and a burst of sunshine would probably convert him into a match-seller. In addition to these recognized classes the pavement was thronged with typical Cockneys eager for business. Here were paraded for sale the most astounding mechanical toys ranging from a clockwork hansom-cab to a poodle which barked. Besides toys

almost everything could be bought on the kerbstones, from walk-
ing-sticks to groundsel for the canary, from shirt-studs to comic
songs. Everything was sold to the accompaniment of an
arresting but unceasing patter. Many of the salesmen were
abjectly poor, and the purchaser of some trifle often had the
feeling that his or her copper might make all the difference
between a night in the open on the Embankment or a tolerably
comfortable bed in a lodging-house. There were in London
alone at this time over a thousand of these doss-houses—some for
women, some for married couples, but mostly for men. For 4d.
a night a man could be assured of warmth and a good night's
rest, but the very number of these places illustrated the uncertainties confronting labour. An analysis of these street
vendors, holding their goods in meek silence or to the accompaniment of a rather reproachful whine, showed that many of
them—here and there they were educated and had even in
happier times owned their own small businesses—were the
weakest who, in the economic struggle, had literally gone to
the wall. Today this race is almost extinct and with the beggars
who sat or drooped against the walls, with their pitiful labels
"Blind", "Crippled", or "Paralysed", they have abandoned
their once profitable pitches.

If occasionally this seamy side of London life made itself felt,
there was, as compensation for the visitor, the varied pageantry
of London life which could be seen free and for nothing. For
those who enjoyed a glimpse of the aristocracy, Hyde Park had
great rewards for the casual stroller. In the morning there was
the pram parade—nurses starched and white, far more proud
and stiff than their employers, pushing the young nobility.
Women would be cantering along Rotten Row for their
morning exercise, while the splendid carriages of elderly ladies
drove slowly along the road, pausing every now and again so
that the footman could get down to give the lap-dog a run on
the grass. If the weather was fine it was usual for the Princess
of Wales to drive through the park at five o'clock in the afternoon, and in anticipation of this the carriages of the leading

members of London society were drawn up by the roadside to give her a respectful greeting.

For those who liked their entertainment a little less exclusive there were the mellow tones of the hurdy-gurdy or barrel-organ which were a constant element in the London streets—apart from a few squares and streets in Mayfair and Belgravia where they were not admitted. While they were a torment to people attempting to concentrate on their work—a distinguished mathematician calculated that one-third of his working life had been ruined by organ-grinders, and when Dickens wanted to give a really scornful description of a schoolmaster he referred to him as a human barrel-organ with a little list of tunes he was constantly churning out without variation—they did provide a not disagreeable background of melody which softened the noise of traffic. With gaudily-dressed monkeys crawling round the organ or with mechanical toys whirling round the top and perhaps a gaily-clad *signorina*, doing a few graceful dance steps and appealing for funds, they, too, were calculated to cheer the spirits of the passer-by. In those days, before the radio brought music to the home, the hurdy-gurdy (especially in the poorer streets) was popular and welcome.

A more sombre change from the barrel-organ with its suggestion of sunshine and the south, was provided by German bands. These bandsmen were for the most part serious gentry almost inevitably wearing glasses and flaunting a curious kind of peaked cap. The band generally numbered about six; they gathered underneath a lamp-post and were occasionally reinforced by a boy singing a sentimental German song. Their favourite tune was "The Blue Danube", with the deep notes of the bassoon steadily and prominently played. They came and went with the swallow, completely disappearing in the winter when they were popularly supposed to be engaged on espionage. If the visitor had followed a barrel-organ or a German band out of one of the popular thoroughfares into a side street of working-class families he or she would have been surprised how quickly the whole street began to dance, until the barrel-organ itself or the instruments were completely obscured by the girls hopping and gliding with unexpected grace. Though they certainly never had the indulgence of a dancing lesson, they seemed to know exactly how to do it—heel and toe, glissade and curtsey, all were correct.

Again, on Bank Holiday on Hampstead Heath married women, in spite of the encumbrance of their full Victorian skirts, would start dancing with wonderful verve, and finish with a lightness of heart which many people might suppose to be limited to a southern people. Although it might be possible to argue that London itself was grim and even gloomy, it was redeemed and cheered by the zest and spirit of those who lived in it. Examples of Cockney wit abounded and ranged from the policeman on point duty to the domestic slut clambering up the area steps for her morning passage of arms with the milkman. In southern towns, with the sun shining, it was perhaps easy to be cheerful, but badinage and repartee helped the Londoner to triumph over adversity.

No picture of London at this time would be complete which did not give some account of life in the public-house and of the part it played in the entertainment of those living there. While it is perfectly true that both the theatre and the music-hall had never been so prosperous and successful as they were in these years, they catered to some extent for a migrant public— visitors and those who came up to London for a conventional night out. In those days before cinemas, wireless, the general spread of libraries, and working-men's clubs, public-houses provided the permanent residents of the town with their sole means of communal recreation. In singling out the undoubted attractions of the public-house, we should keep the picture in proportion by remembering the colossal abuses of alcohol at this time. The various social workers, investigating conditions in the poorest parts of London, were unanimous in condemning drink as the principal cause—often the only cause—of squalor, degradation, and poverty. The hours in which drink could be bought were virtually unlimited, and it was not uncommon to see workmen hurrying into the public-house for a tot of gin on their way to work at six o'clock in the morning. Many enlightened people, especially in the Radical section of the Liberal Party, felt that if the scourge of drunkenness was firmly tackled half the programmes of social reform to which politicians were committed would be unnecessary.

None the less the picture of the drink trade was not wholly black, and the fairer side was shown in the comradeship and cheerfulness of the London "pub". An intelligent foreigner once observed, after a prolonged study of the destination boards on London buses, that the omnibus system of London must have been designed to take the hard-drinking citizens from one public-house to another. This was understandable enough when it is remembered that the commonest termini of buses were "The Angel" at Islington, "The Crown" at Cricklewood, "The Elephant and Castle" at Newington, "The Welsh Harp" at Hendon, "The Manor House" at Finsbury, or "The Swiss Cottage" in Finchley Road. But these were the great renowned houses of London and it was perhaps in the smaller, more secluded establishments that the essence of Cockney friendliness seemed enshrined. Such a place was well described by W. W. Jacobs when he wrote, "A little pub in the turning off the Mile End Road—clean as a new pin, and as quiet and respectable as a front parlour. Everybody calling the landlady 'Ma', and the landlady calling most of them by their Christian names, and asking after their families. There were two poll parrots in cages, with not a bad word between them—except once when a man played the cornet outside—and a canary that almost sang its heart out." In these places (as in so much of London) the best things—the company, the glowing coal fire, the highly-polished mugs and glasses, the cosy nooks were thrown in free. The *habitués* of the public-house have been well described by a survivor from those days. "Cronies as we were none of us knew anything of one another's lives. We knew one another only by nick-names and where each went after leaving for the night was known only to the individual. We had no curiosity in the matter. We met simply to be ourselves for a short time, to throw off the trappings that we necessarily had to wear in civilized society, to discuss affairs of the day, sometimes to be very rude to one another, and for a time we all glowed in the fascinating light of human individuality."

In looking back to London in the days of its plenitude we can all too easily slide into the mistake, made by many who from the somewhat murky present idyllize the years that are gone, of seeing in them those enchantments which are the creation of time and our own imagination. Many an elderly writer looking back to the London of his youth paints a romantic picture of old days in something the same way as Tennyson, eating his solitary chop in a London tavern, looked back to the happy days when he was a personality at Cambridge:

> The gas-light wavers dimmer
> And softly through a vinous mist
> My college friendships glimmer.

Such sentimentalists depict London as a kind of paradise of pleasure in which the shops were bursting with food, and the pockets of mortal men were jingling with golden coins, and in the evening Marie Lloyd was for ever singing, "O Mr. Porter" or "When you wink the other eye", and at night there were perpetual supper parties where champagne was sipped from the heel of an actress's shoe. London is in some danger of being seen through this kind of tender haze of romance which still hangs lightly over the memory of nineteenth-century Vienna. But when we have made every allowance for these sentimental backward glances, we can see that there was a sort of camaraderie about London life which was unique in the large cities of Europe. As the standards of each generation change and expand it is easy to overlook the feelings of our forefathers about things which we take for granted or merely regard as out-of-date and mistaken.

For example anyone coming to London at the end of the nineteenth century would have seen at a glance how immensely proud Londoners were of their town and buildings, which it is difficult for a generation which has grown up with them to understand. Indeed, as has already been suggested here, Londoners did not on the surface seem to have a great deal which was worthy of admiration. They could point to no outstandingly historic streets such as by themselves attracted tourists to Rome or Paris, nor could they point to streets finely planned and laid out such as were to be seen in the great cities of Germany—the only possible exception to this was the work of the great architect, Nash, in his splendid conception of Regent's Street and Portland Place leading up to Regent's Park; nor could they point to those outstanding collections of art or wonderfully embellished churches which also by themselves attracted many a tourist to other European cities at this time. For the Londoner it was different—he was proud of the whole expanse of his town—the whole conglomeration of bricks and mortar, which it was possible to conceive as a monument to the wealth and genius of the citizens who had made their capital the financial and commercial centre of the world.

This was no gradual growth of a thousand years but a sudden spectacular leap forward during the nineteenth century. Nothing illustrates this more clearly than the figures of population. In 1800 there were only 800,000 people in London: in 1820 there were 1,200,000; in 1840 there were 1,800,000: in 1860 there were 2,800,000: in 1880 there were 3,000,000, and by the end of the century the number had reached the figure quoted at the beginning of this chapter. Men of eighty at the end of the century, who had passed their lives in the capital, had seen the face of London change beyond recognition. With the exception of Waterloo Bridge, they would have seen the building or rebuilding of every bridge across the Thames. Such people could also remember the building of the Houses of Parliament, the British Museum, the great markets for meat, fish, and fruit, nearly all the hospitals, the banks, the hotels, the General Post Office, the theatres, Trafalgar Square with its awe-inspiring monument to British naval greatness,

Northumberland Avenue, Kingsway, Piccadilly Circus, Holborn Viaduct, Victoria Street, and the Embankment along the Thames. In addition such people would have watched the creation of most of the docks, all the tramways, the underground railways, and the railway termini. Moreover they would have seen whole tracts of farming land turned into residential areas.

Many years before this, that shrewd and amusing observer of eighteenth-century life—Horace Walpole—was astounded by the housebuilding in London in the 1770's which he attentively watched on his drives up to London from Twickenham. "How much longer is this exuberance of opulence to last?" he asked. The answer would have been that it was to last for nearly a century and a half, though in its later stages it was to take a slightly different form from that which had startled Horace Walpole. The building of private houses which he had noticed was to give way to the great metropolitan improvements which marked the nineteenth century. No doubt, in the process, much that was attractive was swept away, for London in 1800 presented something of that graceful spaciousness which immediately strikes the visitor to Dublin today. That fugitive charm, which can still be traced in parts of Berkeley Square and here and there in the streets leading off Park Lane and Piccadilly, was destroyed but it has to be said that in the nineteenth century they cared less for such things than we do today and that they were not greatly bothered by the fal-lals of architectural prettiness. They would have felt that any beauty which had been lost was amply compensated for in the greater cleanliness and convenience of London.

Although emphasis in this chapter has been rightly placed on the distresses and dire misfortunes of poverty—indeed it could be argued that they were an essential ingredient in the constant propulsion of a thriving and prosperous community—it is also right to emphasize the great efforts which were made during this period to improve the lot of the unfortunate. Some thoughtful observers might argue that these efforts were not less worthy of admiration than the more obvious structural embellishments of the time. Anyone casting back their minds to those filthy streets and alley-ways, described by Dickens, where for instance Mr. Quilp used to collect his rents, and then looking forward to the housing improvements at the end of the century, would at once be conscious of what this advance meant in the amelioration of human suffering. One of the men in the van of the movement to improve the housing conditions of London was an American, George Peabody, who gave half a million for the re-housing of the London poor. In his huge blocks of flats known as Peabody Buildings working men were given homes with baths and laundries attached. The first was built in Spitalfields but others quickly followed in the inner suburbs —Islington, Bermondsey, and Chelsea.

Equally impressive was the expansion of schools during these years. Apart from the Board Schools which, after the introduction of compulsory education in 1870, multiplied with great rapidity, the growth of schools for the middle classes and of establishments for adult education was striking. During the nineteenth century both King's College and University College, together with Bedford College for Women, were founded: St. Paul's School and the City of London School were restarted: the School of Mines, the City Technical and Science College, the Royal Academy of Music, the Royal College of Music, and the Polytechnics all started during these years.

Perhaps, therefore, the most striking and most remarkable achievement of London at its zenith lay in what was done to improve the well-being of the race. Certainly it was to that aspect of their life that Londoners themselves would have pointed as their most considerable triumph for, like all who lived in nineteenth-century England, they believed above all else in progress and improvement. The genius who adorned the City of London in the seventeenth century—Sir Christopher Wren—is buried in St. Paul's Cathedral and on his tomb are inscribed proud words of advice to posterity—*Circumspice, si Monumentum requiris*. So might it have been said to one wandering through the streets of London in search of a trophy to the pioneer work in social reform achieved by the British people in the nineteenth century. Writing at the time of his retirement from politics, Mr. Gladstone expressed his opinion that the half-century from 1840 to 1890 would be known as the "half-century of emancipation". In that work—and it might well be argued that this was the greatest contribution made by the genius of the British people to the civilization of Europe—London played a part which was conspicuous and illustrious.

Yet it is right to point out that with these improvements and with increased respectability disappeared something of the old Cockney character and something of that quick-witted zest for life which had made London famous. This change was accelerated by the spread of London away from the centre and in particular by the growth of suburban life with its somewhat absurd standards of exclusiveness and conventional behaviour, largely based on nervousness of what the people next door might be saying or thinking. These suburbs, which were all developed in the latter half of the nineteenth century, had their own completely independent lives and were in fact distinct communities. The various churches, chapels, and youth organizations provided the suburban girls and lads with organized entertainment from which liquor and loose behaviour were rigorously excluded. This in itself was a remarkable achievement and led to the development of a superior type both intellectually and physically. The counterparts of these young men in early Victorian London, when everyone lived cooped up within two or three miles of Bow Bells, had no organized amusements except to go to those rather disreputable dives and dens so amusingly described in the novels of Thackeray and Dickens. An American observer summed up the youth of London in the 1850's by saying that they were namby-pambies at their work and that after working hours they were "fast young men on the street". By the 1890's, as is clear from the novels of H. G. Wells, these young men had become pillars of their local rambling clubs or bicycling societies. This transformation with all that it meant in the way of increased health, was not the smallest of the achievements of nineteenth-century London.

Many years before this period, in the placid calm of the eighteenth century, Dr. Johnson agreed in conversation with a friend that Fleet Street was full of life, and then he added, "But I think the full tide of human existence is at Charing Cross." Perhaps by the end of the nineteenth century the tide of which he spoke had shifted a trifle farther west and was situated at Piccadilly Circus. This concentration of humanity helps to explain what was to the foreigner one of the most incomprehensible things about London—the way in which the personality of the town was expressed through the crowd. Anyone privileged to see the great Jubilee processions at the end of Queen Victoria's reign would have realized the truth of this. It was not the pageantry of soldiers, not the foreign princes bobbing up and down, not even the queen herself which made the Jubilee: it was the people of London. Queen Victoria describing her drive through London on the occasion of the Golden Jubilee in 1887 (and no one had a keener perception of what was striking or important) wrote in her diary, "Everyone seemed to be in such a good humour."

This kind of ebullient good humour in the citizens of London often broke out with little warning or prompting. For instance, in May 1900, the news of the Relief of Mafeking inspired one of the most astonishing spectacles which even London has seen. The news did not reach the city until nine o'clock at night so there was no possibility of any celebration being arranged or premeditated. The crowd literally seemed to spring from the pavements. Surging and cheering they took possession of the town as they had done in 1887 and in 1897. They seemed to illustrate the essence of London's history during those days— which was, as has already been explained, that London was symbolized rather by human beings than by buildings.

But with the closing years of the century came clear signs that the commercial supremacy of England, which had grown and expanded since Waterloo, was being seriously challenged.

Years before, Disraeli (with remarkable foresight) had said that
the continent of Europe would never allow England to remain
the workshop of the world. The full truth of this was abun-
dantly plain, for both the United States and Germany were
making great advances and were capturing markets where
Great Britain had long been supreme—although even at the
end of the nineteenth century British trade was still double that
of any other nation. In particular the development of coal-
mining in Germany and eastern Europe was a mortal blow.
These were the clouds—admittedly small but yet lowering—
which smudged the sky. Men looking to the future might have
said with the most characteristic of the Victorian poets,
Browning:

> . . . the glimmer of twilight,
> Never glad, confident morning again.

In addition there were clear signs, which became much more
obvious as the twentieth century began, that Englishmen were
more concerned with welfare and social justice at home than
with maintaining pre-eminence in the markets of the world.
Those portents of misfortune moved at a vastly accelerated pace
during and after the War of 1914.

When the First World War began, the people of London
called attention to the hour by marching amid scenes of the
greatest enthusiasm along the Mall to Buckingham Palace.
But the harsh events, ushered in by that August evening, were
to prove unfavourable to the geniality and kindliness on which
so much of the strength of London depended. Henceforward the
history of the capital was to be less smooth and the observer
was to be less conscious of the surging vitality of the town. One
who watched that momentous August evening in London has
well summed up the truth when he wrote: "And I heard the
great crowd roar for its own death." For certainly the War of
1914, which changed the face of Europe, swept away the pre-
eminence of London.

PLATE 43

PRIVATE VIEW AT THE ROYAL ACADEMY, 1888
Painting by H. J. Brook

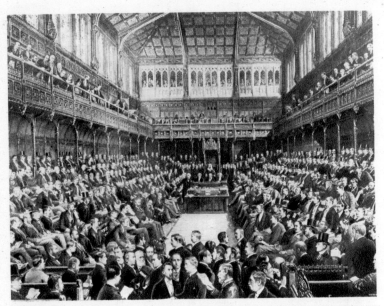

GLADSTONE ADDRESSING THE HOUSE OF COMMONS DURING THE DEBATE
ON HOME RULE
Lithograph by Werner

PLATE 44

RAILWAY STATION
Painting by W. P. Frith, 1863

ST. MARTIN-IN-THE-FIELDS
Painting by William Logsdail, 1888

20th Century New York

ROBERT WAITHMAN

FROM the deck of a ship in New York harbour the towers of twentieth-century Manhattan are so stirring and beautiful that they exert upon the senses a power like the power of poetry. But the mood does not last. As the ship enters the North River the enchantment fades, and there is a long moment when New York seems to be a singularly ugly place. The West Side piers and warehouses the ship slowly passes have the dispirited air of buildings exiled forever from the habitations of beauty and grace. There are hard, unfriendly electric signs and there is the first glimpse of the express highway, along which the upper halves of cars can be seen travelling at a fast speed.

New York is as shabby and depressing at the second look as it was glamorous and thrilling at the first look; and after that, in the taxi that makes its hemmed-in way block by block to the lights at the intersections of the cross-town streets, the city becomes confusing and noisy and (the new arrivals nearly always think) unexpectedly dirty. For the imagination of the new arrivals has nearly always been nourished on pictures of the tall, straight skyscrapers and of elegant hotel dining-rooms or alternatively of white suburban houses surrounded by lawns with no fences. Instead, on the way from the ship, they see grimy brownstone houses and garish drug stores, and trucks and unbeautiful sidewalks; and they hear the nerve-shattering noises; and because the ship has brought them so close they forget the outer squalor of other great cities before the fashionable centre has been reached, and feel uneasy or disillusioned. There have been so many more films about Park Avenue than about Tenth Avenue.

Yet within twenty-four hours or less the newcomer to New York usually finds what he has wanted to find. The dusk descends and the skyscrapers reach up to the heavens in a jewelled pattern of light and shade, stirring and lovely. The Broadway canyon twinkles and glows. Here is the storied 42nd Street. The song spoke of the beat of dancing feet; and if the sound comes out a little differently anyone can see what the song meant. The city roars and pulses, and its memorable sights are mostly free.

There is no charge for walking into Grand Central Station, which has a sort of grandeur and sometimes during the day, when the sun is slanting through the high windows, seems to be playing out a detached and lofty rôle, as though it were the cathedral of a modern faith.

Anyone can stand on Park Avenue and feel its steel floor tremble with the cars on its surface and the trains that are running below it: anyone can watch the traffic-lights all change together, a mile at a time. The sight of the Rockefeller Center, rearing in aseptic splendour in the sunshine above Fifth Avenue, is free to everyone. Harlem is there to be studied—the flow along the sidewalks of 125th Street of the bright, confident, coloured girls, and the shop-windows, and the signs and sounds of a Negro metropolis on the white man's island.

The Empire State Building rears to the sky—the world's tallest building, 102 stories high, with 25,000 occupants, so big that in the earlier days, before the offices were all taken, a man was employed just to go from floor to floor and flush the lavatories to keep them in working order; so characteristic of a generation already past that its designers provided at its summit a mast for mooring dirigibles (a facility that has never once been used).

Central Park is free, and so is the sight of its children in the playgrounds and its old men and young lovers on the benches in the twilight. It costs nothing to walk across the Brooklyn Bridge and look down at the ships in the East River, or to see the sun shining through the tracery of the Third Avenue elevated railway, or to stare up at the moneyed magnificence of the Wall Street office suites.

New York, like America itself, is the product of an immense energy which has been allowed to follow its natural bent. Since the nature of man is infinitely varied his works are an infinite variety of beautiful and ugly things, harsh, gentle, vulgar, and tasteful things. In New York the results of the profuse out-pouring of the natural bent of energetic Americans are the good and bad things, enshrined all together, elbow to elbow, on one of the most crowded patches of the globe.

The island of Manhattan, the heart of New York, is less than thirteen and a half miles long and less than two and a half miles wide at its extreme breadth; but nearly two million people live upon this flat rock. If they had not raised tall buildings, blasted out tunnels, and created a honeycomb of electric mains, gas mains, water mains, and sewers Manhattan would be a night-mare: a place of indescribable congestion, confusion, and squalor. But as it is Manhattan provides for many of its inhabitants about the highest standard of living in the world.

They consume cargoes of food a day, but the food is brought in to them through the tunnels and over the bridges, with-out a hitch. They live, many of them, in layers of apart-ments, one above the other unto the tenth and twentieth story; but each dweller in each apartment has a shower, running hot or cold, beneath which he can bathe in the morning, and there is no lack of electricity to whisk him up and down from the street in an elevator, to give him light and to speed him through the subway tunnels to and from his work. In the state of Nevada, in the American west, the population density is one person to the square mile; in Wyoming there are two to the square mile. But in Manhattan the density is about 62,000 to the square mile. And what is most wonderful about the city is not the Empire State Building or Coney Island or Grand Central

Station. What is most wonderful is the composition and behaviour of the people who live so many in so small a space.

*

It has lately become fashionable among the Americans to patronize or to apologize for New York. Even New Yorkers sometimes behave as though an emotional attachment to the city is a social vice, like keeping a mistress.

The United States is an enormous country where the channels of communication are so wide and run so swiftly that all the cities, once objects of awe and excitement to the country places, are now open books. A farmer in Illinois or California who reads his newspapers and magazines, listens to his radio or watches his television-set can form quite definite opinions about New York without ever feeling the need to go and see it for himself. And he is assisted in the formation of these opinions by a series of contemporary clichés about the town—judgments widely propagated and generally accepted in America.

One of these clichés is so famous that it is listed as an American saying in a book called *Best Quotations For All Occasions*. It runs: *I like to visit New York, but I wouldn't live there if you gave it to me.*

It is a saying often repeated by Americans; but there is next to no sense in it. It is the snap decision of a tourist; superficial and uninformed. It almost certainly owes its currency to the sympathetic echoes it has awakened in the memories of other tourists whose feet hurt and whose heads ached in hotel bedrooms in Manhattan after days of unaccustomed exercise on the sightseeing beat and nights of determined dissipation in the hot spots. But how would they know what is to be said for or against living in New York? They have neither seen nor sought the things for which a city is loved.

It is usually not a good idea to inquire of an American who says "I like to visit New York . . ." and so on, why he feels that way. The question releases a flight of further clichés, such as "Everything moves too fast" and "The whole place is money mad" and "I can never sleep for the noise". There are various replies to these and other denunciations of New York, but they do little good. They lead remorselessly to another and still more chalky bromide, one which is almost infallibly produced for its awesome effect on visitors newly arrived on American soil from abroad. This is: *New York isn't America.*

The observation that the part is unequal to the whole is sound, though not new. If there are any foreign visitors in the United States who are prepared to believe that $314\frac{1}{4}$ square miles, which is the land area of the five boroughs of New York City, is equal to 2,977,128 square miles, which is the land area of the continental United States, then it might be wise and humane to detain them on Ellis Island. To the rest the thought that the American prairies and mountains, the farmlands and deserts may encourage a different sort of life from that lived in the most densely populated city in the nation may well already have occurred. But if, as seems more likely, the bromide is meant to imply that New York City does not represent the essential part, the life and spirit of America, then it is less than half true. For New York is a synthesis of America. The essence of the American achievement is concentrated here.

There is a wide-ranging dispute about the nature of the American achievement. It is a many-sided matter, and Americans themselves, let alone the rest of the world, do not agree on what it is in the American achievement which counts for most. The big, swirling words are used a good deal: such words as freedom and equality. But the habit of examining them to see what they mean has lately been almost abandoned. They have become Fourth of July words, standing for conditions which are recognized to be desirable and good and which are held by common consent to be found in greater measure in America than in any other country in the world.

It is one thing to mean that by comparison with the inhabitants of the twentieth century police states, the Americans enjoy a marvellous measure of political freedom. This is so. It is, however, quite another thing to imply, as Fourth of July orators often do, that because of the political freedom the nation has preserved for a hundred and seventy-five years all Americans are simultaneously and automatically made economically free, socially free, and intellectually free. This is not so. There is a fine tradition of social equality: the boss's son and the char-woman's daughter sit side by side in school and like one another. But there are some suburbs in New York, as in most other big cities, in which some Americans cannot live, and the successful anywhere are apt to enjoy privileges and immunities which are denied to the unsuccessful.

The trouble with the big, swirling words which the Fourth of July orators use as shorthand for the American achievement is not only that they are alarmingly inexact. The trouble further is that they beg the question. If Americans are free and equal, what is it that they have done to obtain this result? The orators say that the competitive enterprise system has produced the highest standard of living in the world. But the real triumphs are not the refrigerators and the television-sets, the telephones and the gas stations. The real triumphs are each of the steps collectively taken which have enabled the Americans to make so many goods and to distribute in such abundance to so many people.

There are cities up and down the United States where one or another of the American achievements can be studied in close detail. Detroit, Michigan, is the place for a student who wants to see in its modern maturity the mechanics of mass-production, which, as has often been pointed out, has done more than all the laws on the statute books to lift the Americans out of the drudgery in which most of the rest of the world is still mired. Washington, D.C., is the place to watch the working of the system of Federal Government which, by virtue of a wise Constitution, has made possible the administration, develop-ment, and enrichment of a continent under one national flag. But whoever would go painstakingly into the fundamentals of the American movement, its elements and its results, will linger upon New York. For the story is here, in the people and the life that is lived among the splendid concrete towers and the Tenth Avenue garbage cans.

New York is where one of the foremost of the American accomplishments is most vividly discernible. The miracle has been slurred over and forgotten, but in New York there is to be observed the best evidence that America alone of all the countries of the world has lifted the curse of the Tower of Babel.

This is the first of the wonders that are greater than the Empire State Building or the Statue of Liberty. When your incoming ship approached the West Side pier the little man who caught the first rope probably was a New Yorker born in Italy and taught from birth to speak Italian—one of 400,000 such New Yorkers. Your trunks were wheeled away by a New Yorker born in Poland, one of 195,000 immigrants from Poland in the city—or he could have been a German-born New Yorker, of whom there are 225,000, or a Russian-born New Yorker, one of 395,000. There is a good chance that the taxi-driver who took you and your luggage from the pier to the hotel was a Greek-born New Yorker, one of 28,000, and the little argument he had on the way was with an Irish-born policeman, one of 182,000 New Yorkers born in South or North Ireland. The clerk you talked to at the hotel desk was one of the 145,000 Austrian-born New Yorkers, and you were taken up in the elevator by one of the 62,000 New Yorkers who were born in Hungary, and shown to your room by one of the 40,000 Rumanian-born New Yorkers. And before long you will have passed in the street, without identifying them, a representative cross-section of the other tens of thousands of New Yorkers who were born Swedes, Danes, Dutchmen, Belgians, Frenchmen, Swiss, Czechs, Yugoslavs, Latvians, Lithuanians, Finns, Bulgars, Turks, Spaniards, Portuguese, Palestinians, Syrians, Mexicans, Cubans, Chinese, and Japanese.

Counting the foreign-born and their children, there are 5,000,000 New Yorkers, or well over half the population, who are of foreign descent. But now they live and work together quite easily, for they have all learned the same language and adopted the same economic and social creed. Elsewhere on earth such a unity of dissimilar peoples is still an insubstantial aspiration. In New York it is a commonplace: it is working, and it has been working for years. And the names of many of the city's greatest men, who dominate and direct universities, financial houses, Press, radio, and many other institutions, are reminders of what New York owes to its foreign stock.

Those who labour for the Parliament of Man, the Federation of the World, might learn much from New York, both about the strains that are inevitable in this fusing of peoples and about the means by which the strains can be successfully borne. They will see in New York better perhaps than in any other part of America that it has been required of the stream of immigrants that each one, on embracing American citizenship, should acknowledge a new loyalty and make it paramount. But they will find too that the further technical requirement that all old loyalties shall be simultaneously renounced is not too literally interpreted. It is on the contrary modified with much good sense, much kindliness, and much toleration. It had to be, or it would not have worked.

For the old loyalties go deep, and a law which said that they must be abandoned and forgotten as from such and such a time or date, under penalty of punishment, would be an unwise and unworkable law. New York does not attempt to impose it. Instead New York lines Fifth Avenue on St. Patrick's Day when 50,000 Irish-Americans parade in honour of the country of their forefathers, the country they have been willing to leave but are not willing to forget. New York watches with frank interest while the American-Poles celebrate Pulaski Day, the American-Italian societies celebrate the days of their saints and heroes, the American-Rumanians mark the day of deliverance from Turkish rule, the American-Spaniards hold the Day of their Race, the American-Serbs, Croats, and Slovenes rejoice in the unity of Yugoslavia, the American-Greeks, the American-Armenians, and the American-Syrians hail their respective Independence Days, the American-Hungarians salute Kossuth, and the American-Danes and American-Swedes keep their days of national celebration.

The orthodox American-Russians and the American-Chinese keep traditional dates according to old calendars which the new life in America has never invalidated. And on St. George's Day men of British birth or stock go decorously to church in the shadow of the monoliths of Wall Street, there to hear read a message from the king and queen. America is big enough and sure enough of itself not to be afraid of these phenomena, and New York is wise enough to respect the emotions that lie behind them.

New York offers good grounds for believing that if the nations of the world are ever to live together under a single government they will need to be treated with as much toleration and as little dogmatism as any one group of immigrants and their descendants in New York displays towards any other group. But that won't be all. There will need to be an abiding reason why the effort of toleration should be made—something which will make it more worth while to live and work together than to yield to the manifold temptations of disunity.

The abiding reason shows clear and strong in the pattern of New York. The Greeks and Turks, Bulgars and Czechs, Poles and Germans, Dutch and Danes, Irishmen, Italians, Frenchmen, Swedes, and all the rest who have come to New York from abroad, all the Americans who have come to New York from another part of the country, and all those who have been born and bred in the city, are unified by a common hope. It is the hope of economic betterment.

Though they rub shoulders together all day and all night long in the streets and subways, the people of New York live in fantastically different environments. He is a New Yorker who sits on a summer evening in a white dinner-jacket on a penthouse roof on the fringe of Central Park, some hundreds of feet above the fevered traffic, and drinks a very cold cocktail and watches Manhattan sparkle into griddles of yellow light in the dusk. And he is no less a New Yorker who climbs from his window to sit in his undershirt a few feet above the garbage cans on the warm iron rung of a fire-escape in Brooklyn, and sees no more than the winking neon sign of a bar and grill.

There is a girl, walking down Fifth Avenue, crisp and smart and desirable, fragrant with perfume, sheathed in nylon, straight and slim and queenly—the American girl of the five-colour ads. And there is another girl pressed into a corner of a Lexington Avenue Uptown express, plump and sweating, chewing her gum, clutching her handbag and evening paper.

The New Yorkers hurry home at the end of the day, jostling and overtaking one another on the sidewalks, pouring into the stations, passing one another in yellow taxis. They are bound for apartments in Park Avenue, rented at $400 a month, and walk-up flats in the Bronx, rented at $40 a month. They live in brownstone houses in the cross-town streets and white Colonial-style houses in the suburbs, and in basements and in rows of ugly brick boxes in Brooklyn and in elegant hotels with tall, velvet curtains at the windows and snowy towels in the bath-rooms. They are the old and young, the rich and poor, the successful and unsuccessful; and they are all New Yorkers, united by the common hope of economic betterment.

*

It is a widely held belief, advanced in many a sociological treatise and laid down as an article of a religious creed by orthodox Communists, that affluence and poverty cannot co-exist without the growing probability of an explosion. But affluence and relative poverty do coexist in New York; and they coexist among a polyglot population in conditions which must sometimes have appeared to the confident theoreticians in Moscow to be conducive to the most awe-inspiring social explosions.

It is, in fact, a long time since there has been any considerable danger in New York of a conflict based on the dissatisfaction of the poor with their condition in relation to that of the rich. There was little sign of that sort of feeling even in the darkest days of the depression in the early thirties. The charges subsequently brought by opposition politicians against President Franklin D. Roosevelt that he was inciting this sort of class warfare in the nation do not bear any close examination. The truth almost certainly is that the rich and prosperous have been and are less resented by the poor in America than in any other industrial country in the world, and that in all America the least resentment of the rich and prosperous is encountered in New York.

Is this because the standard of living is so much higher in America in general and in New York in particular that even the relatively poor are conscious of their economic blessings and contented with their lot? The standard of living is high. The words poor and poverty are almost never applied by Americans to other Americans: they are nearly always used to describe conditions in other parts of the world. For less well-heeled fellow-citizens there is the more respectable word under-privileged. And while the conditions in which some of the underprivileged in the south and some of the underprivileged migrant workers in the southwest live out their days are so close to poverty as to be indistinguishable from it, the American standard of living does indeed make a comparative rarity of the sort of economic misery that is commonplace in Asia and Africa and even in some parts of Europe.

It seems to be entirely reasonable to believe that in this sense the higher living standard helps to make less likely social explosions of the kind the Communists have wanted to see and must have expected. But the related conclusion that the poor in America are contented with their lot is about as wrong as it could be. The poor, the near-poor, the middle class (only the Americans, disliking the word class, prefer to call them the middle income groups) and even the upper class (or high income groups) all want to improve their lot. There is nothing remarkable about that. What is remarkable is that all Americans, and none more than the poor, also *expect* to improve their lot.

This is at the very heart of the American story. It is what makes it worth while to resist and overcome the greatest of the temptations to disunity. It is what enables the temperamentally different peoples of New York to live together in amity and in fundamental agreement. It is what does most to protect America in general and New York in particular from the sort of social explosion the propinquity of riches and poverty might otherwise encourage.

America is a country where a man can readily believe that he is able to raise himself to a different and better condition of life. New York is a city where a man can readily believe that he is in the best local situation to accomplish that transition.

The conviction Americans share is that there is no insuperable obstacle to any one man's economic and social improvement, that there are no conditions anywhere that cannot be changed, and that not slow, little gains but very big and very swift gains may be made by anyone, by one or more of a number of processes—by hard work, by good judgment, or by luck, for instance. When some of those Americans from the easier-going towns visit New York and then return to report that the whole place is money-mad, most of them mean that they have been surprised by signs that the effort towards economic betterment is pursued in New York with more application and intensity than is exhibited in their home towns—more than they themselves are prepared to exhibit.

It would be a different and graver criticism of New York if any American, back from a visit, said to his home-town audience: "The place is full of startling contrasts between the conditions in which the rich and successful live and those in which the poor and unsuccessful live. The rich exploit the poor, and the poor allow it to go on and work themselves to shadows in the hope that they will somehow be able to move out of the lower class into the upper class. But of course that is a terrible delusion, for the poor will always be poor." But no American says anything like that, for no American believes in his heart that anything of the kind is true.

And it is indeed not true: not in America, not in New York. Anyone who thinks that it is in only a few exceptional cases that the son of poor parents, who sold newspapers or worked behind a grocery counter or hauled ice or coal in his youth, has become the owner or managing director of a business with a turnover of millions of dollars should take the trouble to read the obituary notices in, say, the *New York Times* for a few months.

The rich and famous in America are rarely those who have inherited either their money or their fame: the overwhelming majority of them are those who earned their way out of insecurity and anonymity. This has gone on in America for a long time, and it is going on still; and so long as it goes on there will be more than an appreciation of liberty and justice to make living and working in America seem to be worth while. And the knowledge that the lightning of fame and wealth may strike anyone, anywhere, at any time—that there is no regulation or prejudice which might deny even to an unlettered immigrant the satisfactions of substantial material betterment—is itself a great force for unity.

It draws the lower, the middle, and the higher income groups together into a readiness to defend a system each wishes to continue. It goes a long way to explain why nine out of ten Americans, or more, have not only refused to accept Socialism but have not even troubled to understand it, thereby creating the circumstances in which a Federal or State Government cannot put the most beneficial and necessary Socialistic measures into effect until it has fervently denied that they are Socialistic.

*

The municipal government of New York City is engaged in about as many of the Socialistic activities—the activities of a co-operative society—as are other great cities in the twentieth century. Subways, parks, schools, hospitals, and health clinics are among the public services it polices, regulates, and controls, and to the extent that it makes provision for its poor out of the taxes collected from its well-to-do, it lends itself to a more equitable sharing of wealth—a thoroughly Socialistic concept.

Almost to a man, however, the politicians who direct these activities declare themselves at election times to be unalterably opposed to Socialism; and the people of New York continue to regard Socialism in all its forms as an alien doctrine to be resisted with might and main. What the politicians and the people both mean is that they want to keep the Socialistic activities of their city and nation down to the minimum necessary to ensure safety, order, and the humanity which a Christian conscience dictates, and to continue now as in the past to place their hope and faith in the competitive free enterprise system. For they are able with justice to point out that the results in terms of material wealth, comfort, and leisure achieved by following the capitalist American way have been phenomenal.

New Yorkers like to remember that the island of Manhattan, which at the mid-century had a total assessed property value of $8,291,241,400 and contained at least one building site (at the corner of Wall Street and downtown Broadway) which had changed hands at $1,070 a square foot, was bought from the Indians in 1626 for trinkets worth $24.00.

This satisfactory transaction was completed—a few years after the island had been discovered by Henry Hudson, an English explorer in the service of the Dutch India Company —by Peter Minuit, who had been appointed Director General of New Netherland, as the Dutch government had named its new possessions in the New World. For fifty years (1614–1664) Manhattan was called New Amsterdam. Then the British took it and called it New York, because Charles II had granted all the Dutch land in America to his brother, James, Duke of York. Nine years later the Dutch recaptured the city and renamed it New Orange, but in the following year all of New Netherland was ceded back to the British. New York the city then became again, New York it was after the War of the Revolution had been fought, and George Washington was inaugurated in 1789 on the steps of a Wall Street building called the New Federal Hall; and New York it has been ever since.

And though it has been the very centre and symbol of private enterprise the city has been improved and enhanced by a series of public planning operations which Socialists in any country might take as a model. Especially since the end of the First World War—through the period of the Regional Plan Committee under Charles D. Norton and Frederick A. Delano, through the period of the Municipal Housing Authority and the zoning committees, and by way of the recent imaginative schemes of Robert Moses—New York has been planned, zoned, and equipped so that the city now has parkways and arterial roads, bridges, tunnels, parks and playgrounds on a scale that is probably unmatched anywhere else in the world.

The municipal history of New York during most of the nineteenth century and well into the twentieth has been notable for a series of thoroughly corrupt local governments, directed by political bosses (Fernando Wood in the eighteen-fifties was one of the toughest, but William Marcy Tweed in the eighteen-sixties was probably the most notorious) and by a succession of ruthless chieftains of Tammany Hall, the local headquarters of the Democratic Party.

It seems doubtful whether there can have been any other city in the world whose administration was so completely and so consistently taken over by political racketeers, or whose taxpayers were so regularly swindled out of such large sums of money. But New York, the gateway through which the immigrants were streaming by the tens of thousands, year after year —the poor and the not-so-poor, the hopeful and credulous, ready to begin a new life in a land whose rules and language they had still to learn—offered unique opportunities for graft to politicians who thought faster and had fewer scruples than their fellows. And even much later, in the Prohibition era, there was enough dirty work in New York to establish a pattern of gang warfare, police and judicial corruption and other elements of misgovernment, the stories of which have shocked, fascinated, and entertained much of the civilized world ever since.

It is by no means certain, though, that the people of New York, who were the collective victims of such villainies, found them so very shocking at the time when they were being most energetically practised. And it is beyond doubt that in retrospect the wide-open twenties have a rare, nostalgic charm for those who lived through their worst excesses.

The New York custom had been to rebel in time against city administrations which had grown too corrupt or too greedy. Reform mayors had come, had wrought changes, and had stayed a while in the nineteenth and earlier twentieth century; and in the nineteen-thirties Mayor Fiorello La Guardia, probably the most vigorous, successful, and popular reformer New York ever did produce, was elected and re-elected. He was an honest man, and he arrived on the scene at a time when large Federal funds were being made available for relief and for public works in pursuit of the New Deal plans of President Franklin D. Roosevelt, by which the nation was being pulled out of the depths of the depression. Tammany Hall had never had this sort of money to spend for the benefit of needy voters. So La Guardia gained and held a commanding political lead, and he used it well. District Attorney Dewey and his colleagues greatly reduced if they did not altogether destroy the contemporary underworld. Brothels and burlesque houses were closed, and the highways, playgrounds, and parks which Mr. Robert Moses created gave New Yorkers something to see for their tax money.

It was a purer and better New York City from 1934 on. And yet it was not uncommon in the nineteen-forties to detect in the voice of a New Yorker, as he talked of the bad old days, a wistful note of regret. An objective outsider might have come to the conclusion that it was in the nature of many New Yorkers to find a fascination in the lawless, to regard almost with admiration a man smart enough to procure the election of his friends and to swindle the city on a really handsome scale.

The argument used to be that there was not much anyone could do about it, anyway. An objective outsider was often encouraged to conclude that there was not much that the majority greatly wanted to do about it. New York in the old days was a great show: and if some of the city fathers were dishonest you had to hand it to them—they were not dull, and everyone had a lot of fun. That was the view many a New Yorker would take in the reformed forties, with a faint, fond, reminiscent grin. And the objective outsider was left wondering whether New York's notable lapses of corrupt government were not to a considerable degree hereby explained.

The heat was on again in 1951. When Senator Kefauver's Senate Crime Investigating Committee came to New York, and peopled the nation's television screens with many of the dubious underworld characters who had hitherto been no more than names read about in the papers, there was a perceptible public groundswell. The racketeers were an unattractive crowd to watch and listen to, and though there were some reservations in some part of the public about the justice with which they were being handled in this televized semi-trial, and some frustration at the loose ends that were left—the not-quite-proved charges, the imperfectly rounded out hints of official malpractices—it seemed to be clear enough that public sympathy was over-whelmingly with the hunters and against the hunted. Thereafter there were some sentences in court, and a quite extraordinary number of New York policemen thought it prudent to resign from the force.

There was a public growl, but there was no public cry angry enough, loud enough, and consistent enough to produce full explanations of what had gone unexplained or half explained. This might well have been in part because the evidence had not been strong enough to leave the impression that there were radical wrongs which needed to be righted. And almost certainly it was also in part because New Yorkers saw about them many signs that the city was now being efficiently run.

New York had never been more crowded, more bustling,

22

more prosperous. It was a prosperity now as always founded on the opportunities and rewards of competitive free enterprise; but that did not make it any less dependent on the smooth functioning, twenty-four hours a day, of the city-run services.

The Mayor of New York has always had formidable responsibilities and formidable powers; and his responsibilities and powers have expanded side by side through the first half of the twentieth century. The city now pays the mayor a salary of $40,000 a year and furnishes him with one of its most desirable houses, Gracie Mansion, to live in. There is an elected City Council of twenty-five members, but the real decisions which determine the manner of the city's governing are taken either by the mayor personally or by the Board of Estimate of eight members, over which the mayor presides.

The mayor begins by assuring himself of effective control of the departments and bureaux of the city government by appointing men of his own choice to direct them. Thereafter he exerts by far the most potent influence of any of the members on the Board of Estimate, which handles the city's billion-dollar budget. With the mayor on the Board of Estimate are the Comptroller, President of the Council and presidents of each of the five boroughs—Manhattan, the Bronx, Brooklyn, Queens, and Richmond. All these are elected officials. But while the Borough Presidents of the Bronx, Queens, and Richmond have one vote each, the Borough Presidents of Manhattan and Brooklyn have two votes each, the Mayor, Comptroller, and President of the Council have three votes each. The mayor, in short, is enabled mainly to get his own way.

He will get the chief credit for the good things the city does; but he will get the blame, too, if anything goes badly wrong. It is the mayor who is expected to surmount the recurrent crises the city can expect to face. If it is buried under snowbanks—and it very quickly can be: in 1947 twenty-five inches of snow fell in twenty-four hours—the decision how much money to spend on clearing the streets in how much time must be made or approved by the mayor. There are 4,000 miles of streets and a snowstorm has been known to cost New York City $9,000,000.

The mayor may be grumbled at if anyone has any reason to think that a big fire was not tackled fast enough or skilfully enough. The mayor was expected to do something about it when a water shortage in 1950 prevented New Yorkers from washing their cars and brought in a brief era of no-bath-on-Thursdays appeals to the citizenry (and indeed the mayor did something about it, in the sense that he took a hand in the enterprising but inconclusive experiments to produce rain by seeding clouds with dry ice and silver iodide).

The subway trains must make 13,000 trips a day, the city markets must be filled and emptied of fish and produce, the schools must take in and instruct their 850,000 children a day, the city hospitals must be ready with 24,000 beds for every sort of patient from the tubercular to the alcoholic, there must be no serious increase in the population of rats and mice and no undue flowering of ragweed to afflict the sufferers from hay-fever: otherwise the mayor will soon know about it.

The government of the Port of New York is in other hands. The states of New York and New Jersey agreed in a treaty signed in 1921 to appoint six commissioners each to the board of a Port Authority which has the duty of regulating and improving the commerce that is a large part of the sustenance of both states.

But the commissioners are not alone concerned with immense water-borne traffic which ceaselessly moves through New York harbour. They have held since 1947 fifty-year leases on the three big airports in the New York metropolitan area—the La Guardia Airport on Long Island, the Newark Airport across the river in New Jersey, and the new, big International Airport at Idlewild—and have owned since 1949 a fourth airport, Teterboro in New Jersey. It is their duty to operate and develop these restless way-stations.

The Port Authority looks after two of the road tunnels and four of the road bridges, through or over which cars, buses, and trucks make well over 50,000,000 crossings to and from Manhattan in a year. In its building on Eighth Avenue, Manhattan, the administration forces for huge railroad, grain, marine, and truck terminals are housed. And the Port Authority in 1951 opened in mid-Manhattan the most elaborate bus terminal in the world—a steel and concrete edifice 800 feet long and 200 feet wide. Into this great air-conditioned depot and out of it there now pour more than 2,000 buses a day; and there are drug stores, bars, restaurants, bowling-alleys and news-stands, with barbers, florists, grocers, and other shops and a laundry. There are sweeping ramps and concourses and swift escalators and a vast roof for parked cars.

The new bus terminal was fitted smoothly into the city's daily routine and was quickly taken for granted, like any other product of the energy and imagination of prosperous Manhattan.

*

As to the mid-century prosperity of New York there were abundant statistics. New Yorkers were maintaining 5,769,065 individual savings accounts, the total of which came to $9,908,353,000 (the President of the Commerce and Industry Association noted in the spring of 1950). This indicated an average of $1,544 for an account and an average of $1,113 *per capita* of the population. Nobody was going to pretend that everyone in New York had savings of more than $1,000 to draw upon: a lot of people on the lower East Side and elsewhere had never seen as much money as that at one time in all their lives. But for the whole of America the average sum *per capita* in savings accounts was less than $400, so that it seemed fair to assume that New Yorkers as a whole were farther along the road to prosperity.

Rather more than 234,500 business firms were counted in New York at about the half-century, and of them 41,300 were manufacturers. The average weekly wage of production workers in these manufacturing industries was about $56.00. The

PLATE 45

NEW YORK'S WATERFRONT
from the Hudson River

FULTON FISH MARKET
with wharf on the East River

PLATE 46

WHERE THE BOWERY AND CHINA
TOWN MEET

WALL STREET SKYSCRAPERS
and elevated railway

UNITED NATIONS HEADQUARTERS
The Secretariat building

BUS TERMINAL
built by the Port Authority in 1951

average weekly wage of a New York stenographer was $46.00 (£16 10s.).

These were among the modest wages. A bricklayer, plasterer, electrician, printer, electric welder—the practitioner of any one of dozens of skilled trades—was often earning a little more or a little less than $100.00 a week.

From one end of the metropolitan area to the other there were thousands upon thousands of dwellers in the suburbs who, without thinking of themselves as unduly privileged, would have shuddered at the idea of living on as little as $100.00 a week. Beyond them were the people who were making what was usually described as real money. In some New York circles $20,000 a year was real money; but in others a man with only $20,000 a year was pitied or derided.

The stores were selling something in the neighbourhood of $8,000,000,000 worth of goods a year. The largest of them, Macy's department store, was reporting that it was being visited by about 150,000 customers a day—and at Christmas-time by 350,000 a day.

The shops were the most varied, the best-stocked, and the most elaborately filled shops in the world; and they were busy and thriving. They sold some of the most attractive articles in the world, and they sold most of them in enormous quantities.

In the garment district in mid-town New York there were being turned out by the thousands frocks that were both smart and cheap: frocks and underclothes, blouses and skirts and coats, made in a multitude of sizes, so that they would fit beautifully. The department stores had them, and though prices went up wages went up too, so that the stenographers and sales-girls, the coloured housemaids and the waitresses and factory workers could always afford to buy them. The smart, cheap frocks and coats appeared in the subways in the morning and evening rush hours, and in the afternoons and evenings on Fifth Avenue and Broadway and in the restaurants and night-clubs the expensive clothes from the elegant shops were on view, all the time, even when almost everyone was complaining about inflation.

In New York, in the least lovely streets amid the ashcans and the fire-escapes, all year round through the freezing winters, through the sweltering summers, the relatively poor in the drug stores and diners and delicatessens were eating and drinking a good many of the things that in most of the rest of the world —and not least in Moscow—the rich still regarded as luxuries.

As to the future, there were economists who were unsure that the Americans could keep up the pace and who worried lest there should be recessions to come and wondered what limit was to be placed on American industrial expansion. But as to the present, by all the criteria—by statistical evidence and on the evidence of what could be seen, touched, and tasted—New York at the mid-century was the most prosperous city civilization had yet produced.

This phenomenon, though it was denied or misrepresented in the sealed-off Communist countries beyond the Iron Curtain, was not as a rule questioned in the better informed countries of western Europe or elsewhere in the free world. It was not pretended there (except in the places where the view was adjusted to the Communist Party line) that the American capitalist system had failed to produce a remarkably high standard of material well-being.

What was more often said was that the Americans were hopelessly materialist in their outlook; that the gospel of economic success had distorted their values; that refrigerators and washing machines, smart frocks, shining cars and ice-cream in twenty flavours were being naïvely accepted as the ultimate good; that spiritual and intellectual values had been submerged in the tide of material prosperity. And of all places in America New York was cited as the most abysmally materialist, the most spiritually and intellectually abandoned.

This was not true: it was a long way from being true. New York in fact was and long had been a place of immense cultural and spiritual vigour.

A teeming life was centred in its universities—in Columbia (established 200 years ago by a grant of George II), New York

University (120 years old), the College of the City of New York, Fordham, Hunter, Manhattan, St. Francis Xavier. The New York Public Library, richly endowed, was one of the greatest in the world: it had a reference section containing 2,000,000 volumes, and there were over sixty branches in various parts of New York as well as the imposing Manhattan headquarters. Any city, anywhere, would have been proud to possess the Metropolitan Museum of Art, the biggest and most important of the American museums, with great resources not only of art but also of energy.

New York held the Frick Museum, housing one of the really great art collections, the American Museum of Natural History, the Hayden Planetarium, and a dozen other temples of art or science that might have been more famous if they had been situated in a city which made it less easy to forget them. New York was constantly performing and producing good music and opera, and these performances were constantly being listened to lovingly by thousands or (when they were broadcast) millions of people. And New York was continuously bringing out the best books and plays in America, and some of the best magazines and at least two of the best newspapers in the world.

New York, in fact, had produced and was producing a modern culture marked with its unmistakable stamp. It was a lively and popular culture: most of the writing, music, and art were for the many, not the few. Europeans often and Americans occasionally looked down their noses at it; but intellectuals had been known in the past to have judged wrongly, and it might be reasonable to believe that some at least of the books, plays, tunes, and pictures would turn out to be not less worthy or durable because they had been well-used by the generation for whom they had been produced.

Were there any great novels among those of Sinclair Lewis, Hemingway, Steinbeck, Sherwood Anderson, Thomas Wolfe, Dreiser? Were, say, Robert Frost or Archibald MacLeish or Carl Sandburg great poets? Nobody could be sure what other generations would find in them.

There was a good deal for coming generations to examine. They would have to look into the plays of Eugene O'Neill, Elmer Rice, Thornton Wilder, Maxwell Anderson, Robert Sherwood, William Saroyan. They would have to listen to an enormous amount of music: that of Virgil Thomson and Deems Taylor, that of Gershwin, and that of the men who had written for theatre, cinema, radio, and television the music that had its brief day and was then more or less discarded—men like Richard Rodgers, Cole Porter, Irving Berlin, Jerome Kern, and a hundred others. A lot of it had seemed to be uneven stuff, a lot of it was pathetic, but some of it was wonderfully inventive and effective.

The two American painters best known by the mid-century Americans probably were Grant Wood and Thomas Benton. But nobody knew yet whether among the many who were now painting in and out of New York there was someone who, long hence, would be called the master of his day. There had not been time to be sure which of the architects had contributed most to New York and America; or what manner of magic would cling to the names of the Barrymores, or the Lunts, or Helen Hayes or Katherine Cornell; or whether the lyrics of Oscar Hammerstein would come to be loved as were W. S. Gilbert's.

Because so much writing, music, and art was produced in or inspired by New York and because so much of it was plainly shoddy and second-rate, it had become harder to know what among it was good and enduring. In any case, however, the mid-century world was in no position to deride what was coming out of the American metropolis. For the mid-century world read the writings of New York and played and sang the music of New York all the time, in nearly all latitudes and longitudes, and did so with much pleasure and (it could easily be argued) some profit.

This was one of the phenomena, evoking images of lights and theatres and dance-floors, which gave a good deal of the world its mental view of New York. It was a more entertaining than a complete view. It omitted, for example, the truth that in New York religious observances were regularly and widely carried out. An uncertain enquirer might watch the crowds of Roman Catholic worshippers in St. Patrick's Cathedral and the Protestants in the Cathedral of St. John the Divine, and in Baptist, Christian Science, Congregational, Jewish, Lutheran, Methodist, Presbyterian, Protestant Episcopal, Quaker, Reformed, Roman Catholic, or Unitarian churches or in those of any of a dozen other religious denominations. To call the Americans—among whom were the descendants of families with a lifetime preoccupation with the religious truths and mysteries —a hopelessly materialist nation was perhaps the silliest generalization of them all.

There were times when western criticism of the American civilization seemed to reveal undertones of jealous resentment, and there were times when it showed itself to be based upon doctrinaire prejudice; but it could not always be dismissed on those or kindred grounds. A traveller in, for example, Britain and the western European continent in the years after the Second World War—the years of recognition that the seat of power had now shifted from the Old World to the New—could feel among honest people a great uncertainty about the Americans, and a great uneasiness.

When it had been conceded that they were rich, and they were energetic, and that they had food and houses and material comforts which surpassed anything else on earth, honest people were inclined still to ask whether that was enough to qualify a nation for the leadership of the world. The teaching of centuries had denigrated wealth: it had exalted other values. In what the rest of the free world heard of America there seemed to be too much about wealth and energy and too little about the qualities in which men and nations had always long and rewardingly put their ultimate faith—the qualities of dedication, self-discipline, fortitude, and the things of the spirit.

The honest question was whether rich and energetic Americans were worthy of their sudden inheritance. The honest doubt was whether it would be good for the world that power and leadership should be transferred to the Americans.

Well, it would be comforting to many people in many parts of the world if it had been possible truthfully to say that New York is little different from London or Paris or New Delhi, and that the new world leaders can be relied upon to feel, think, and behave as the old world leaders did. But in fact neither of the two simple alternative propositions turns out on examination to be true. It is not true that the Americans are just transplanted Europeans who will be disposed, when they have settled down to it and acquired a bit more experience, to exercise the old international responsibilities in the old ways. Nor is it true either that the Americans are so crude and so violent, so brash and so impulsive that all the rules must now be changed and the old world's most cherished values must be jettisoned.

One of the principal reasons for the widespread uneasiness about Americans of honest people abroad is that the Americans often project themselves to the rest of the world in approximately the same way as they advertise what they have to sell to one another at home. Advertising in America is a tremendous game, with huge stakes to be won and lost, intensively played according to regulations with which all the players—the sellers and the buyers alike—are familiar by a sort of instinct.

The regulation it is always most important to bear in mind is that, within rather vaguely defined limits, any technique of salesmanship which succeeds is a good technique. Anyone who finds a way of persuading large numbers of people to buy what he has to sell is entitled to whatever profits he can thereby make. If he is downright dishonest he will defeat his own ends: nobody will buy his product. But he may exaggerate his virtues, cloak his deficiencies, distract attention from an unfavourable quality and focus attention on a favourable quality, build himself up, enter claims he can be reasonably sure will not be seriously disputed, employ any device of salesmanship that will not arouse positive resentment; and if he succeeds in selling what he has to sell in the face of public resistance and scepticism then he is entitled to his winnings.

This is all right—or at least it is not so dreadful—when the right adjustments have been made by all concerned. The trouble is that so many millions of people who, mainly since the war, have turned their eyes towards America and the Americans for the first time have not been coached in the rules and have not made the adjustments. When an American advertiser, addressing an American typist in print or by radio or television says: "My product will make you lovelier, more glamorous, irresistible to men!" both parties know well enough that in the case of most typists it is unlikely to do anything of the sort, but that the raising of so pleasurable a possibility is in itself an acceptable gesture.

But only a few European or Asiatic observers of American films, or readers of American novels or magazines, or even the foreign followers of American political debates are automatically aware of the allowances that should be made when the great selling game is in progress. And the Americans themselves often show a notable unawareness that effects they have created abroad—effects which would be highly appreciated in America—have done them more harm than good.

The tough and rough things, the shootings-from-the-hip both by gangsters and politicians, are shocking and therefore (when the right allowances have been made) mildly attractive to the Americans. They are usually shocking and not even mildly attractive to the rest of the world. For the rest of the world does not know how much there is in America to balance them.

The rest of the world hears about human rats who have been caught selling narcotic drugs to schoolchildren, and about the occasional excesses and the underworld characters with picturesque names; it hears about American buying panics and the revelations of Congressional investigations, and strange, illiberal witch-hunts in the groves of learning. These stories are true in themselves: there *was* this despair, degradation, dishonesty, hysteria, fear.

What Americans know and what most of the rest of the world does not know is that at the same time, and all the time, millions of quiet, well-adjusted, unhysterical people were going about their work, attending church, sitting in their living-rooms or on their porches, planning their children's future, listening, reading, ruminating and automatically putting the shocking things into perspective.

*

It was undeniable that there were manifest dangers in America at the mid-century: the dangers of the fashionable propaganda, which induced in too many places a terrible tendency to conformity of thought, the dangers of demagoguery, of public impatience, and of the failure to discriminate between the true and the false. But it was true too that these were not new dangers, and that when they had appeared before they had nearly always been overcome.

There was this to be said for the comfort of honest men who felt unsure of the capacity of the Americans to exercise wisely the world leadership they had inherited: that America still was a country where the ultimate power resided in the unrecorded, unsensational people, and that in the testing times these same people had mainly chosen well.

They had chosen well, moreover, when every habit and training had urged them to take an easier course. For generations they had believed in the doctrine that came to be called Isolationism: they had believed that the well-endowed continent their ancestors had carved out of a wilderness was inviolable and self-sufficient. But they were capable, before they went to war, of Lend-Lease, which Mr. Winston Churchill called "the most unsordid act in history", and after they had been to war they were capable of the Marshall Plan and the Atlantic Pact and of a brave and unprecedented effort in Korea.

They often sounded self-righteous and more often still they sounded irresponsible: they were volatile and undisciplined, and their frequent noisy arguments and the threats they uttered

PLATE 47

THE STATUE OF ATLAS

Rockefeller Center. The sphere carries on its outer ring the twelve signs of the zodiac and its axis points to the North Star

PLATE 48

THE GRAND CENTRAL TERMINAL
with raised roadway

THE LINCOLN TUNNEL
New Jersey Approaches

made the world tremble. But they assumed burdens and responsibilities and they made voluntary sacrifices such as no nation
in history had ever matched.

They sold the world its best dance-music and its most entertaining films; but they gave away thousands of millions of
dollars' worth of food and oil and machinery. They were
employing 90,000 of their citizens in an atomic energy programme which was mainly designed to produce the most
frightful weapons of war so far conceived; but they were also a
nation whose Chief of State could say:

> "If peace could be made sure the American people would
> be glad to invest a part of the resources we must now allocate
> to defence to a large-scale programme of world-wide econo-
> mic development. . . . With such a programme we could, in
> co-operation with other peoples, inaugurate the most hopeful
> and fruitful period of peaceful development the world has
> ever seen."

Whether peace could be made sure was the question the
Americans were living with at the mid-century. Many of them
expected war, or said they expected war: a poll in May 1950
indicated that 22 per cent thought the United States would be
at war within a year, and 57 per cent expected war within five
years. When General Eisenhower took command of the defence
forces in Europe and the feeling grew that the North Atlantic
Pact was beginning to mean something more, people were inclined to take a rather more hopeful view of the future. But
there was almost no dissent from the argument that everything
should be done to prepare for war: for atomic war.

New York expected to be attacked and atom-bombed if war
should come. Horrific predictions were published of what could
happen in that event—of the fire and devastation that would
sweep Manhattan, of the 75,000 or 150,000 who might be killed
in a few seconds.

Civil Defence measures were now under way. Foreign visitors
found it startling to see in New York signs pointing the way to

public bomb shelters: signs such as had not appeared so far in the European cities. But there was a difference about the talk the visitor heard in New York. It was the talk of anxious people to whom bombing was a nightmare not of the memory but of the imagination, with all the fascination of the awful unknown.

Nobody could know the future of New York; but while the thought of New York under the conditions of atomic warfare was a matter for imaginative guesswork, there was a lot less guesswork in the thought of New York under a sure peace.

The city would change swiftly with the swiftly changing times; it would grow greater and more beautiful, and it would experiment and seize upon the new achievements of science and technology. That was a discernible public belief in New York, where the men and women of the Old World had learned how to live together and how to assure themselves that nobody's condition was hopeless and that everything could be made better for everyone. There would be little reluctance to abandon the present things for the future things: no inhibitions of sentimentality, no fear of something fresh. The skyscrapers could be pulled down and newer and better ones could be built.

BOOKS
RECOMMENDED FOR FURTHER READING

ATHENS: THE PERICLEAN AGE

A. Zimmern, *The Greek Commonwealth*
J. D. Beazley and B. Ashmole, *Greek Sculpture and Painting*
M. Schede, *The Acropolis of Athens*
    Cambridge Ancient History, Vol. V
T. Zielinski, *The Religion of Ancient Greece*
W. S. Ferguson, *Greek Imperialism*

ROME UNDER THE ANTONINES

Roberto Paribeni, *Optimus Princeps*
B. W. Henderson, *The Life and Principate of the Emperor Hadrian*
M. Rostovtzeff, *The Social and Economic History of the Roman Empire*
    Cambridge Ancient History, Vol. XI
Samuel Dill, *Roman Society from Nero to Marcus Aurelius*
Johnston, *Private Life of the Romans*
Jérôme Carcopino, *Daily Life in Ancient Rome*

CONSTANTINOPLE

N. H. Baynes, *The Byzantine Empire*
    Cambridge Medieval History, Vol. IV
D. T. Rice, *Byzantine Art*
S. Runciman, *Byzantine Civilization*
E. H. Swift, *Hagia Sophia*
A. A. Vasiliev, *History of the Byzantine Empire*

MEDIEVAL PARIS

H. Belloc, *Paris*
H. Rashdall, *The Universities of the Middle Ages*
A. Luchaire, *Social Life in France at the Time of Philip Augustus*
A. Tilley, *Medieval France*
J. Evans, *Life in Medieval France*
R. H. de Villefosse, *Histoire de Paris*

MEDICEAN FLORENCE

Bernhard Berenson, *The Florentine Painters of the Renaissance*
Jacob Burckhardt, *The Civilization of the Renaissance in Italy*
F. A. Hyett, *Florence: Her History and Art to the Fall of the Republic*
Walter Pater, *The Renaissance, Studies in Art and Poetry*
Janet Ross, *Lives of the Early Medici*
J. A. Symonds, *The Renaissance in Italy*

THE VENETIAN REPUBLIC

Horatio F. Brown, *Venice: an Historical Sketch of the Republic*
Alethea Wiel, *Venice ("Story of the Nations" series)*
Pompeo Molmenti, *La Storia di Venezia nella vita privata*
Bernhard Berenson, *Venetian Painters of the Renaissance*
Ruskin, *Stones of Venice*

MADRID UNDER THE HOUSE OF AUSTRIA

R. B. Merriman, *The Spanish Empire*
R. Trevor Davies, *The Golden Century of Spain*
M. A. S. Hume, *Spain: Its Greatness and Decay*
Carl Justi, *Diego Velazquez and his Times*
B. C. Erskine, *Madrid Past and Present*
Louis Bertrand, *Philippe II, une tenebreuse affaire*

ROME OF THE POPES

John Addington Symonds, *The Renaissance in Italy*
Ferdinand Gregorovius, *History of Rome in the Middle Ages*
Ludwig Paster, *History of the Popes*
Jakob Burckhardt, *The Civilization of the Renaissance in Italy*
Rodolfe Lanciani, *The Golden Days of the Renaissance in Rome*

PARIS, VERSAILLES, AND THE 'GRAND SIÈCLE'

J. E. Farner, *Versailles and the Court of Louis XIV*
  The Cambridge Modern History, Vol. V
F. Funck Brentano, *The Old Regime in France*
P. Gaxotte, *La France de Louis XIV*
G. Hongredien, *La Vie Quotidienne sous Louis XIV*

VIENNA UNDER METTERNICH

Mrs. Trollope, *Austria and the Austrians*
Algernon Cecil, *Metternich*
Harold Nicolson, *The Congress of Vienna*
Charles A. Gulick, *Austria from Habsburg to Hitler*

JUBILEE LONDON

Sir Walter Besant, *London in the Nineteenth Century*
Robert Harling, *London Miscellany—A Nineteenth Century Scrap-book*
G. M. Young, *Early Victorian England*
Charles Booth, *Life and Labour of the People of London*
Ernest L. Woodward, *The Age of Reform*
Robert C. Ensor, *England, 1870–1914*

TWENTIETH-CENTURY NEW YORK

E. B. White, *Here is New York*
Francis Marshall, *An Englishman in New York*
Cleveland Rodgers and Rebecca B. Rankin, *New York: The World's Capital City, its Development and Culture*
George H. Johnston, *Skyscrapers in a Mist*
New York City Guide—the Federal Writers' Project, New York City
Hulbert Footner, *New York: City of Cities*

23

INDEX